MasterWorks

MasterWorks

decorative and functional art

Compiled by Sally Milner

MILNER CRAFT

MasterWorks

decorative and functional art

First published in 2000 by **Sally Milner Publishing** Pty Ltd

PO Box 2104 Bowral NSW 2576 AUSTRALIA

© In this collection, Sally Milner Publishing Pty Ltd 2000

Design by Ken Gilroy

Editing by Sally Milner and Donna Hennessy

Printed in Hong Kong

National Library of Australia Cataloguing-in-Publication data:

Masterworks: decorative & functional art. Embroidery,

cross-stitch, lacework, quilts

ISBN 1 86351 275 6 (bk. 1).

1. Cross-stitch. 2. Lace and lace making. 3. Embroidery.

4. Handicrafts. 5. Quilts. I. Milner, Sally.

(Series: Milner craft series).

746.4

Main photography by Andrew Sikorski, Art Atelier

Cover photograph: detail of work by Annemieke Mein,

untitled, based on the shapes, venations and markings

commonly found on the wings and moths of

butterflies; 45cm x 55cm (18" x 22"); materials used: silk,

mohair, rayon which have been dyed, felted, plied, combed,

teased or spun, synthetic metallic fibres; surface materials:

black crystal organza, embroidery threads of silk, rayon

and cotton, machine threads varying from thick, thin, dull

or shiny, variety of glass beads; techniques: layering, plying,

collage, trupunto, couching, machine embroidery (free

sewing), hand embroidery including French knots, stem

stitch, rope stitch, beading.

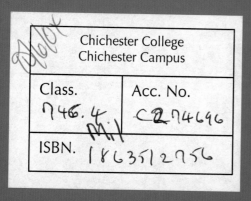

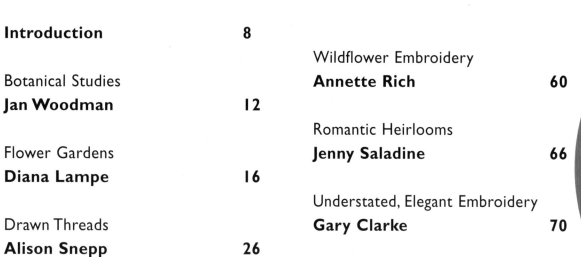

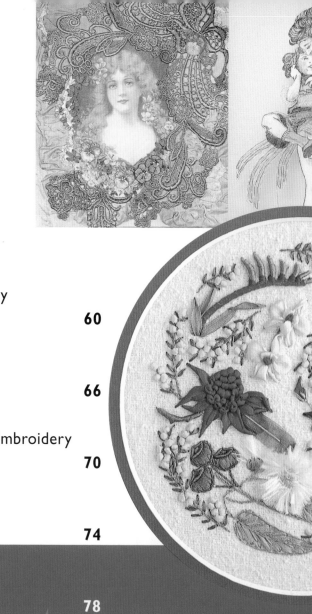

Contents

Contents

Beryl Hodges

THIS COLLECTION is the result of a request to leading designer-makers to contribute to a book which would display the quality and range of work being undertaken in the fields of decorative and practical arts at the turn of the century and millennium. The response was enthusiastic, and, while some artists were unable to create new work specifically for this project, because of other pressing commitments and our timetable, almost every one was willing to share their work in some way. Some have given detailed instructions on how the work could be recreated, others have given a general description which would enable experienced workers to create something similar, while others have allowed us to display their current work and ideas. All will provide inspiration to admirers, collectors and practitioners. The aim of this book, and its companion volume, is to excite the reader by the extent and scope of the work being created at this time, and we feel this anthology far exceeds our aim.

No collection, however, could ever be comprehensive, or contain a full survey of activity and creative talent today. There are other artists who should have been included. These omissions are a consequence of the gaps in my own knowledge and experience. I apologise to those artists, particularly those new and emerging designers, whose work I may have overlooked.

This volume contains crafts which use fabric and thread in their construction. It includes embroidery, both machine and hand worked; lace making in many forms, including bobbin, needle and knitting; quilting; weaving; rag rug making and the creation of collectables – teddy bears and dolls. These have been called the 'gentle arts', practised mainly by women through the centuries and so often undervalued. The companion volume to this one contains découpage, painted finishes, glass, ceramics, wood, jewellery.

There are few formal institutional courses or training available for those wishing to work in these fields. Many of the skills displayed have been handed down informally between generations, and practised of necessity. Others have been acquired through the dedication of experienced teachers, operating individually or through needlework suppliers, or under the auspices of the various Guilds and groups, such as the Lace Guilds and the Quilters' Guilds, non-profit groups run by the members for the members.

The Embroiderers' Guilds are wonderful examples of the way in which these skills are passed on. Guild teachers are qualified before they can start, the courses offered are comprehensive, proficiency certificates are

Beryl Hodges
Grid III: Solar Flare
132cm x 132cm
(53" x 53")

awarded, exhibition work is judged to the highest standard, sholarships for study overseas are offered. The role of the Guilds has been, and continues to be, inestimable in rejuvenating and keeping alive the techniques for each craft.

As well, hundreds of informal groups meet daily throughout the country to share their skills, or simply to set aside time to work on their craft together. There may be no leader or teacher, just a true sharing of the experience of the work.

Canberra Quilters Inc, well represented in this book, shows the amount of activity in a small area. Formed 24 years ago, it has hundreds of members, at least 200 of whom attend each monthly meeting. It runs a full teaching

Annemieke Mein
Thornbills
High relief wall
sculpture with relief
leaves extending
beyond the frame.
65cm x 92cm x 6cm
(26" x 37" x 2¹/₂")

programme of approximately 20 courses each year, holds an important annual exhibition, and groups of members work together on their quilts on a regular basis. Its success shows the level of dedication of all the members, not only to practise their skills but also to share their knowledge and expertise. As a result, many of its members are recognised internationally for the quality and originality of their work and design.

Very few artists have chosen to formalise their training, however, some have undertaken tertiary research and achieved qualifications. Many more have travelled overseas at their own expense or under the auspices of the Guilds or the Churchill Fellowship, to study the crafts which in the main originated in Europe. Many of the artists included in this volume exhibit and teach regularly overseas, bringing back and disseminating new ideas, materials and techniques.

Some of the artists represented may seem to be interested only in recreating the work of the past. It may indeed be their aim to preserve patterns and techniques. However, the wide range of colours in threads, the quality of the threads and fabrics they use, and, most importantly, the subject matter they choose, give the work a definitively contemporary feel. Other artists have taken their hard won and well grounded skills and have used them to create modern, eclectic, vibrant designs. Almost all have been influenced in some way by the environment in which they live, featuring gardens, landscapes, the natural flora and fauna and geography of place in their work.

The use of modern equipment has allowed new techniques in most of these fields to develop, and quicker results have led to a greater willingness to experiment. Embroidery by machine is perhaps the best example of this. Yet still many choose to work by hand, even where machines can be employed. Hand quilting a bed size quilt may take months of full-time work, but it gives a softer, gentler look and feel, highly valued. Life-like embroidered flowers, each different in form and hue, can only be worked by hand, delicate laces by needle, shuttle and bobbin.

What do such different artists have in common? Certainly very few are remunerated well and must rely on family support, or undertake rigorous teaching and writing programmes which keep them away from their workrooms. More importantly though, years of learning, dedication and constant working and practising have honed their skills and techniques to near perfection. The hours of labour required have imbued each piece of their work with their personality and show us the quality of their workmanship and affinity to their design and materials.

Each one is an inspiration.

Coastal Wild Flowers of South Australia

Botanical Studies

Jan Woodman

A passionate love for Australian wildflowers, in particular for the smaller herbaceous plants and ground orchids, combined with an incredible eye for detail, inspired Jan Woodman to paint botanical studies. In addition to studying flower painting between 1983 and 1987, using the demanding medium of pure watercolour, she studied plants and their structure under the tutelage of botanists at the State Herbarium of South Australia in the Botanic Gardens.

Jan says, 'By painting life-size botanically accurate plant studies I hope to show their fragility and beauty, to promote interest in their conservation and help the flower lover identify the different plants. It is a pleasure and privilege to record these flowers.' Jan is perhaps better known for her painting than her embroidery, but she began to reproduce her beloved plants in petit-point and later in cross stitch. Since 1986, she has often exhibited watercolours and embroideries together. Her attention to detail and colour allows her to translate her paintings into needlework with accuracy and her charts are ever-popular.

Jan is now working some of her wildflowers in surface stitchery. The freedom of varied stitches and threads will, she feels, allow her even more accuracy and realism.

The works shown here are in cross-stitch. The large piece, *Coastal Wildflowers of Southern Australia*, is a reproduction in cross-stitch of part of an earlier watercolour. The smaller piece is worked as a detail from one section of this larger work.

Common and botanical names (from left to right): Sandhill sword-sedge (*Lepidosperma concavum*), Coast velvet-bush (*Lasiopetalum discolor*), Coast swainson pea (*Swainsona lessertifolia*), Native yam (*Microseris lanceolata*), Pink fairies (*Caladenia latifolia*), Erect guinea flower (*Hibbertia riparia*), Running postman (*Kennedia prostrata*), Native flax (*Linum marginale*), Old man's beard (*Clematis microphylla*), Australian trefoil (*Lotus australis*), Yellow microcybe (*Microcybe pauciflora*), Common sea heath (*Frankenia pauciflora*), Common riceflower (*Pimelea humilis*), Coast speedwell (*Veronica hillebrandii*), Sweet apple-berry (*Billardiera cymosa*), Salmon correa (*Correa pulchella*), Silver goodenia (*Goodenia affinis*), Stalked ixiolaena (*Ixiolaena supina*), Australian bindweed (*Convolvulus remotus*), Bower spinach (*Tetragonia implexicoma*), Lavender daisy (*Olearia ciliata*), Coast logania (*Logania crassifolia*), Eyebright (*Euphrasia collina*), Lavender grevillea (*Grevillea lavandulacea*), Variable groundsel (*Senecio lautus*), Billy button (*Craspedia uniflora*), Cockies tongue (*Templetonia retusa*), White correa (*Correa alba*), Dryland tea tree (*Melaleuca lanceolata*), Love vine (*Comesperma volubile*), Spiny wattle (*Acacia spinescens*), Coast twinleaf (*Zygophyllum billardierei*), Round-leaved pigface (*Disphyma crassifolium*).

Lavender daisy,
Eyebright and Coast
Logania
Botanical names:
Olearia ciliata,
Euphrasia colina and
Logania crassifolia
24cm x 18cm
(9³/₄" x 7¹/₄")

Symbol		DMC	Colour
•	•	White	White
ø	ø	316	antique mauve medium
↖	↖	327	antique violet dark
6	6	470	avocado green light
V	V	471	avocado green very light
—	—	472	avocado green ultra light
N	N	553	violet medium
O	O	554	violet light
∅	∅	612	drab brown medium
▽	▽	676	old gold light.
<	<	743	yellow medium
+	+	778	antique mauve light
▯	▯	780	topaz very dark
R	R	783	Christmas gold
▲	▲	937	avocado green medium
F	F	987	forest green dark
✕	✕	988	forest green medium
=	=	3052	grey green medium
⁄⁄	⁄⁄	3778	terra cotta medium light

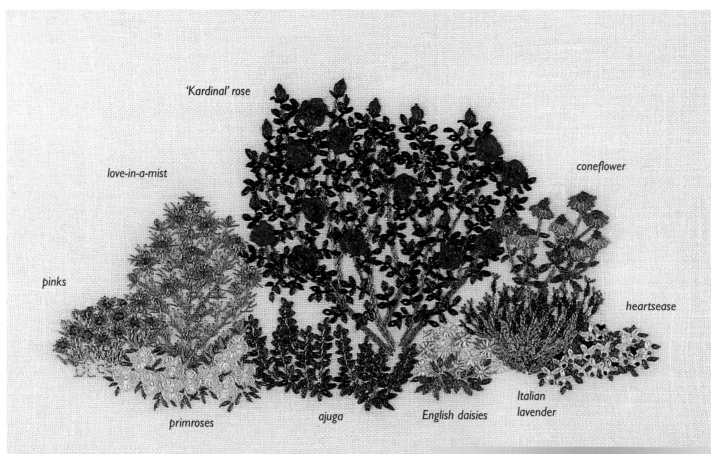

'Kardinal' rose

love-in-a-mist

coneflower

pinks

heartsease

primroses

ajuga

English daisies

Italian
lavender

Above: 'Kardinal' rose garden'
9.5cm x 17.5cm (3 ³/₄" x 7")
Far right: Crazy patchwork evening bags 25cm
(10") deep and 20cm (8") deep
Right: 'G' made for Georgina Lampe
10.5cm x 9.5cm (4¹/₈" x 3³/₄")

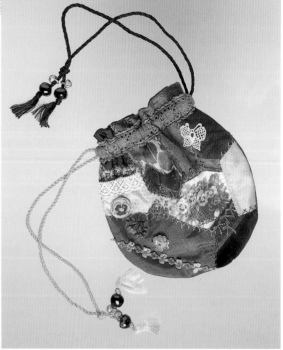

Flower Gardens

Diana Lampe

Crocus, primula, daisies, roses, primrose, pinks, foxgloves, delphiniums. These, and all the perennials and bulbs of the garden, are the subjects of Diana Lampe's exquisite embroideries which she began designing and teaching in 1986.

Diana had loved and collected fancywork from the '30s and '40s and planned to experiment with this type of embroidery one day but was worried it was stylised and that true colours were not used. Her embroidered flowers, in contrast, look alive and recognisable.

Diana is meticulous in her research and preparation as she works her flowers in a detailed and realistic botanical style. She always works with a specimen in front of her and will often grow a flower especially to embroider it. She matches the threads to the flowers in daylight and often mixes two colours together to achieve a colour or effect. She also draws the plant in detail, often at different stages as it is growing, and takes numerous photographs to keep the image fresh after the blooms have faded. Sometimes she presses a specimen or photocopies a part of it, such as a leaf. Then all the details needed to work, from botanical name, thread number, how many petals etc, are recorded. The next step is to embroider a sample. She has now designed more than 250 flowers in this way.

Diana is careful too, in her embroidered gardens, to combine plants which would, in a real garden, flower at the same time, a care she extends to her garlands and initials and smaller projects.

Before 1986 and her passion for embroidered flowerers began, Diana was a patchworker. Now, crazy patchwork is a passion, too, as it combines both patchwork and embroidery. Crazy patchwork brings together everything Diana really loves – fabrics and textures, embroidery and beautiful embellishments.

'S' made for Sophie Harper
11.5cm x 10.5cm (4^1/2" x 4^1/8")

'Kardinal' rose garden

Requirements

embroidery linen 40cm x 30cm (16" x 12")

DMC Stranded Cottons:

208 lavender very dark	210 lavender medium	211 lavender light
223 shell pink light	224 shell pink very light	316 antique mauve medium
327 violet very dark	333 blue violet very dark	400 mahogany dark
444 lemon dark	445 lemon light	469 avocado green
471 avocado green very light	503 blue green medium	522 fern green
550 violet very dark	611 drab brown dark	726 topaz light
727 topaz very light	793 cornflower blue medium	814 garnet dark
815 garnet medium	936 avocado green very dark	3041 antique violet medium
3051 green grey dark	3346 hunter green	3347 yellow green medium
3363 pine green medium	3685 mauve dark	3687 mauve
3689 mauve light	3722 shell pink medium	3726 antique mauve dark
3740 antique violet dark	blanc neige	

Needles:

No 8 crewel needle (for 2 strands thread)
No 8 straw needle (for bullion stitch)
No 9 crewel needle (for 1 strand thread)

2B pencil and embroidery
small embroidery hoop 10cm (4")
scissors

Wash and press the fabric. Fold the linen up one third from the lower edge. This garden is 17.5cm (7") long; centre this measurement on the crease line and mark the ends with a pencil. This will ensure you have ample fabric around the finished embroidery for framing. Work a small running stitch between the pencil marks and along the crease line with one strand of 471. This will form a lasting guide for the ground and can be stitched over and left in your work.

Lightly draw the rose branches freehand with a sharp 2B pencil or place a photocopy of the design onto a light-box or tape to a sunlit window. Position the fabric over the design and trace with the pencil.

As you work, follow the individual instructions for each plant and use the colour photograph as a guide to help you position the flowers and leaves in the design.

Work rose branches first and then the roses, buds and leaves. Stitch the ajuga and English daisies in front of the rose with the lavender and heartsease to the side. Add coneflowers behind the lavender. Work love-in-a-mist on the other side of the rose with primroses in front and pinks at the end.

Bugleweed or Blue bugle

Ajuga reptans 'Purpurea'

DMC Stranded Cotton: 327, 333, 3041, 3051

Stems

Two strands 3041, stem stitch

Draw short straight stems for the flower spikes and work them in stem stitch.

Leaves

One strand each 327 and 3051 blended, chain stalks

Work the leaves on the stems (in pairs) with small chain stalks and with a tiny one at the top. Work rosettes of larger leaves on the 'ground' coming back to the stems.

A chain stalk is a lazy daisy stitch worked with an extended anchoring stitch. Ajuga leaves are worked in the opposite direction to lazy daisy stitch, ie back towards the stem.

Flowers

Two strands 333, French knots

Add the flowers to the flower spikes with French knots, one in the axil of each leaf.

English daisies

Bellis Perennis

DMC Stranded Cotton: blanc neige, 223, 224, 444, 471 3346

Flowers

petals: One strand each 223 and blanc neige blended, straight stitch

one strand each 224 and blanc neige blended, straight stitch

centre: Two strands 444, French knot

Draw small circles for the flowers with a dot for the centre.

Work petals with straight stitches from the outside circle down into the centre (leave space for centre). Work petals in quarters first and fill in between these with two or three more petals. Add in French knot centres.

Stems

Two strands 471, couching

Add short stems from the flowers with couching.

Leaves

Two strands 3346, lazy daisy stitch

Work the leaves with lazy daisy stitches at the base of the stems.

Pinks

Dianthus plumarius

DMC Stranded Cotton: 3685, 3687, 503, 522

Flowers

petals: Two strands 3687, straight stitch.

Draw small circles with a dot in the centre for the flowers. Work the flowers with straight stitch from the outside edge down into the centre. All stitches are worked into the same hole in the centre. Don't work too many stitches for each flower and vary the length of the stitches to achieve a ragged edge like a carnation.

flecks: Two strands 3685, back stitch.

Add flecks of deep pink around centre of flower with tiny backstitch.

Stems

One strand each 503 and 522 blended, stem stitch.

Work short stems for the flowers with stem stitch.

Leaves and stalks

One strand each 503 and 522 blended, straight stitch.

Add straight stitch leaves up and down the stems and from the ground, forming a clump. Some of these straight stitches will form the stalks for buds.

Buds

Two strands 3687, lazy daisy stitch.

Add some buds to the stalks with lazy daisy stitch.

Coneflower

Echinacea purpurea

DMC Stranded Cotton: 316, 400, 469, 3722, 3726

Stems

Two strands 3722, stem stitch.

Draw the stems and work them in stem stitch.

cone – French knots

petals – lazy daisy stitch

stem – stem stitch

leaves – double lazy daisy stitch

axillary leaves – lazy daisy stitch

Flowers

Petals:	Two strands 3726, lazy daisy stitch.
Faded petals:	Two strands 316, lazy daisy stitch.
	Draw cone shapes for the flowers. Work the petals with lazy daisy stitch. Use 316 for the more
	mature, faded and drooping petals and 3726 for the newer flowers.
Centre (cone):	Two strands 400, French knots.
	Fill in the cones with French knots.

Leaves

Two strands 469, double lazy daisy, lazy daisy stitch and straight stitch.

Work the leaves in pairs with double lazy daisy stitch and attach to stem with a straight stitch stalk. Add smaller axillary leaves with lazy daisy stitch.

Italian lavender

Lavandula stoechas
DMC Stranded Cotton: 208, 522, 550, 3740

Lavender bush

Branches and foliage: two strands 522, fly stitch.

Lightly mark the branches for the foliage. Start at the top of the bush and work each branch with fly stitch down to the 'ground'. Overlap some branches and stitch some smaller branches for a well-shaped bush. The fly stitch branches can only be worked down so you will have to finish off your thread at the 'ground' and start again. You can weave a short distance up the back for the smaller branches.

stems:	One strand each 522 and 3740 blended, straight stitch.
	Work straight stitch stems (5mm, $^1/_4$") for the flowers at the top of the bush and amongst the foliage.

Flowers

flower heads:	One strand each 550 and 3740 blended, bullion stitch (five wraps).
	Work the flower heads, with bullion stitch attached to each stem.
bracts:	Two strands 208, straight stitch.
	Add the petal-like bracts above each flower head with two or three small straight stitches.

Love-in-a-mist

Nigella damascena
DMC Stranded Cotton: 793, 3347, 3363, 3740

Stems

young stems:	One strand 3347, stem stitch.
mature stems:	One strand each 3347 and 3363 blended, stem stitch.
	Draw stems and work them with stem stitch in the thread combinations above.

Flowers

petals: Two strands 793, lazy daisy stitch.

Work the five petalled flowers with small lazy daisy stitches, leaving a space for the centre. Add some side-view flowers with just four petals.

Centre: One strand each 3740 and 3363 blended, French knot.

Add French knot (two twists) to the centre of flowers.

Buds

 One strand each 3347 and 3363 blended, lazy daisy and straight stitch.

Add a few buds to some of the minor branches. Work a small straight stitch with a lazy daisy stitch around it.

Sepals and foliage

One strand 3347, feather stitch and straight stitch

Add straight stitch sepals for flowers to the gaps between petals, and for buds from the stem just below.

Add the tufts of foliage quite freely to the stems with feather stitch and the odd straight stitch. To achieve the effect of flowers peeping through a ferny mist, work an occasional stitch over a flower.

Pods

One strand each 3740 and 3363 blended, bullion stitch.

Spikes: one strand 3347.

Add some pods to the plant if you wish, with 2 bullion stitches (three or four wraps) side by side, with three or four spikes above.

Rose of Mexico or pink evening primrose

Oenothera speciosa
DMC Stranded Cotton: 445, 471, 3346, 3689

Flowers

petals: One strand 3689, buttonhole stitch.

Draw four petalled flower shapes with a dot in the centre.

start

Stitch each petal from the centre, leaving a tiny space in the centre. Work four or five small buttonhole stitches and then take the needle and thread to the back of your work. The first stitch will look like a lazy daisy stitch. Come up again in the centre to start the next petal and work the other three petals in the same manner. Stitch opposite petals first to make positioning easier.

finish

centre: Two strands 445, French knot.

Add a French knot centre.

Stems

One strand 471, stem stitch.

Work stems with stem stitch.

Buds

One strand 471, bullion stitch (nine wraps)

Add some buds with bullion stitch amongst the flowers. Work each bud with nine wraps and take the needle out a little further when anchoring the bullion stitch to form a point.

Leaves

One strand 3346, lazy daisy stitch.

Work the leaves with lazy daisy stitches attached to the stems below the flowers. Leaves should be longish and worked with firm tension to make them thin.

'Kardinal' *Rosa X*

Hybrid Tea Rose

DMC Stranded Cotton: 611, 814, 815, 936, 3346

Branches

Two strands 611, stem stitch.

Mark the branches for the rose. Work the major branches with two rows of stem stitch and smaller branches with one.

Rose

Before you begin thread up all the needles you require. Work several roses and buds amongst the branches.

full-blown rose: Two strands 815, buttonhole stitch.

One strand each 814 and 815 blended, buttonhole stitch.

Mark a circle for the rose with a small circle within. Work each petal from the inside circle with three or four buttonhole stitches forming a scallop shape. The first stitch will look like a lazy daisy stitch. Take the thread to the back of your work to complete the petal.

Work five petals (more for a bigger rose) around the circle with 815, and then work three or four inner petals to overlap the first with 814/815. If you have a little space left in the centre and can't fit another petal, fill with a French knot.

Buds

One strand each 814 and 815, lazy daisy stitch.

Add several rose buds amongst the branches and roses.

Work each bud with four lazy daisy stitches to form a nicely shaped bud. Work two lazy daisy stitches side by side; from the middle of these add another lazy daisy to form the tip of the bud. Work the fourth lazy daisy from below the bud into the centre of the bud.

Stems

Two strands 3346, couching.

Add stems to all roses and buds attaching them back to the branches with couching.

thorns: One strand 3346, backstitch.

                  Add thorns to the stems and branches with tiny backstitches, angled down from the stem.

Leaves and sepals

Two strands 936

leaf stalks: Backstitch.

                  Work curving stalks for the leaves with three or four small backstitches.

Leaves: Lazy daisy stitch.

                  Add lazy daisy stitch leaves in pairs along the stalks and one for the tip (five to seven leaves).

sepals: Fly and straight stitch.

                  Work a tiny fly stitch or straight stitches around each bud and a straight stitch into the bud depicting the sepals.

Add stalks and leaves to the branches amongst the roses and buds stitching over existing embroidery.

Heartsease or Johnny jump-up

Viola tricolor

If you look closely at a heartsease plant in the garden you'll find the intensity of colour varies considerably from flower to flower. The newly opened flowers are vibrant and those which have been out for a while have faded to softer hues. Try other thread combinations for even more variety using the threads listed.

DMC Stranded Cotton: 208, 210, 211, 333, 444, 469, 550, 726, 727

Flowers

These flowers are very tiny, so the stitches need to be kept as small as possible. Work one or two flowers at a time in each thread combination. This makes it easier to position the flowers. Some flowers may overlap another. Be sure to keep all threads on the top of your work whilst working.

lower petal: buttonhole stitch

vibrant: Two strands 444.

faded: One strand each 444 and 726 blended.

                  Draw small triangles for the lower petals. Work each lower petal with three tiny buttonhole stitches. Start stitching at the left-hand side of the lower edge and work each stitch into the same hole (in the centre of the flower).

top petals and spot:

                    Lazy daisy stitch and French knot.

vibrant: Two strands 550.

faded: One strand each 208 and 333 blended.

                    From slightly above the central point, work the two top petals (pointing upwards) in lazy daisy stitch. Add the spot with a French knot to the bottom edge of the lower petal.

side petals: One strand each 727 and 211 blended or two strands 210, lazy daisy stitch.

                    Work the side petals at a slightly upward angle. They will overlap the upper petals a little.

Leaves

Two strands 469, lazy daisy stitch.

Work leaves with lazy daisy stitch beneath and amongst the flowers.

Finishing

The work can be personalised by adding another flower or an insect to the design. It can also be signed in stem stitch or backstitch using one strand of pale green thread.

The back of the work should be tidied up ensuring there are no tags, which could show through when framed. The piece can then be handwashed in cool water with soft soap. Don't soak or leave wet, as some deeply shaded threads might bleed. Rinse well, but don't wring, as creases can be hard to remove.

The embroidery is then placed face down on a towel, overlaid with a pressing cloth and carefully pressed with a hot iron until dry, taking care not to scorch it.

The finished embroidery can then be taken to a good framer who knows the correct way to frame needlework. The framer will help choose a frame to enhance the design.

Drawn thread on pillowslip and sheet by Alison Snepp
with Smocked girl's dress and smocked bishop's baby gown by Wendy Findlay

Drawn Threads

Alison Snepp

University trained in the social sciences, Alison Snepp was always a keen and talented embroiderer. Twenty-five years ago she was able to take the step to become a 'freelance embroiderer', creating and working original designs, teaching and writing. She has published numerous books ranging over counted thread, needlepoint, soft furnishings and surface stitchery, sharing her skills and designs with thousands.

Four years ago, Alison bought a highly successful needlecraft shop in Sydney where she continues to introduce her own ideas, to stock beautiful fabrics, threads and other essential supplies, but also to find and introduce to her customers new, talented embroiderers and their work.

Pillowslip and sheet

Requirements

3 metres (120") white tracing linen, 137cm (54") wide
3 skeins DMC Broder 35 cotton white
tapestry needle No 28
ruler
pins
fine embroidery scissors and fabric scissors
sewing machine thread in a medium colour

General notes: All the hemstitching and four-sided stitch are worked with one full thickness of Broder 35 thread.

It is important to remember that all the hemstitching is worked from the wrong side of the work, while all the four-sided stitch is worked from the right side of the work. Both the hemstitching and the four-sided stitch are pulled firmly.

Pillowslip

Pull a thread across the width of the linen to ensure it has a straight edge. Even up the linen by cutting carefully along the line of the drawn thread. Measure 55cm (21$^{1}/_{2}$") from the evened-up edge and pull another thread across the width of the linen. Cut along this drawn thread. The smaller piece of linen is for the pillowslip and the larger for the sheet.

Measure 5cm (2") in from the selvage at one short side of the linen and withdraw six fabric threads. Note the withdrawn threads will be parallel to the selvage. Turn in and pin a doubled 2cm ($^4/_5$") wide hem using the 5cm (2") of fabric. The hem should be folded level with the edge of the drawn threads. Tack the hem in position with sewing machine cotton. Hemstitch around four threads to secure the hem. Note that all the embroidery on the pillowslip is parallel to the fabric selvage.

Leave four fabric threads and withdraw the next six fabric threads. Work a row of four-sided stitch onto the four threads remaining in the fabric using the same bundles of four threads drawn together with the hem stitch. This will give a ladder-like appearance.

Leave four fabric threads and withdraw the next six fabric threads. Work a row of four-sided stitch onto the four threads left behind, again using the same bundles of four threads to give another ladder-like row.

Work a row of hemstitching over the same bundles of four threads to complete the ladder-like row.

Leave 12 fabric threads and withdraw the next seven threads. Work a row of hemstitching on the side of the drawn threads closest to the embroidery already completed using the same bundles of four threads.

Leave four fabric threads and withdraw the next seven threads. Work a row of four-sided stitch onto the four threads left, but this time each four-sided stitch should be worked around two threads from one hemstitching bundle and two threads from the adjacent hemstitching bundle (making a total of four threads). This will give a serpentine effect.

Work a row of hemstitching along the other side of the gap where the seven threads were withdrawn. Again the hemstitch should be worked around two threads from one four-sided stitch bundle and two threads from the adjacent four-sided stitch bundle to give a serpentine effect.

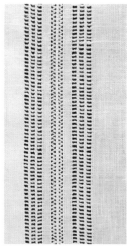

Detail of drawn thread work on pillowslip

Leave 12 fabric threads and withdraw the next seven threads. Work a row of hemstitching on the side of the drawn threads closest to the embroidery already completed using the same bundles of four threads.

Work a row of four-sided stitch over the same bundles of four threads to complete the ladder-like row.

Leave four fabric threads and withdraw the next six fabric threads. Work a row of four-sided stitch onto the four threads left behind, again using the same bundles of four threads to give another ladder-like row.

Work a row of hemstitching over the same bundles of four threads to complete the ladder-like row.

Steam press the embroidered fabric well on the wrong side of the work. Fold the pillowslip in half (to make the normal pillowslip shape) with wrong sides facing. Machine stitch a 6mm ($^1/_4$") seam along the long sides. Press the seam and turn the pillowslip inside out, so that the right sides of the embroidery are facing. Pin a 9mm ($^3/_8$") seam along the long sides of the pillowslip to complete the French seam. Turn the pillowslip right side out and press well.

Sheet

The sheet is embroidered at one end only and the pattern of the embroidery is the same on the sheet as on the pillowslip, except the embroidery and the drawing of the threads are worked from the selvage at one side of the fabric to the selvage at the other side of the fabric.

Start the embroidery by withdrawing six fabric threads 7cm (2 $^3/_4$") from the cut edge of the linen. Turn in and pin a doubled 3cm (1 $^1/_5$") hem along this edge of the sheet. The hem should be folded level with the edge of the drawn threads. Tack the hem in position with sewing machine cotton. Hemstitch around four threads to secure the hem.

To embroider the sheet, follow the steps given in the pillowslip.

To work the hem at the other end of the sheet withdraw four fabric threads 5cm (2") in from the even-up cut edge of the fabric. Turn in and pin a doubled 2cm ($^4/_5$") wide hem using the 5cm (2") of fabric. The hem should be level with the edge of the drawn threads. Tack the hem in position with sewing machine cotton. Hemstitch around four threads to secure the hem.

Turn in a doubled 1cm ($^2/_5$") hem down each long side of the sheet and work a slip-stitched hem to finish these sides.

Steam press the sheet well on the wrong side of the embroidery.

Stitches

Hemstitching along hem

1. Bring needle out in the hem one thread above the hem fold.

2. Pass the needle beneath four threads in gap where threads have been withdrawn. Note the needle comes out level with where the thread lies in the hem fold.

3. Pick up edge of hem fold one thread up from the fold itself. Note position above where the diagonal stitch ends. Don't stitch through to the right side of the fabric - only the hem fold.

Pull embroidery thread firmly.

Hemstitching on single layer of fabric

1. Bring the needle out two fabric threads above the drawn threads.

2. Pass the needle beneath four threads in the gap where the threads have been withdrawn. Note that the needle comes out level where the thread lies in the fabric.

3. Pass the needle vertically beneath two fabric threads. Note the position is level with where the diagonal stitch ends.

Pull embroidery thread firmly.

Four-sided stitch

Leaving an 8 – 10cm (3" – 4") length of thread at the back of the work, bring the needle out of the fabric to the right side at 1.* Put the needle into the fabric at 2 and bring it out at 3. Put the needle back into the fabric at 4 (the same hole as 1) and bring it out at 5. Insert the needle at 6 and bring it out at 7 (the same hole as 3)**. Repeat from * to **. All stitches should be pulled firmly so that bundles are formed.

To end off a thread, work a running stitch over one thread and under one thread close to the embroidery stitches within the pulled section.

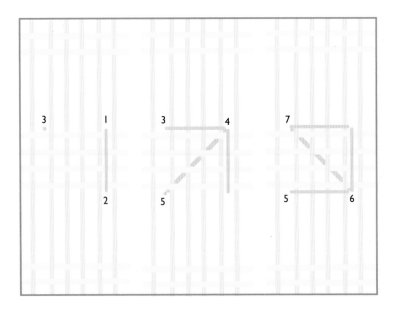

Smocking

Wendy Findlay

The gentle art of smocking was introduced to Wendy Findlay as a small girl when all her own 'special' clothes were smocked, some in cotton, some in linen and others in crêpe de chine. These were worked by the women of her family, sharing their experiences and designs, and laboriously pleating by hand.

Now Wendy is dedicated to passing on the skills and techniques of smocking to others, treasuring the methods and patterns of the past while creating new designs. Smocking still evokes a sense of luxury and care and is still used on children's clothes, particularly those worn on special occasions.

The smocking designs shown previously and on the following pages are worked on garments made from standard, readily available patterns.

Girl's dress

To suit a three year old.

Requirements

dupion silk soft pink

Madeira Silk using two strands for smocking:

      4 packets in main colour, soft pink

      1 packet in second colour (one shade darker than the main colour)

1 box Mill Hill seed beads

needles: milliners needle No 9

      crewel needle Nos 7 or 8

Pattern

A basic square yoke pattern with puff sleeves designed to fit a three year old girl has been used to construct this dress, with a number of simple variations.

After cutting the bodice yoke pieces for back, front and sleeves, the following pieces will be required.

Skirts. Pull a thread across the fabric to obtain a straight cutting line and cut two pieces of fabric for skirt front and skirt back using full width of fabric x 80cm (32") in length.

Neck frill. Cut one piece of fabric 5cm x 45cm (2" x 18").

Sleeve binding. Cut two pieces 6cm x 32cm (2^{1}/$_{4}$" x 12^{1}/$_{2}$")

Neck binding. Cut one piece 6cm x 22cm (2^{1}/$_{4}$" x 8^{3}/$_{4}$") on the cross.

Placket. Cut one piece 3cm x 36cm (1^{1}/$_{4}$" x 14").

Sashes. Cut four pieces 10cm x 90cm (4" x 36").

Lining. Using yoke blocking guides, cut lining areas for front and back smocked areas.

Preparation for smocking

Pleat 13 rows of full spaces in front skirt fabric.

You will need 126 pleats for the front smocking pattern. Each 'diamond' pattern requires 12 pleats with four extra pleats used in the centre pattern and two pleats for end cables.

Remove pleating threads back from outer edges to coincide with armhole shaping on front blocking guide. Be sure to leave 126 pleats. Adjust pleats and tie off threads in pairs.

Fold skirt back in half lengthwise and run a tacking thread from waistline down 18cm (7"). Pleat 13 rows of full spaces in this back skirt piece. Gently draw out threads along tacking line of centre back and snip. Remove these threads back from centre line for 1cm (^{2}/$_{5}$").

This unsmocked 2cm (^{4}/$_{5}$") area will form the seam line for the back placket of the skirt. Do not cut this seam line until smocking has been completed and it is time to sew in the placket, then cut down 17cm (6 ^{3}/$_{4}$") along centre line. Tie off these centre threads in pairs.

Remove pleating from each side of fabric to coincide with armhole shaping on back blocking guide leaving the 62 pleats required for each side of the back skirt. Adjust pleats and tie off outer sets of pleating threads.

Smocking

The pattern for this smocking was designed to use the texture of the silk fabric to advantage, with the use of beads for a third dimension. It will be necessary to use a milliners (or straw) needle for rows with stitches using beads. A No 7 or 8 crewel may be used for other smocking.

Backsmocking needs only a single thread.

In the centre of each diamond pattern in rows 3 and 9 there are highlight single flowerettes using a seed bead on each cable of the flowerette.

Girl's dress to suit a three year old

Each side of the back skirt takes five full diamond pattern repeats requiring 12 pleats each. The front of the dress has 10 full diamond pattern repeats requiring 12 pleats each plus two extra pleats for end cables.

When all smocking has been completed it should be blocked to fit the guide so dress construction may begin. To block smocking undo pleating threads at each end of smocking and place piece on ironing board. Gently ease out smocking to the size required and pin to hold in place along each outer edge of smocking. Holding steam iron above, not on, steam the smocking well. Allow to dry thoroughly before moving.

Never remove top holding row of thread. This row acts as a seam guide and gathering thread for attaching skirt to bodice.

Smocking graph

Row 1:	alternating cable - basic cable row using a seed bead on each centre cable of the alternating cable stitches.
Row 1$^1/_2$:	single feather stitch beginning from right hand side.
Row 2 to 2$^3/_4$:	3 cable 2 step wave 5 cable combination.
Row 2$^1/_4$ to 3:	3 cable 2 step wave 5 cable combination.
Row 3 to 3$^3/_4$:	mirror image of row 4 – cable wave combination.
Row 3$^1/_4$ to 4:	mirror image of row 3 – cable wave combination.
Row 4$^1/_2$ to 5:	1 step wave.
Row 5$^1/_4$ to 4$^3/_4$:	3 cable 1 step wave, 1 cable combination – using a seed bead in conjunction with the three cables.

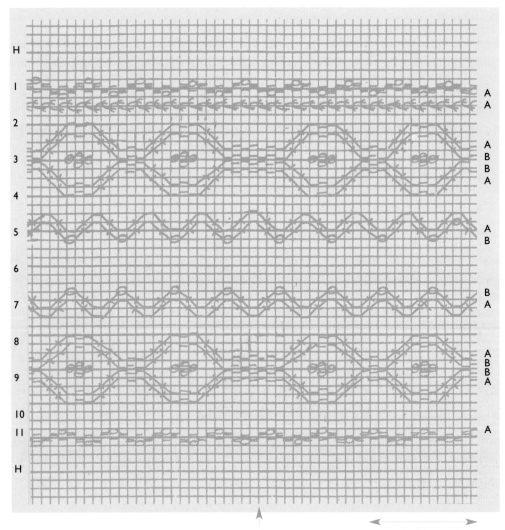

A = main colour

B = contrast colour

centre

pattern repeat

Row 6:   backsmock with cable stitch.

Rows 6^3/$_4$ to 7^1/$_4$: mirror images of 4^1/$_2$ to 5^1/$_4$.

Rows 8 to 10:   repeat rows 2 to 4.

Row 11:   repeat row 1.

In the centre of each diamond pattern on rows 3 and 9 there are highlight single flowerettes using a single seed bead on each cable of the flowerette.

In the centre front there are extra cable stitches used as a design variation at the junction of the diamonds in rows 3 and 9.

Dress construction

The dress should be constructed in the usual manner, bodices joined, skirts attached, sleeves inserted. The following variations apply.

Pipe lower edges of bodices with a fine self-covered piping.

Fold neck frill piece in half lengthwise with right side together. Seam short ends, trim and turn to right side and press.

Gather raw edge of frill and adjust gathers to fit neckline. Attach to neckline.

Fold neck binding in half lengthwise with wrong side together, carefully measure length of neckline and fold in short edges of binding to fit neckline accurately. Press in place.

Attach binding to right side of neckline, which already has frill in place. Turn binding over to wrong side and slip stitch in place.

Sleeve binding

Join together two short edges of sleeve binding. Fold in halves lengthwise with wrong sides together and press.
After gathering lower edges of sleeves, adjust gathers and attach binding to right side of sleeve. Trim seam and turn binding over to the wrong side and slip stitch in place.

Sashes

Hand roll and stitch raw edges of sashes, leaving one short edge unfinished.
Half a centimetre from alongside the last row of smocking on front and at side seam edges of back make a 4cm slit towards the top of the skirt. A total of four openings.
Take a fold in the top raw edge of each sash and slide one into each opening taking care to have hems facing in towards dress.
Carefully, using a half centimetre seam allowance, sew in place. Finish off with oversewing.

Buttons

Make 2 1.5 self covered buttons. Using a back stitch and one thread of silk attach 8 beads evenly around outer edge of each button. Attach buttons to back right yoke and make buttonholes on back left yoke.

Embossed

Jane Nicholas

In 1982 Jane Nicholas, from a background of dressmaking and practical crafts, became fascinated by stumpwork embroidery, the raised or embossed embroidery practised originally in England between 1650 and 1700. Some might say that a form of endeavour popular for such a short time was of limited interest today, but Jane has proved stumpwork could capture the hearts and minds of embroiderers worldwide in the twentieth and twenty-first centuries. Jane is constantly travelling between Australia, the United States, New Zealand, her books and classes in constant demand, and her family's business swamped with orders for all the small and delicate, hard-to-find items needed for this craft. Such kits as Jane and her husband John provide were also sold in the seventeenth century, the design printed or painted on the ivory satin background. A tantalising assortment of material was therefore available to the home embroiderer, as Jane has ensured today.

Jane was intrigued originally by the extremely fine nature of the work and the subjects depicted. Also, brilliant colours were used, as she was able to discover when she saw pieces which had been stored properly, away from the light. She began her stumpwork with the sampler shown on these pages, *Homage to the Seventeenth Century*, which contains as many elements of those original embroideries as she was able to depict: two figures dressed in period costume on a mound, an arbour of flowers, fruits and insects, a border of fish, shells and seaweed, lion and stag, a castle, tent, sun, clouds and stars. Now her designs tend to be simpler, deliberately bringing the work into the present day, while still honouring the work of the past.

Garland of Berries

Requirements

15cm (6") embroidery hoop	3 x 10cm (4") embroidery hoops
tracing paper	fine (0.5mm) HB lead pencil
red marking pen (to colour wire – optional)	dressmaker's carbon paper (white or orange)
small sharp pointed scissors	fine tweezers for bending wire
wire cutters (or old scissors)	ivory satin 20cm x 20cm (8" x 8")
purple cotton homespun 15cm x 15cm (6" x 6")	red cotton homespun 15cm x 15cm (6" x 6")

quilter's muslin or calico two pieces each 20cm x 20cm (8" x 8")

Vliesofix (paper-back fusible web) two pieces each 8cm x 5cm (3" x 2")

Homage to the seventeenth century
40cm x 32cm (16" x 12¹/₂")

cream felt 8cm x 5cm (3" x 2")

straw needles Nos 1 and 9

chenille needle No 8

Mill Hill pebble beads No 5025 col ruby

fine flower wire 50cm (20")

Mill Hill frosted beads Nos 62056 boysenberry and 60367 garnet

Mill Hill petite beads Nos 42028 ginger and 42014 black

crewel/embroidery needles Nos 5 – 10

tapestry needles Nos 24 – 26

sharps/applique needle No 12 (or beading needle)

Mill Hill seed beads Nos 367 garnet and 330 copper

stuffing

Enlarge to 155%

Vine and leaf outline

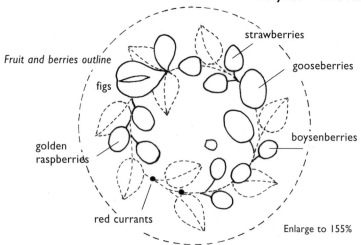

Suggested threads (these are listed below for main use but are also used elsewhere in design):

Vine – DMC No 937 dark green and No 469 lighter green (or Soie d'Alger Nos 2126 and 2125 green)

Figs – Au Ver à Soie d'Alger Nos 4636 plum, 3326 dark purple,

4136 dark brown (or DMC No 3371 dark brown) and DMC No 433 mid brown

Strawberries – DMC No 817 dark coral red

– Kanagawa (YLI) Silk 1000 denier 4 dark red twisted

– DMC No 3819 pale green

– Madeira Metallic No 40 gold – 4

Golden Raspberries – Soie d'Alger No 611 gold , DMC No 3854 light gold (or Madeira Silk 2307)

– Kanagawa (YLI) Silk 1000 denier 113 green twisted

Boysenberries – Soie d'Alger No 3326 dark purple/plum

– Kanagawa Silk 1000 denier 113 green twisted

Red Currants – DMC No 75 red variegated (or Floss Overdyed 153)

Ladybird – DMC No 310 black, DMC No 900 red/orange (or Soie d'Alger No 646)

Fruit and berries outline

figs

golden raspberries

red currants

strawberries

gooseberries

boysenberries

Enlarge to 155%

Order of work

1. Mount satin and muslin/calico backing into (15cm) 6" hoop, stretching both layers as tight as a drum.

2. Transfer the vine and leaf outline to the right side of the satin as follows: trace vine and leaf outline onto tracing paper with lead pencil. Draw over the outline again on the back of the tracing paper; turn the tracing to the right side and place over the satin in the hoop. With a board or lid under the fabric for support, draw over the vine and leaf outline with pencil, stylus or empty ball-point pen, thus transferring a pencil outline to the satin.

3. Embroider the vine outline in chain stitch with one strand of dark green thread (937 or 2126). Embroider the stalks after all the fruits and berries have been applied.

4. The leaves are embroidered with one strand of dark green thread as follows:
   work the central veins in chain stitch;
   pad the leaf surface with straight stitches;
   embroider each side of the leaf with close buttonhole stitches, the buttonholed edge just covering the pencil outline.

5. Transfer the fruit and berries outline to the muslin/calico backing as follows:
   add fruit and berries to original tracing, using the leaves as a guide;
   place the design right side down on the muslin/calico backing, making sure that the leaves are aligned;
   draw over the fruit and berries outline with pencil or empty ball-point pen, thus transferring a pencil outline on to the muslin/calico backing.

6. Work the figs, strawberries, golden raspberries, boysenberries, red currants and the ladybird and apply to the satin, using the outline on the muslin/calico backing as a guide.

Figs

Mount purple fabric in hoop and trace fig shapes using dressmaker's carbon paper.
Leave a 2cm ($^4/_5$") space between the shapes.

Large split fig

1. With one strand of plum thread (4636) work each side of split with small chain stitches, then cover with buttonhole stitch, the ridge towards the split. Work the fig outline in split backstitch then embroider shape in long and short stitch, starting at the base with a dark brown (4136 or 3371) then blending in purple and plum (3326 and 4636). Add a few stitches in green if desired.

2. Carefully cut out split close to buttonhole stitches. Run a row of gathering stitches close to shape then cut out, allowing a small turning. Apply fig with small stab stitches, pulling gathering stitches to turn in raw edges and following the pencil outline

Garland of berries
10cm x 10cm
(4" x 4")

on the back. (It is important to follow this outline as the embroidered shape is slightly larger to allow for the stuffing.) Pad the sides of the fig through split with a little stuffing, using a sate stick. Stitch beads into the fig one at a time, with mid-brown (433) thread, until the shape is filled. If necessary, cover the stab stitches around the outside with straight stitches, blending colours.

Small fig

3. Outline in split back stitch with one strand of plum thread (4636). Embroider fig in long and short stitch, starting at the base with dark brown (4136 or 3371) then blending in purple and plum (3326 and 4636) at the top.

4. Run a row of gathering stitches close to the shape and then cut out, allowing a small turning. Apply fig with small stab stitches, pulling gathering stitches to turn in raw edges and following the pencil outline on the back. Leave a small opening at the base of the fig to insert stuffing, then stitch opening closed. If necessary, cover the stab stitches with straight stitches, blending colours.

5. Work a French knot (two wraps) at the base of each fig with two strands of mid-brown (433) thread in a No 1 straw needle.

Strawberries

1. Using paper-backed fusible web, cut two pieces of red felt to pad the strawberry, one the actual shape of the strawberry, and one slightly smaller.

2. Using one strand of red thread (817), stab stitch the smaller shape in place. Using the same thread, apply the larger shape on top with buttonhole stitch. Work a row of small back stitches around the strawberry (close to felt) in the red twisted silk thread.

3. Using red twisted silk and tapestry needle No 26, embroider the strawberry trellis stitch (see instructions at end), working rows in alternate directions to produce desired texture. Work first row of trellis stitch into five back stitches at the top of the strawberry. At the end of each row, insert the needle through to the back of the work, then bring it up again slightly below, to commence the next row. Increase or decrease stitches at each end of row if required.

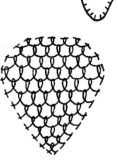

4. With two strands of green thread (469 or 2125), work three or four chain stitches at the top of the strawberry to form the sepals.

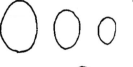

Gooseberries

1. Using paper-backed fusible web, cut three pieces of cream felt to pad the gooseberry – one piece the actual size and two pieces successively smaller.

2. With one strand of pale green thread (3819), apply three layers of felt with stab stitches, starting with the smallest layer. Outline the shape with buttonhole stitch around the top layer of felt.

3. With one strand of pale green thread (3819), cover the padded shape with satin stitch, covering the buttonhole outline. Concentrate the needle's entry and exit points at each end of the gooseberry to give a rounded shape.

4. With Madeira metallic gold thread in a No. 9 straw needle, embroider the veins in feather and single feather stitch, starting and ending each row at the same points at the top and base of the gooseberry.

5. Work a tuft at the top of the gooseberry with a turkey knot, using three strands of brown (433) thread.

Golden raspberries

1. Mount calico or muslin into hoop and draw raspberry outlines.

Embroider raspberries with a layer of closely worked french knots (one wrap). Use five strands of Soie d'Alger (611) and six strands of Madeira/DMC (2307/3854). Use a No 1 straw/milliners needle and mix the threads to vary the shading, if desired.

To apply raspberries

Run a row of gathering stitches close to the outline then cut out, allowing a small turning. Pull gathering stitches to turn in raw edges.

2. With one strand of thread, stitch raspberry into position with tiny stab stitches around edge. Cover the edge, if necessary, with french knots (as above). Press gently around edges with fingernails to shape the berries.

scrap thread

Sepals

Using green twisted in silk in No 26 tapestry needle, work three sepals in needleweaving, at the base of each raspberry.

Boysenberries

1. Mark the centre of the berries with a short line (3mm or $^1/_8$"). The berries are formed by stitching beads to the main fabric, using one strand of purple/plum thread (3326) in No 10 crewel needle, in two layers as shown. Apply the beads (62056, 60367 and 367) one at a time and mix the colours as desired.

Lower layer

a Stitch two beads on the centre line.

b Backstitch nine beads around the centre then run three rounds of thread through these beads to draw them into a tight oval.

Upper layer

c Stitch one bead in the centre (take the needle between the beads in the lower layer through to the back.)

d Backstitch seven beads around the centre then run three rounds of thread through these beads to draw them into a tight oval. Secure thread at back.

2. Using green twisted silk thread in a No 7 or 8 milliners needle, work three sepals at the base of each berry. Each sepal is a bullion stitch with about ten wraps.

Red Currants

1. With a long strand of red variegated stranded thread (75) thread 1 metre, (40") in a No 26 tapestry needle, stitch through the hole in the pebble bead (5025) until covered, leaving a thread tail on either side of head.

2. To form the top of a currant, thread on a seed bead (330) then bring the needle through the pebble bead to the base (two tails of thread). Make six currants.

3. Apply currants in two groups of three – insert thread tails through one hole and secure at the back for each group.

Small ladybird

Wings

1. Mount red cotton homespun in hoop and trace wing outline.

2. Colour wire with marking pen if desired. With one strand of red/orange thread (900 or 646), couch, then overcast the wire to the fabric around the wing outline, leaving the ends of the wire free at the top of the wings.

3. Pad stitch then satin stitch the wings, inside the overcasting.

4. With one strand of black thread, embroider spots on the wings in satin stitch (across wing stitches).

Body

With one strand of black thread, outline the body with small backstitches, then embroider with padded satin stitch (worked from side to side).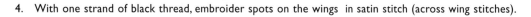

To complete ladybird

1. Cut out the wings and apply by inserting wires through • using a chenille needle. Bend wires towards tail of the ladybird and secure at the back of the work with a few stitches. Trim the wire.

2. With one strand of black thread, work legs and antennae in straight stitches Apply two black beads for eyes. Gently shape the wings with tweezers.

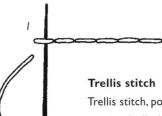

Trellis stitch

Trellis stitch, popular in the 17th century, is a needlelace filling stitch, attached only at the edges, and is most easily worked with a twisted silk thread. The first row of trellis stitch is worked into a foundation of backstitches, the size depending on the effect desired – close together and the trellis stitches resemble tent stitches in canvas work, further apart and an open 'trellis' is the result.

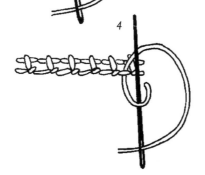

Bring the needle out at 1, slip it under the first backstitch (forming a 't' – a good way to remember this stitch), pull the thread through holding the resulting loop with the left thumb. Slip the needle through this loop (2) then pull the thread down, forming a firm knot. Repeat, to work a row of firm knots with loops in between. Insert the needle into the fabric at the end of the row.

To work a second row, bring the needle out at 3 and slip the needle through the loop between two knots, pull the thread through holding the resulting loop with the left thumb. Slip the needle through this loop (4) then pull the thread down, forming a firm knot. Repeat to the end of the row, insert the needle and continue as above.

Chief eunech from ballet 'Shéhérazade'
9cm x 15cm
(7^{1}/$_{2}$" x 6")

Tablelands in summer 15cm x 21cm (6" x 8^1/$_2$")

Embroidered Landscapes

Judy Wilford

Fifteen years ago when Judy Wilford first began working, developing and experimenting in this medium, she came to it as a painter and object maker, not as an embroiderer. She explains further. 'There were certain painterly qualities I wanted to capture in my work. I wanted to achieve the quality of distance, the translucent qualities of light and the timeless quality which is to me the essence of the Australian landscape. I also wanted the work to have the qualities of a watercolour painting with the low relief texture of hand embroidery and, above all, I wanted the landscapes to be depicted in a way which the viewer could relate to.'

Judy has achieved these qualities with the choice and use of specific fabrics and colour, and with the use of adapted techniques of fabric layering and shadow applique to build layer by layer the background of the work. This is followed with the use of layered surface stitchery to form the detail of the foreground. It is the combined layering of fabric, thread and stitch that gives the distance and dimension of the work.

The landscape which Judy has explained here in detail is a naturalistic depiction of the Northern Tablelands of New South Wales, with the summer vergeside flora of lace flowers and daisies. Judy chose this particular landscape as the Tablelands are very suited to some of the techniques she uses when working with embroidered landscapes, with its defined natural lines such as the ranges, the tree and grass lines. The finished work is shown on page 50.

Northern Tablelands

Requirements

1 rigid frame with minimum internal dimensions of 20cm x 30cm (8" x 12") and approx 2cm ($^3/_4$") deep. This is a simple, flat wooden frame. (Note: this work cannot be done using a hoop or roller frame)

1 pair of 'C' or Fretsaw clamps. (Note: the clamp size must accommodate the edge of your table, plus the depth of the frame)

leather squares to protect your table when it is clamped

masking tape 4cm ($1^1/_2$") wide

scissors: paper; fabric; sharp, long-bladed embroidery

needles: assorted sizes and types as preferred or required

pins

tissue paper, 2 strips 4cm x 21cm ($1^1/_2$" x $8^1/_4$")

light weight card 21cm x 21cm ($8^1/_4$" x $8^1/_4$")

Vliesofix (paper-back fusible web) 3 strips 2cm x 21cm ($^3/_4$" x $8^1/_4$")

1 H Pencil

ruler

eraser

fine ink drawing pen

Fabrics

unwashed calico, sufficient to cover the frame size being used

Sky	Sky Blue	100 per cent cotton	11cm x 21cm (4^{1}/$_{4}$" x 8^{1}/$_{4}$")
Range line 1	Deep Blue	silk organza	4cm x 21cm (1^{1}/$_{2}$" x 8^{1}/$_{4}$")
Range line 2	Deep Blue	100 per cent cotton	4cm x 21cm (1^{1}/$_{2}$" x 8^{1}/$_{4}$")
Tree line 1	Mid Green	100 per cent cotton	4cm x 21cm (1^{1}/$_{2}$" x 8^{1}/$_{4}$")
Tree line 2	Dark Green	100 per cent cotton	4cm x 21cm (1^{1}/$_{2}$" x 8^{1}/$_{4}$")
Grass line 1	Cream	lining silk	3cm x 21cm (1^{1}/$_{5}$" x 8^{1}/$_{4}$")
Grass line 2	Pale Green	lining silk	3cm x 21cm (1^{1}/$_{5}$" x 8^{1}/$_{4}$")
Grass line 3	Mid Green	lining silk	3cm x 21cm (1^{1}/$_{5}$" x 8^{1}/$_{4}$")
Foreground	Mid Green	100 per cent cotton	9.5cm x 21cm (3^{3}/$_{4}$" x 8^{1}/$_{4}$")
Overlay	White	silk organza	21cm x 21cm (8^{1}/$_{4}$" x 8^{1}/$_{4}$")

Note: All silk fabrics must be 100 per cent silk. All cottons used are of 'Homespun' weight. Do not pre-wash any of the fabrics.

Threads

All threads listed are DMC Stranded Cotton

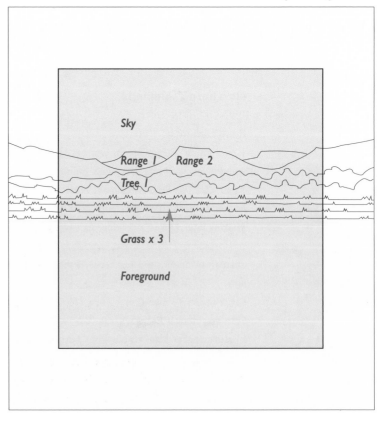

Enlarge drawing to 200%

Backstitching	No 3022 brown grey medium
Grasses	Nos 3024 brown grey light,
	524 fern green light, 522 fern green
Stems	No 3051 green grey dark
Flowers	white, Nos 743 medium yellow,
	742 tangerine
Leaves	Nos 3051 green grey dark,
	3012 khaki green medium
Trees	Nos 3787 brown grey dark,
	3051 green grey dark,
	3012 khaki green medium

strong thread for lacing both the frame and the work on completion.
polycotton thread of a pale colour.

Preparation

The Frame

Cut the unwashed calico slightly larger than the outer dimensions of the frame. Dampen and then steam iron calico dry. Lay the frame on the straight grain of the calico, draw around the outside edge using a pencil. Cut away excess fabric. Fix the calico to the frame with masking tape by taping the long sides first and then the short sides. Tension the calico as you tape.

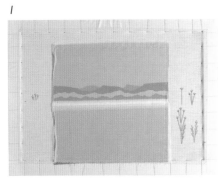

1

2

Clamp the frame to the table with one long edge protruding 9cm – 10cm (3^1/$_2$" – 4") beyond the edge of the table. Using a strong thread and blanket stitch 2cm – 3cm (^{3}/$_4$" – 1^1/$_4$") apart, lace the calico to the frame. Begin by pulling the thread through the calico at one corner and tie it tightly around the frame and stitch to the end pulling the fabric tightly to the inner edge of the frame. Finish with a stitch through the top of the last stitch which should fall at the corner. Turn the frame and lace the opposite long side, this time placing the stitch about 5 – 10mm (^{1}/$_8$" – ^{1}/$_4$") into the calico and pull it firmly towards the edge of the frame. This will tension the calico. Finish off as before. Stitch the short sides of the frame in the same way. Tie corner threads together and clip close to the knot. The finished frame should be drum tight.

Refer to photographs which show the way the calico is tightly sewn over the frame.

The Window

Cut a central window of 15cm x 15cm (6" x 6") in the light weight card. This will leave a border/lacing allowance of 3cm (1^1/$_5$") on all edges. This window will be used throughout the working of this project.

Refer to photograph 2 which shows the frame in use.

The Fabrics

Iron all fabrics.

Cut and prepare the fabrics as below. Note all fabrics will be the sizes stated in the requirements list regardless of preparation.

The Sky	Cut to size
Range line 1	Cut to size
Range line 2	Cut to size. Apply a Vliesofix strip to the top (long) edge
Tree line 1	Cut to size. Apply a Vliesofix strip to the top (long) edge
Tree line 2	Cut to size. Apply a Vliesofix strip to the top (long) edge
Grass line 1	Tear silk and fray 2 – 3mm (^{1}/$_{10}$") of one long edge. Trim short sides to size.
Grass line 2 & 3	Tear silk and fray as above.
Foreground	Tear cotton and fray 2 – 3mm (^{1}/$_{10}$") of one long edge. Cut other edge to size.

3

Photograph 1: The work in progress, showing: lacing of the calico to the frame; layering stage of the work; tacking; isolation stitch; examples of 'practice' stitches – to the right is the lace flower structures and feather stitch.

Photograph 2: The same as photograph 1 but showing the window in position.

Photograph 3: A sampler of the work showing completed backstitched lines; progression of stitching of the three grass layers; stitched lace flower structures and flower heads as they will appear when stitched over the grass layers; the stitched trees.

Note: The Vliesofix is used purely to prevent fraying. It is never used to fuse layers together. Use a dry iron at a cotton setting, lay the rough side of the Vliesofix face down on the edge of the fabric and press for 8 – 10 seconds. Ensure the adhesive has melted onto the fabric. Wait until cool or until you are ready to use the section of fabric before removing the paper backing.

Tissue paper

Two pieces cut to size 4cm x 21cm ($1^1/2$" x $8^1/4$"). Make a tracing of each of the two Range lines.

Use the fine ink pen and number them 1 and 2.

When tracing Range line 1, trace the Range area which is showing. Connect these areas with a dotted line which dips below Range line 2. Trace Range line 2 as in the design.

With both, continue the line to the outer edge of the border and mark the inner edge on the tracing. This will help you to position both Ranges. Do not make tracings of the tree lines as these will be cut 'free-hand'.

The Working Procedure

When layering in the background, it is important to cut and position one layer at a time, using the design and the window as a guide for placement. This will prevent over-handling of the fabric strips and therefore fraying of the cut edges.

Always begin at the top of the work, the sky, and layer to the base of the work.

Layering in the Background (Refer to photographs 1 and 2).

Take the window and place it centrally on the frame with the outer base edge on the inner edge of a long side of the frame.

Lay in the Sky fabric so it covers the upper and side outer edges of the window. Carefully remove the window and place it into position on the top of the sky. Check that all borders just cover the Sky fabric. Leave the window in this position.

Pin the tracing of Range line 1 to the blue organza and carefully cut along the traced line. Check the design and use the window to place the range into position.

Pin the tracing of Range line 2 on to the right side of the Vliesofixed edge of the dark blue cotton, remove the paper from the back, the Vliesofixed edge or the wrong side, and carefully cut along the traced line. Lay Range line 2 into position by superimposing over Range line 1. Make sure both Ranges are in place by checking the design.

At this point the window can be removed. Hold the Range lines down with one hand and slip the window away, making sure you do not move the Range line while you are doing this.

The Tree lines, the mid and dark green cottons, are cut and layered one after the other. Remove the paper backing from the Vliesofixed edges. With this side uppermost, cut the Tree lines by drawing the fabric backwards and forwards against the blades of the embroidery scissors as you slowly close them. This will give you a complex waving line which resembles distant trees. It takes a little time to get it right and it might be an idea to have a practice run first on a similar fabric.

Layer the Tree lines into position, mid green first followed by dark green, and nestle them up against the ranges. Because these lines have been cut 'free hand' you may find that the dark green will, in some places, completely cover small areas of the mid green. This is fine and will add to the natural appearance of the work.

The Grass lines have been frayed during the fabric preparation stage and are therefore ready to be layered into position. Layer them from the lightest colour to the deepest.

The First layer is positioned so that it nestles under the second Tree line and the following lines are placed so that the top of the frayed section lies at the bottom of the frayed section of the line before. This means that only the frayed sections are showing.

The Foreground of mid green cotton also forms the last grass layer and is now layered in the same manner over the silk layers.

Replace the window on the work. The edges of all borders should be at the outer edge of the window. Check against the design and adjust if necessary. Remove the window.

Carefully lay the white silk organza over the top of the background so that it is completely covered. With a pale polycotton thread tack the organza into place in the following way. Tack the top edge, the Sky, first, then tack the bottom edge, tensioning the silk organza layer as you tack. Tack the sides in the same way. Use a medium sized stitch. Refer to photographs 1 and 2.

Place the window into position and outline the Foreground area with three long straight stitches. Do not place any part of these stitches in the sky area. These stitches define the area you will work within. If you stitch into the border you will find it difficult to lace the work when it is completed. These stitches are called isolating stitches. Refer to photographs 1 and 2.

The layering of the background is now complete. You are ready to begin the surface stitching.

The Foreground - Surface Stitchery

Clamp the frame to the table so that it overhangs the table and allows easy access from the Foreground to the Range lines. All stitching will be done with the frame clamped.

Begin stitching in any way you prefer. Judy uses a small knot. Finish with a tiny backstitch into the base of a stitch or into the last stitch of a line. Clip off at the back of the work or bring the thread up into the calico edges and clip off on the surface. Tidy up the back when you finish work each day.

Backstitching (Refer to photograph 3).

Backstitching of the tree and range line will hold the layers into position and will begin to give a sense of distance to the work. It is important to stitch in the following sequence:

Begin at the centre of Tree line 2, backstitch along the edge of the line to 2mm beyond the isolating stitch. Return to the centre and work out to the other side. Repeat for Tree line 1 and Range line 2. Do not backstitch Range line 1.

Use a single strand of DMC Stranded Cotton 3022 throughout. Keep the stitches small and even and do not pull them too tightly. They should lie close to the surface without distorting the silk organza.

Surface Stitchery

There is a process which must be followed while working the stitched layers of the foreground.
1. Completely stitch the grass layers.
2. Stitch all of the stems for all of the flowers you intend to work. This will form a lattice upon which you will work the flower heads.
3. Stitch all of the daisies, scattering them throughout the lower foreground. Make sure their heads are placed on the point of one of the stems. Do not stitch the centres.
4. Stitch in all of the lace flowers.

Northern Tablelands
15cm x 15cm
(6" x 6")

5. Stitch in the leaves at the base of the stems as needed to fill the base of the foreground.
6. Stitch in the trees across the middle ground.
7. Finally, stitch in the daisy centres.

The Grass

Refer to photograph 3.

There are 3 layers of grass in this piece of work. The colours are graded from light to dark. Single strands of DMC Stranded Cotton colours 3024, 524 and 522 are used. Begin in the centre, bringing the 3024 thread up into the frayed area of the lower grass lines. Stitch to the edge of the isolating stitch, making these stitches approximately 5 – 10mm ($^1/_8$" – $^1/_4$") apart and 2.5cm – 3.5cm (1" – 1$^1/_4$") long. Return to the centre and repeat out to the other side. Do not pull your thread tightly. It should lie on the surface of the organza. From whichever side you prefer to work, fill in this line of grass so that the stitches lie side by side. The top and the base of this layer are completely irregular. Note that the stitch is a 'laid' stitch, not a satin stitch, which means there will be no build up of thread on the back of the work.

The second layer is begun from your preferred working side using 524 and worked to the other edge as above, and again the top and base of this layer are completely irregular.

The third and last layer is begun as before using 522 and worked to the other edge. However, with this layer the top is completely irregular while the base is stitched to the isolating stitch giving a completely even line. Check the photograph and you will see the progression of stitching.

The Flora (Refer to photograph 3).

Practise your stitches on the frame as all stitches are stitched as stab stitches and therefore the method of stitching may be different from that which you normally use. Refer to photos 1 and 2.

Stitching this way gives you more control over the thread and the stitch as you have both hands free. Your left hand controls both the direction and the tension of the thread as you stitch and your right hand controls the placement and position of the stitch.

The stems are stitched using a single strand of 3051 throughout. The stitch is a combination of fly and feather stitches which are stitched from the top of the grasses to the base. The stem and branch stitches are superimposed upon each other to form a complex lattice. It is important that the area is closely stitched otherwise the flowers will appear very sparse indeed. The process of stitching the stems in this work is to place all of the lace flower structures across the surface of the stitched grasses. You should be able to fit between ten and twelve structures in the foreground area. The base area below these structures is filled in with feather stitch lines. Use the worked example to note the placement of the flora and use the calico sides on the frame to practise the stitches from the diagrams if you wish.

The flower heads use simple stitches of French knots for the lace flowers, detached chain stitches and French knots for the daisies and the leaves are detached chain stitches with varying sized catch stiches placed into the stems of the plants. These simple stitches are arranged in such a way as to depict the flowers used in the work.

Leaves are a 'filler' used to deepen and give further structure to the base line of the foreground. They are formed with detached chain stitches with the catch side angled into the 'stems of the daisies' or the feather stitches. Use two strands, one each of 3051 and 3012. This combination gives a lovely natural play of colour across the work.

The tree trunks are a combination of fly and three pronged feather stitches scattered across the middle-ground. The top of the stitches begin in the tree lines and the trunks are placed in the frayed areas of the silk grass lines. Use one strand of 3787.

The canopies are groupings of French knots giving the rounded appearance of tree tops. Use two strands, one each of 3051 and 3012 with one or two wraps for each knot.

Finishing the Work

When you are happy with your landscape and feel it is finished, leave it for a day or so to be sure, then carefully remove it from the frame by undoing the lacing and removing the masking tape. Place the window over the work and draw around the outside edge with a hard pencil. Cut the excess calico and other fabric away (but don't forget to save for your records any stitch practices you have worked.) Trim off any thread on the back to the edge of the work. Remove the tacking, do not iron the work.

Re-measure the stitched area at the base of the work. You may find it has pulled in slightly during the stitching. It often does. Cut a piece of foam core board or 3 – 4mm ($^1/_{10}$") thick craft board to the size of the final measurement. Glue a wool based felt to one surface of the board and trim away any excess. Do not use Pelham or any other puffy wadding.

Fold over sides, pin corner folds, lace and tension firmly as before.

Each corner must be oversewn to give firm corner edges to the laced work. Take the thread through to the point of the corner and stitch back towards the centre of the board. Do not pull the thread tightly at the corners. Use a pale blue or green polycotton. The landscape is now ready to be mounted and framed.

Wildflower emblems 12.5cm (5") diameter

Silk Ribbon Wildflowers

Jenny Bradford

A chance mention in 1986 of silk ribbon embroidery classes to be given by expatriate Australian Melva McCameron led to Jenny Bradford not only attending the class, but becoming fascinated by this form of embroidery. Already the author of books on smocking she went on to become a highly acclaimed author of numerous texts on silk ribbon embroidery and is said by many to be responsible for the resurgence of interest in this craft form. Certainly she is renowned for her skill as a teacher, her attention to detail and her development, and clear explanations, of different techniques. Assisted by her husband Don, who draws most of her diagrams, she is always able to produce clear, readable and easy to follow instructions.

Jenny was born in England and came to Australia in 1964. Since her arrival she has been intrigued by Australian wildlife and wildflowers. In the main piece shown here she has depicted the wildflower emblems of each state and territory of Australia, based on the design of a commemorative coin from the Australian Mint. She shows how this work can be displayed inside the lid of a box, or, with minor variations, as a framed work.

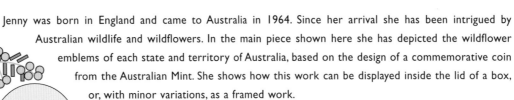

Requirements - general
noil, or raw silk backed with Soft-Sew Vilene
hoop just large enough to take the complete design
needles:
chenille No 20 for 4mm ribbon
chenille No 22 for 2mm ribbon
crewel or straw Nos 7 or 8 for embroidered stems, etc.

This design diagram shows the flowers true to size and may be used to gauge stitch size where necessary.

Waratah (emblem of New South Wales)

50cm (20") 2mm YLI Silk Ribbon No 140 brown
1 metre (40") each 2 & 4mm YLI Silk Ribbon No 49 dark red
15cm (6") 9mm spark organdie ribbon in olive green
DMC Stranded Cotton No 3346 green

First work stem in whipped chain using 2mm brown.

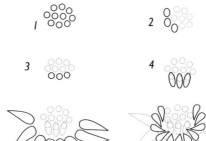

Flowers

Work a tight cluster of 10 colonial knots in 2mm red ribbon for the top of the cone (1), cover each knot with a straight stitch (2).

Work three more knots in the centre front (3) and cover with longer straight stitches (4). Work petals in bullion lazy daisy, two wraps of 4mm ribbon, around the base of the cone (5).

Finish with pistil stitches in 2mm ribbon, filling in the area between the cone and lower petals (6).

For framed piece only, work a leaf with double straight stitch in spark organdie between the petals. Add a vein in straight stitch worked with a single strand of cotton.

Cooktown Orchid (emblem of Queensland)

Requirements:
50cm (20") each 4 & 7mm YLI Silk Ribbon No 7 pale pink
15cm (6") 4mm YLI Silk Ribbon No 49 dark red
No 18 chenille needle

Flowers

Work two side petals using 7mm ribbon, straight stitch and a No 18 chenille needle (1). Follow with three smaller petals in 4mm, using ribbon stitch (2).

Work a French knot in dark red for the centre of the flower.

Work a hood around the centre knot in 4mm pink with two small looped straight stitches around the top half of the knot and a longer looped petal under the knot for the throat (3).

Gum leaf and blossom (emblem of Tasmania)

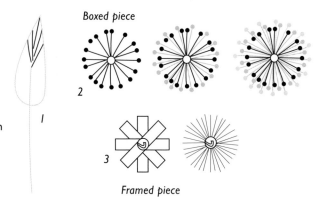

Boxed piece

Framed piece

Requirements:

1 metre (40") each 2mm YLI Silk Ribbon No 32 green & 140 brown

20cm (8") 4mm YLI Silk Ribbon No 156 cream

DMC Stranded Cotton Nos 3363 green, No 523 col fern green, No 918 brown & No 712 cream

machine embroidery thread in bright yellow

Mill Hill Pebble beads in black or clear

Leaf

Draw leaf shapes from main diagram onto fabric. Work stems in whipped chain using two strands
of DMC Stranded Cotton No 3363 green.

Fill in leaves in straight stitch using 2mm Silk Ribbon No 32 green, starting with a stitch about 1cm ($^1/_5$") long from the top of
the vein to the tip of the leaf. Spread the ribbon carefully to prevent rolling at the edges. Space stitches to cover the fabric, but
do not overlap too much and maintain a good angle on each stitch as shown in diagram.

Outline the leaf in stem stitch with a single strand of No 3363. Complete veins in stem stitch with the same thread.

Flowers (boxed piece only)

Work in pistil stitch in a single strand of No 712 (2). Divide the flower circle into quarters with a single long pistil stitch at the
quarter points then work a few stitches of equal length in each quarter. Work a light scattering of medium stitches over the
area. Finish with a third layer of shorter stitches.

Using machine embroidery thread, work a French knot into the centre of some of the knots on the tips of the pistil stitches.

Finish the centre with a looped bullion stitch in a single strand of green No 523 .

Flowers (framed piece only)

Cut four 2cm ($^4/_5$") lengths of cream 4mm ribbon. Using a single strand of green thread, bring the needle up in at the centre
point of the flower, pass through the centre of each of the 2cm ($^4/_5$") ribbon lengths and fan the ribbon into a circle before
attaching to the fabric by taking the needle back down through all the layers.

Work the centre of the flower with green thread, filling in a small circle with straight stitches and finishing with a looped bullion
stitch (3). Fray ribbon carefully with a sharp needle then trim evenly into a circle.

Gumnuts

Draw the outline of the nut shape and fill in with straight stitches in brown 2mm ribbon. Work a single stitch across the top of these stitches (4).

Work a whipped straight stitch, making the foundation stitch very slightly longer than the width of the group of stitches, across the top of the nut. Finish the wrapping in the centre of the bar and pull the stitch into a slight curve before anchoring at the base of the group of stitches (5).

Work two more whipped stitches, positioning them as shown in (5). Using two strands of No 918, couch around the base of the nut and join them to the main stem with stem stitches in one strand (6).

Note: Pebble beads can be used for the nuts if preferred. Wrap beads with 2mm brown ribbon, leaving tails for attaching to the work. Bring both ends of the ribbon together at one end of the bead and wrap firmly with a single strand of No 918 cotton to form a stalk. Thread ends to the back of the work, adjust length and sew securely.

Bluebell (emblem of the Australian Capital Territory)

50cm (20") 4mm YLI Silk Ribbon No 118 blue
10cm (4") 4mm YLI Silk Ribbon in No 3 white
DMC Stranded Cotton No 522 green

Work stems in whipped chain with one strand of No 522 green.

Mark the centre of each flower with a small dot. Work five petal flowers in ribbon stitch in blue and finish with a French knot in white for the centre.

Work a single bullion lazy daisy stitch for the bud, finishing with three straight stitches around the base of the bud in two strands of No 522.

Sturt's Desert Rose (emblem of the Northern Territory)

50cm (20") 2mm YLI Silk Ribbon No 21 green
50cm (20") 13mm YLI Silk Ribbon No 7 pink
Au Ver à Soie Stranded Silk No 945 red
DMC Stranded Cotton No 3362 green
No 18 chenille needle

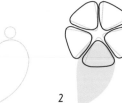

Draw a 3mm (¹/₈") diameter circle for the flower centre. Draw a leaf shape starting close to the edge of the circle (1).

Using 2mm green ribbon, work the leaf as described for the gum leaf outlining with a single strand of 3362.

Using a No 18 chenille needle work five petals in looped straight stitch around the centre, taking a stitch length of about 3mm (¹/₈") and leaving a loop about 10mm (³/₈") long (2).

Using a single strand of red silk, work straight stitches about 3mm ($^1/_8$") long from the centre into the base of the petals (3). Take care to arrange the petals evenly, overlapping them symmetrically.

Work a looped bullion stitch in the centre of the flower for the pistil, using two strands of silk thread (3).

Sturt's Desert Pea (emblem of South Australia)

1 metre (40") 4mm YLI Silk Ribbon No 2 red
30cm (12") 4mm YLI Silk Ribbon No 74 green
30cm (12") 4mm YLI Silk Ribbon black
DMC stranded cotton No 522 green
3mm ($^1/_8$") black beads

Work stems in whipped chain with one strand No 522.

Work centre four stitches in bullion lazy daisy stitch, picking up about 4mm ($^1/_6$") of the fabric and wrapping the ribbon twice around the needle. Leave a 2mm ($^1/_{10}$") space between top and bottom row (1). Pull the points of the top stitches toward each other and the bottom ones away from the centre.

Position the outer four petals as shown in diagram 2.

3mm ($^1/_8$") black beads can be used for the centres of the flowers (as used in the box insert embroidery) or work with 4mm black ribbon following the instructions for the wattle flowers and making the base stitch 3mm ($^1/_8$") long.

Work the leaf with straight stitches in green ribbon.

Heath (emblem of Victoria)

1 metre (40") 2mm YLI Silk Ribbon No 91 medium pink
50cm (20") 2mm YLI Silk Ribbon No 20 green
DMC Stranded Cotton No 3032 green

Work stem in whipped chain with a single strand of cotton.

Work pink bells in bullion lazy daisy with a 2mm ($^1/_{10}$") stitch with a single wrap around the needle. Use one right and one left handed stitch, pulling the points of the stitches away from the centre line (1). Work a ribbon stitch for the centre petal (2).

Attach each bell to the stem with a single straight stitch in the centre petal and a fly stitch around the outside. Anchor the fly stitch to form a short stem (3).

Small straight stitches form unopened flowers at the top of the stem.

Leaves are worked in ribbon stitch pulled firmly to create a spiky leaf.

Wombat sleeping
A study in raised embroidery
techniques
Worked around bronze button by
Marylyn Verstraeten
9cm deep x 7cm wide (3^1/$_2$" x 2 ^{3}/$_4$")

Wildflower emblems – inset for box
12.5cm (5") diameter

Kangaroo Paw (emblem of Western Australia)

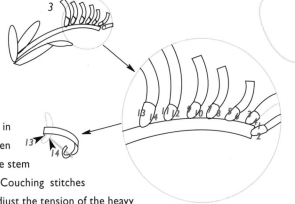

1 metre (40") 4mm YLI Silk Ribbon No 20 green

30cm (12") 4mm YLI Silk Ribbon No 49 red

Coton Perle No 3 red

Au Ver à Soie Stranded Silk No 945 red

No 26 tapestry needle

Thread Perle No 3 into a large needle and lay down in stem position. Do not fasten off until couching has been completed and the length has been adjusted. Couch the stem into place using a single strand of silk thread (1). Couching stitches should be evenly spaced at about 2mm ($^1/_{10}$") apart. Adjust the tension of the heavy thread to give a smooth curve. Sew the end firmly on the back of the work.

Using a No 26 tapestry needle and one strand of silk thread, work rows of stem stitch to cover the stem, picking up the couching threads only (2).

Work the flowers in whipped stitch starting at the bottom with the largest stitch. Wrap these stitches firmly with as many wraps as are necessary to give the required bulk. Finish each stitch in the centre and pull into a curve before anchoring the ribbon. Fit these stitches as close to the stem as possible (3).

Work a backstitch in red over the end of each wrapped stitch where it touches the stem.

Leaves are worked in ribbon stitch overlapping and couched in places to show a twist (3).

Wattle (emblem of Australia)

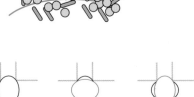

2 metres each 2mm YLI Silk Ribbon No 15 yellow & 32 green

DMC Stranded Cotton No 3032 green

Work stem with a single strand of cotton in whipped chain.

Add clusters of flowers in straight stitch working each bloom with three tiny stitches, one vertical stitch 2mm ($^1/_{10}$") long (1), a second stitch in the transverse direction across the first stitch (2) and a third stitch worked in the same direction as the first one and pulled down firmly to form a tiny ball shaped flower (3). Keep the stitches small and spread the ribbon carefully for each step.

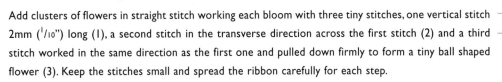

Leaves are worked in ribbon stitch pulled firmly to give a spiky look.

"Celebration"

Telopea Speciosissima
"OLYMPIC FLAME"

Acacia Pycnantha
GOLDEN WATTLE

Annette Rich Jan. 2000

Telopea speciosissima Olympic Flame and Acacia pyncathia Golden Wattle
30cm x 30cm (12" x 12")

Annette Rich

The wonderful sheen of Annette Rich's embroidery is obtained from the American rayon threads she uses. She also admires their textures and array of colours. Using surface stitching and many elements and techniques from traditional forms of needlework, Annette creates her own designs and delights in working with the intense colours of the threads to reproduce Australian wildflowers in a style similar to botanical art.

Living all her life in country New South Wales, Annette has devoted endless hours to studying the flora of Australia and working on innovative ways to depict their brilliant colours and distinctive forms.

Telopea speciosissima **Olympic Flame and Acacia pyncathia Golden Wattle**

Requirements
cream trigger cloth 50cm x 50cm (20" x 20")
red homespun or poly/cotton approximately 21cm wide x 44cm long (8^{1}/$_{4}$" x 17^{1}/$_{2}$")
fine blue transfer pen
10 lengths #30 gauge white covered wire
blocking board (see below for details)
crewel needles Nos 2, 3, 4 & 5
straw needle No 7
milliners needle No 4
darner needles Nos 1, 3 & 18
wooden embroidery hoops, 10cm (4") and 16cm (6^{1}/$_{2}$"), with inner ring bound with white cotton tape
fine scissors, such as used for hardanger or carrickmacross
stiletto

Threads for wattle:
1 hank of Iris No 317 variegated golden yellow to dull green
1 hank Glory No 215 medium avocado
3 hanks Iris No 203 bright golden yellow
2 hanks Divine Zeta No G-20 olive green

Annette Rich

Enlarge to 185%

Threads for waratah:

1 hank Lola No 45 medium brown

1 hank Zeta No G-20 olive green

1 hank Cire No 50 medium to light avocado

1 hank Glory No 305 variegated very pale grey green to grey green

1 hank Nova No 200 poppy

2 hanks Cire No 152 Christmas red

2 hanks Nova No 101 light/dark red

6 hanks Cire No 101 light/dark red

Overlock the edges of the fabric then transfer the design to the fabric. Trace or photocopy the design. Fold fabric in four to determine the centre and fold the copied design in four also.

Place paper under the fabric, centring the design, and, using the fine tip blue transfer pen, carefully trace the design onto the fabric.

Wattle

Begin the embroidery by working the branch of the wattle. Using Iris No 317 in the crewel No 5 needle work two rows of outline stitch (thread down) close together along the stem line. Begin at the base on each row. Then whip stitch the two rows together. Always watch the colour change and shadings of this thread and use to advantage.

Branches for the flowers

With Iris No 317 in a crewel No 5 needle, backstitch the little branches, working each stitch from joint to joint. With the same thread work tiny straight stitches out from the joints to each flower point. A straight stitch is also required from the main stem to the top point of each leaf.

Leaves

Using Zeta G-20 in a crewel No 4 needle, work each wattle leaf in very sloping satin stitch. Begin with a long straight stitch at the point of the leaf and watch the slope of the stitching all the time. Work a two wrap French knot at the top of leaf where it joins the little straight stitch. The veins are couched with Glory No 215 in the straw No 7 needle. First couch the centre vein and then small straight stitches from centre vein to the leaf edge.

Flowers

All the wattle flowers are worked with Iris No 203 in the milliners No 4 needle. Each flower is a bullion stitch, made by taking a very small bite of fabric and twisting the bullion around itself and couching the stitch in place. The tiny flowers at the tip on the sprays of wattle are made with ten wrap bullions, then 15 wraps, then 20 wraps. (Increasing the wraps increases the flower size.) Always couch carefully. Occasionally, Annette has worked a 35 wrap bullion and then placed a two-wrap French knot in the middle and couched down the bullion circle. Use one- and two-wrap French knots for the very tiny flowers at the tip of the flower branch.

The waratah

The stem is worked in raised stem band. Using Lola 45 in the darner No 1 needle, pad the stem with four rows of chain stitch worked close together. Over these chain stitches, work straight bars, from side to side approximately 3mm ($^1/_8$") apart all along the length of the stem. Next work stem stitch over the bars only. Watch the tension all the time to achieve even stitching. Also watch the colour change of this thread and use to the best effect. There should be six rows of stem stitch worked over the bars and begin each row of stitching at the base of the stem, concealing the thread well at the back.

Bracts of the flower head (on fabric)

For easier handling of the work it is best to embroider all the bracts which protrude into the leaves before working the leaves. Using Cire No 152 and the crewel No 2 needle, work all the bracts on the fabric in very sloping satin leaf stitch.

Leaves

Begin by working the upper section of the left leaf. Using Zeta No G-20 and the crewel No 4 needle, pad the stem area of the leaf with running stitch first. Start at the main stem and using a very sloping satin stitch begin on the main stem and stitch over it. Move onto the leaf stem and continue working satin stitch. When the leaf stem is complete change to buttonhole stitch, placing the loop of the buttonhole stitch on the edge of the leaf. Work a sloping buttonhole stitch very carefully along the upper leaf, working from the centre of the leaf to the outside edge. Next, work the small area between 'centre vein' and the edge of the underside of the leaf, changing the angle of the sloping satin stitch.

The turned up underside of the leaf is worked with Cire No 50 and the crewel No 2 needle. Again, use very sloping buttonhole stitch with the loop of the stitch on the leaf edge. Watch the angle of the stitches all the time. Then work one row of detached buttonhole loops into the loops of the previous row of stitching, only on the underside leaf edge. The veins are worked in couching stitch using Glory No 305 in a straw No 7 needle. Couch along the centre vein first and then make small stitches out to the points of the leaf on the topside of the leaf.

The two leaves on the right are worked in the same manner. The leaves close to the flower head are worked with Zeta No G-20 also, with the veins in Glory No 305.

Flower head

Using Nova No 200 and the Darner No 3 needle, cover the flower head up to the line as marked with rows of waratah stitch. Work a small twisted chain stitch and then a normal chain stitch around the first stitch. It is best to turn the work upside down and work across the base of the flower head first, with the first part of the stitch going into the bracts a little bit. Work approximately five rows of the combination stitch, leaving the area at the top unworked. With Nova No 101 and the darner No 18 needle, work 15 wrap bullions on top of the chain, fixing stitch into the area between the stitches of the next row. Work the next row of bullions with 15 wraps and place them alternately compared to the previous row, but still working the bullion over the fixing stitch of the chain stitch. This thread is lightly shaded, so work the thread so that the shadings are used to best effect.

The top of the flower head is worked with Cire No 101 and the darner No 3 needle. Do not work the chain stitching base, but proceed with bullion stitches placed alternately as before and placed carefully to mould and fit to the flower point. This Cire No 101 was a different dye lot from the thread used on the bracts. The paler section was more obvious, so Annette used it to advantage to give a lighter look on the top of the flower.

Bracts (the slips)

Trace the bract slip designs onto the red poly/cotton and then put one circle into the 16cm (6 $^1/_2$") hoop. Using Cire No 101 with a Crewel No 3 needle couch a length of wire onto the bract outline marked A. Place the stitching approximately 1cm ($^2/_5$") apart, then continue right around the shape, couching wire onto the design line. Make sure the stitching is even and firm. Fill the bract with the normal satin leaf stitch, beginning with a long first stitch and keeping a very good slope on both side of the centre. Work the nine slips (A – I) in the same manner.

When finished, soak the worked slips for two to three minutes in warm water with a little white vinegar added. Rinse well and roll in a towel and apply pressure to remove excess moisture from the fabric. Do not twist the towel. Pin fabric taut onto the blocking board, flatten out the slips and leave to dry.

Washing and blocking

The 'red' thread of this work will run and leach out quite a bit, so a long soaking is required. First, rinse the whole work with cold running water to remove all blue transfer pen marks. Half fill a plastic basin with fairly warm water and $^1/_4$ cup of a soaking solution suitable for coloured fabric (e.g. Napisan).

Soak the embroidery in the basin and move it around a little. If there are any soiled areas rub gently. Leave in the water until it

Enlarge to 215%

is cold (overnight). Rinse work very well in chemical free water, then place in tepid water with $^1/_2$ cup white vinegar added. Leave to soak for a while and then rinse again well in chemical free water.

Remove from the water and place on a very thick towel, and then roll the towel up tightly. Place on the floor and tread all over the towel to remove as much water as possible from the work. It is very important to remove as much moisture as you can from the work and do not wring out the embroidery.

The next step is to stretch the work out on a blocking board (see below). Pull each corner, stretch out and pin right around the work every 1cm ($^2/_5$"), pulling the fabric all the time until there are no wrinkles visible. Leave to dry on the board and leave board flat.

If the thread colour has run into the fabric, you need to repeat the whole washing and blocking process again (and maybe again) until background fabric is absolutely clean.

Applying the slips

Iron all the slips carefully, before they are cut out. Mark on pieces of paper the letters 'A' – 'I'. Cut each slip out. Trim the fabric close to the couching stitches and neaten all the edges. When 'A' is finished, pin to the paper marked 'A' and proceed to cut all the slips out in this manner.

Using a stiletto and observing the diagram, push through the fabric and stitching at base of flower head and at wide section of bracts which have been worked on the main embroidery, then push one wire of 'A' through to the back, then the other wire, and twist together at the back. Position all the slips in this manner. Using red sewing thread (double) attach the slips to the work with a few stitches from each slip to the fabric, just to secure them a little. Cut off the long wire ends, once they have been secured well.

Next cut four pieces of red felt as per the patterns (A-D). Place them, in order of size, on top of each other and stitch together carefully. Now position the felt on the back of the waratah, covering the wire ends, then stitch onto the work with the red sewing thread. This pads the back of the flower head and makes it look more prominent from the front.

Now your work is ready to be framed, either by yourself or by a professional framer.

To make a blocking board

The blocking board is a very important piece of equipment to have when finishing off any of this type of very heavily embroidered and dimensional work.

Obtain a 1 metre x 1 metre (40" x 40") piece of lining board with a soft surface, or corkboard, and cut out piece of lighweight wadding approximately 10cm (4") larger all around than the board. Cut some old sheeting or any white fabric the same size as the wadding and overlock the two pieces together around the edges. Fold over the board and secure at the back with wood staples.

Enlarge to 200%

A

B

C

D

E

F

G

H

I

A

B

C

Enlarge to 230%

D

Jenny Saladine

The most delicate of embroideries with the finest tracery of stitches, sometimes worked on or around a printed scene – these are the hallmarks of Jenny Saladine's work. Although her output is not great, Jenny's designs are sought after, not only by her regular pupils in Western Australia, but by others worldwide through her exposure in international magazines. Her husband, Ian, paints the beautiful originals of the scenes in her work and Jenny prints them up herself, so there is no limit to the images she can incorporate into her designs.

Jenny's embroidery is very fine, usually worked with one strand of stranded thread, using the finest needles on the sheerest of fabrics. Her colours are soft and romantic, and her designs are deceptively simple. Perhaps her greatest skill is in her seemingly perfect execution of each individual stitch, no doubt the result of working for seven years for a couturier in Sydney where she undertook beading and embroidery on high fashion garments.

Spring romance garland

Requirements
cream voile
DMC Stranded Cottons as set out in the chart on the next page
straw No 9 needle
crewel No 9 needle
tapestry No 26 needle
embroidery hoop

Left: Spring romance garland 15cm x 13cm (6" x 5")
Right: Rose wheelbarrow 10cm x 14cm (4" x 5¹/₂")

Jenny Saladine

Colours, stitches and needles for garland

Section	stitches	colours	position	needles
Bow	shadow	775 pale blue		tapestry
Roses	bullion	pink combinations 223 deep pink 224 mid pink 225 light pink creamy combinations 677 pale gold 746 cream	 centre bullion first row petals outside row petals centre bullion first and outside row of petals	straw straw
Leaves around roses	lazy daisy	3011 dark green 3012 mid green 3013 light green	pink roses (little) pink roses (main) cream roses	crewel
Rosebuds	bullion	223 deep pink or 224 mid pink		straw
Leaves around buds	extended fly	223 deep pink with 3011 224 medium pink with 3012	buds and leaves buds and leaves	crewel
Forget me nots	Granitos French knots	775 pale blue 742 yellow and 3756 palest blue 677 pale gold	petals centres petals centres	crewel straw
Leaves around forget me nots	lazy daisy	524 pale green		crewel
Wound roses		225 pale pink		straw
Wisteria	French knots	3042 deeper mauve 3743 pale mauve		straw
Butterfly	bullion pistil buttonhole	640 brown 775 pale blue or 3042 deeper mauve	body antennae wings	straw crewel
Bees	Granitos French knots bullion buttonhole	3790 dark brown 3790 dark brown and 676 rich yellow DMC gold thread 1 strand	head eyes body wings	crewel crewel
Spider	Granitos French knots straight	3790 dark brown	body head legs	crewel
Web	straight	DMC gold thread 1 strand		crewel

Using photograph as a guide, mark design onto centre of your fabric using a 2B pencil, pressing very lightly. Place material firmly into hoop. Note: all embroidery is worked with one strand only.

Shadow work

Using one strand and tapestry needle, work the shadow work ribbon. To commence, hold the thread at the back of the work and catch as you do the shadow work, making sure the thread is lying towards the edge so you can't see it when you hold your work up to the light.

To finish off the shadow work slide the thread along the edge on the worn side and catch over two threads at the back.
Buds on the bow: Using 223 make one bullion stitch of six wraps clockwise.
Outside petals: Using 224 make one bullion

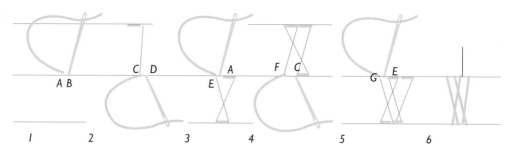

stitch of nine wraps either side of centre working anticlockwise. Place tiny lazy daisy leaves either side using 3012.

Pink and cream roses
Make centre with one bullion stitch of six wraps clockwise. Make the first row of petals with bullion stitch of nine wraps, placed in an anticlockwise direction. Make three of these bullions around the centre making sure they are very close and alternating directions of placement as necessary. Finally make outside petals with bullions of 11 wraps, commencing half way along last bullion stitch made. Some roses may need only two or three of these bullions to make them appear finished while others may need five.

Buds
Work these with two bullion stitches of six wraps each side by side, one placed clockwise, one anticlockwise. Place an extended fly stich around these.

Wisteria
Make a series of five French knots in 3743 with two twists. Then thread up 3042 and, commencing with two twist French knots, taper down to one twist. Leaves around are in straight stitch in 3013.

Wound rose
Pick up a small amount of fabric. Wind thread around the needle four times clockwise. Then pull the needle through gently and ease to bring the stitch up to a small circle. Catch either side with a small stitch.

Granitos – Forget me nots
Placing thread in the same two holes, move the thread from one side to the other. Keep building on stitch until big enough. (Always commence stitch from the centre and work out.) Do the same until you have four petals and finish with a French knot in the centre.

Butterfly
Make one bullion of 13 wraps for body and add two pistil stitches for antennae. Add wings by making a small buttonhole stitch.

Bees
Make a small Granito to form the head and add two French knots to form the eyes. Place one bullion stitch of two wraps for the body, then, leaving a space between each bullion, place another bullion of three wraps. Repeat adding another two wraps to make five, then decrease again to two wraps. e.g. first = two wraps, second = three wraps, third = five wraps, fourth = three wraps, fifth = two wraps, sixth = two wraps. Thread up again with yellow and place a bullion in between each of the brown bullions, increasing and decreasing in size as before. Make wings in gold thread and buttonhole stitch.

Spider and web
Make web with straight stitches for spokes and stem stitches to join the spokes. Attach the spider, which is made of a Granito for the body, French knot for the head and eight straight stitches for the legs, to the web with a straight stitch of gold.

Woman and child 18cm x 13cm (7" x 5")

Understated, Elegant Embroidery

Gary Clarke

Professional art training led Gary Clarke to textile design and from there he moved on to needlework in 1990. Based in Tasmania, he has managed several needlework stores, written many articles for magazines, taught throughout Australia and written five needlework books. Now he travels extensively, demonstrating and teaching and his designs are in great demand as they show the true eye of an artist and he is always generous with information and support.

Woman and child

Requirements

white synthetic organza 40cm x 50cm (16" x 20")

YLI Silk Floss: Black

33 cornflower blue

34 blue

78 gold

112 green

165 mid green

166 light green

182 cream

quilting needle as small as comfortable

pine frame 35cm x 35cm (14" x 14") – see instructions below

Vleisofix

sharp scissors

soft pencil

masking tape

Making the frame

The key to this type of organza embroidery is in the frame. The organza is stretched onto a work frame before it is worked. After the embroidery has been completed the work frame, with its embroidery still in place, is then framed.

4cm (1¹/₂")

1cm (²/₅")

staple the organza to the back of the frame

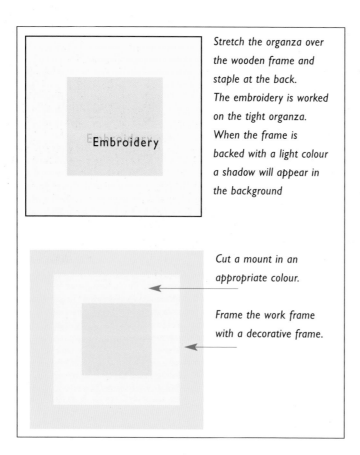

Stretch the organza over the wooden frame and staple at the back.
The embroidery is worked on the tight organza.
When the frame is backed with a light colour a shadow will appear in the background

Cut a mount in an appropriate colour.

Frame the work frame with a decorative frame.

Framing the work frame, and at no time removing the fabric, prevents puckering and distorting of the embroidery.

Organza is very strong and may break the frame joints as it shrinks in changing temperature. Therefore the frame must be as strong as possible. I recommend 4cm x 1cm (1 $^{1}/_{2}$" x $^{2}/_{5}$") dressed pine. This gives strength to prevent bowing, yet the 1cm ($^{2}/_{5}$") thickness is ideal for a spacer between the organza and the back of the frame.

Transferring the design

Make a black and white photocopy of the line drawing and a colour copy of the watercolour painting.

Position the line drawing on the back side of the organza and hold it in place with adhesive tape. Place a book at the back of the organza to give support when tracing the design. Trace the design with a soft lead pencil.

Cut

Enlarge diagrams to 145%

Fastening the colour copy

Fuse the printed side of the colour copy with Vleisofix (fusible webbing). With sharp pointed scissors cut out the area of the design as shown in the illustration, (i.e. the exposed flesh areas or the woman and child.)

From the wrong side position the cut out pieces, place the book as before and iron from the front. Caution: The iron must be as hot as possible without melting the organza.

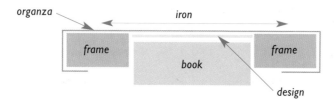

organza *iron*
frame *frame*
book
design

Embroidering the design

Although the organza is a very fine fabric it is not difficult to work on. Use two strands of YLI Silk Floss or one strand of Madeira Silk. Start the stitch with a small knot and finish by threading through the back of your work. When the piece is completed sew in any of the knot tails that might be seen from the front.

Very few stitches are needed in organza work because the underneath stitch is also visible. The stitches are best kept simple and open to enhance the sheerness of the fabric. Be careful not to pull the thread too tight. If the thread in the fabric should become compressed, forming a hole, simply rub over the hole with the back of the needle. Work over a light background to help you see the pencil line.

Begin by following the stitch diagram for an indication of the direction and spacing of the stitches.

Work the striped dress in colours 33, 34, 78. Use the coloured photograph for an indication of the colour placement. Work in Stitch 1. The diagram shows how the stitch is worked.

Work trousers in colours 165, 112 using stitches 1 and 2. Use the coloured photograph for an indication of the colour placement. Stitch 2 is blanket stitch.

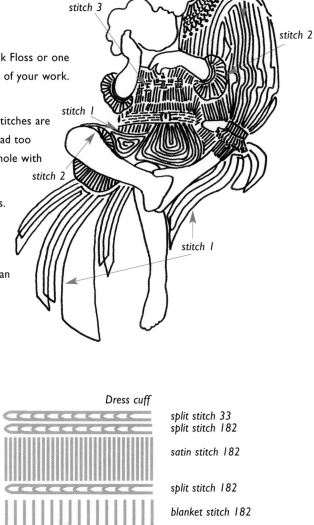

stitch 1

stitch 3

stitch 2

stitch 1

stitch 2

stitch 1

Stitch 1

main stitches on front

thread

organza

small catching stitch on back

thread on the top of the fabric

Stitch 3

thread under the fabric

Dress cuff

split stitch 33
split stitch 182

satin stitch 182

split stitch 182

blanket stitch 182

needlelace c182

satin stitch 78

split stitch 78

Dress collar

blanket stitch

needlelace

open-ended lazy daisy

pistil stitch

Work shirt in colour 166 using stitches 2 (blanket stitch) and 3. The diagram shows how stitch 3 is worked.

Work the dress collar in one strand of 182, using the following stitches.

Work the dress cuffs in one strand of colours 33, 182 and 78. Use the colour photograph as a guide. Work in split, satin, blanket and needlelace stitches, as shown in diagram.

Finish the embroidery by adding shading, using small straight stitches between the existing stitches. Use the coloured photograph as a guide.

Cream on Cream
detail from blanket
36cm x 24cm (14" x 9½")

Soft and Delicate

Christine Harris

The tiniest of stitches and the finest of thread are the hallmarks of much of Christine Harris' embroidery, as shown here in The Parterre Garden. However, she is also a keen embroiderer in wool, loving its soft feel and quick results. Christine, living much of her life in country New South Wales, has developed lovely designs for both her fine work and wool work and has spent recent years as a professional writer and editor of patterns and designs for magazines and books, following a brief time running a needlework supply store.

The Parterre Garden

The inspiration for this design comes from Van Gogh's painting *The Garden of the Hospital at Arles* (1889). The garden is laid out in a traditional pattern of radiating segments surrounded by a 'plante bande'.

Requirements

DMC Stranded Cotton, one hank each of:

211 lavender light	341 blue violet light
369 pistachio green very light	422 hazelnut brown light
472 avocado green ultra light	677 old gold very light
726 topaz light	727 topaz very light
746 off white	762 pearl grey very light
951 sportsman flesh very light	963 dusty rose ultra very light
3052 green grey medium	3053 green grey
3078 golden yellow very light	3363 pine green medium
3722 shell pink medium	3726 antique mauve dark
3743 antique violet very light	3747 blue violet very light
3779 terracotta ultra very light	

30cm (12") 3mm YLI Silk Ribbon No 113 col rose

30cm (12") 2mm YLI Silk Ribbon No 154 col sage

hank of 'Waterlilies' by Caron col eggshell

20cm x 20cm (8" x 8") calico which has been washed and ironed

sharp 2B lead pencil

10cm (4") embroidery hoop

Nos 8, 9 and 10 crewel needles

No 10 chenille needle

The Parterre Garden
5.7cm x 5.7cm (2¹/₄" x 2¹/₄")

Special notes:

With the exception of the straight lines in the path, all the embroidery is worked in single twist French knots. When instructions are given for a certain number of knots in an area, this is meant as a guide only. Each embroiderer works at a different tension. Use the No 10 crewel needle for a single strand of thread, No 9 for two strands of thread and No 8 for three or more strands. Use the chenille needle for the silk ribbon. Where two or more colours are given for particular knots, these colours are blended in the same needle to give subtle shading. Use the sharp lead pencil and your preferred light source and lightly trace the design onto the calico, taking care to keep the straight lines of the design on the grain of the fabric. Place the fabric into the hoop and stretch until taut.

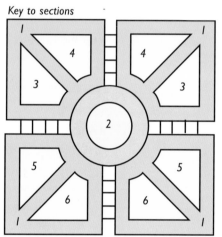

Key to sections

Section 1. Combine a single strand of 3052, 3053 and 472 and work knots closely together along the centre of the area so that approximately half the area is filled. Then, using a single strand each of 3053 and 472, work knots closely along both edges of those already worked, so that almost the whole area is filled.

To finish these little hedges, use a single strand of 3053 or 472, fill any small gaps along the edges, taking care to maintain the straight lines.

Section 2. Fill the area with knots using 3mm rose silk ribbon, concentrating the knots towards the centre of the circle and staying within the dotted line. Then, using 2mm sage silk ribbon, scatter about five knots through those already worked. Using a single strand each of 341 and 3747, fill the remaining area with knots. To finish this garden bed, use a single strand of tiny knots around the outer edge of the circle.

Section 3. Using three strands of 726, together with one strand of 727, work clusters of knots though the area. Then, using two strands each of 3779 and 951, scatter knots at random between those already worked.

Scatter eight to ten knots between those already worked, using three strands of 3722. With a single strand of 3052, fill any small spaces with tiny knots.

Section 4. Using two strands of 727 together with one strand of 677, work approximately 16 – 18 knots, evenly distributed throughout the area. Then, using two strands of 3726 together with one strand of 963, work as above.

Using two strands of 963 together with one strand of 677, repeat, as above, however, as the area is filling, sit a few knots on top of those already worked to give a little dimension to the work.

Finish this section by filling any small gaps with tiny knots using a single strand of 3363.

Section 5. Using two strands of 762 and 3743, work approximately 10 knots through the area. Using two strands each of 3743 and 775, work approximately 25 knots throughout the area. Then, using one strand each of 211 and 3053, scatter knots throughout the section. Using two strands of 369, work about 20 knots over those already worked. Work some tiny knots over the whole section using a single strand of 3363.

Section 6. With two strands each of 3078 and 727, work four clusters of three knots. Then, using two strands each of 963 and 746, work as above. Scatter some knots through those already worked using two strands of 746. To finish the section, use a single strand of 3053, work tiny knots between and over those already worked.

Section 7.   The Paths. Work the straight stitch lines on the pathways where indicated, using a single strand of 422. Then, using a single strand of Caron eggshell, work tiny knots over the whole area, taking care not to cover the straight stitches. Do not work these knots as closely together as previously worked. The knots in the pathway should not quite touch.

Cream on Cream

Requirements

purchased satin-bound basinet blanket 120cm x 80cm (48" x 32")   two hanks Appletons' Crewel Wool No 991 cream
DMC Stranded Cotton: ecru and No 5282 metallic gold   No 7 crewel needle
Nos 18 & 22 chenille needle   No 1 straw needle

Special notes:

Use the straw needle for the French knots, the No 7 crewel needle for the small satin stitch flowers, the No 22 chenille for the stems and leaves and the No 18 chenille for the large satin stitch daisies and the small straight stitch flowers .

Use the Appletons' Crewel Wool for all embroidery unless otherwise stated. The large satin stitch daisies and buds, the straight stitch flowers and the bow are worked with two strands of Appletons' 991. The stems and leaves are worked with a single strand of wool. Transfer the design from the photograph and enlarge to 140 per cent. Be careful if using lead pencil as this may mark the blanketing and leave smudge marks. Tacking lines are recommended for the bow and perhaps just a knot through the tracing paper to mark the position of the large daisies. It is not necessary to mark in the small flowers as they are there to fill any small spaces. You may choose to draw in some naturally curved lines for the stems. If you feel that you need to trace the design, use tacking stitches rather than any type of pen to avoid any soiling.

The bow: To work the padded satin stitch, outline both edges of the bow with a running stitch and work another running stitch through the centre of those just worked. Satin stitch over the padding keeping the stitches as even as possible.

Large satin stitch daisies: Each flower has seven or eight petals and each petal has five stitches. Depending on your tension you may have more or less petals, however, do try to keep the number constant. Tip the edge of each petal with fly stitch using two strands of ecru stranded cotton. The centre of each flower is filled with French knots worked with six strands of ecru together with one strand of metallic gold. Use a single strand of metallic gold in a No 7 crewel needle to work the straight stitch between the petals. If you work part flowers in the design, finish each partial flower with two or three French knots for the centre and work a straight stitch on the outside of the petals.

Straight stitch flowers: Work five small petals. Each petal consists of two stitches side by side. The flower is finished with a French knot centre.

Stems and leaves: These are worked with a single strand of wool. The stems are worked in stem stitch and the leaves are closed fly stitch. Begin each leaf with a long stitch for the tip of the leaf.

Daisy buds: Each bud is worked at the end of a stem and is stitched in the same way as the daisy petal but taking six or seven stitches into the same holes to make a firm, plump bud. The stitches are slightly longer than those for the petals. To finish the buds, take six strands of ecru and strip the thread. Work two straight stitches, side by side, across the base of the bud and then two more straight stitches across the base from the opposite side. Use a single strand of ecru to work a fly stitch at the tip of the bud. Fill any small spaces in the design with small satin stitch flowers worked with two strands of ecru.

Old Ivory and Gold

Helen Eriksson

Three dimensional ribbon embroidery has had a renaissance in recent years, and Helen Eriksson has led the way with her original designs and stitching. She uses only the richest, most delicate and luxurious silk ribbons, linens and velvets to create her realistic work. Her passion is flowers, and she creates lifelike versions in perfectly colour matched ribbons. The ribbons available today, some hand dyed, some double sided, some edged, and all in beautiful silks and with threads to match, make her work possible, as she carefully colour matches each flower to her ribbons and threads.

Requirements

cream damask 50cm x 45cm (20" x 18")

1 packet Madeira Metallic Thread No 5017 black/gold

YLI Fine Metallic Thread No 601 gold

Kacoonda Silk Ribbon:

     2 metres (80") 13mm No 303 variegated cream pink

     2 metres (80") 7mm No 303 variegated cream pink

     5 metres (5^1/2 yards) 7mm No 4 variegated cream

     4 metres (4^1/2 yards) 7mm No 307 variegated dark greens

     5 metres (5^1/2 yards) 4mm No 307 variegated dark greens

     4 metres (4^1/2 yards) 4mm No 104 variegated greens

     4 metres (4^1/2 yards) 4mm No 4 variegated cream

     4 metres (4^1/2 yards) 4mm No 8J variegated pale green

     5 metres (5^1/2 yards) 4mm No 107 variegated taupe/cream

2 packets Kacoonda Fine Silk Thread No 104 variegated greens

4 metres (4^1/2 yards) YLI Silk Ribbon 4mm No 54 old gold

2 metres (80") ^{7}/16" (10mm) Hanah Silk Ribbon Mossy Rock, yellow green

4 metres (4^1/2 yards") ^{7}/16" (10mm) Hanah Silk Ribbon Old Ivory, cream with tan edges

1 skein Marlitt Thread No 1140 tan

1 skein Marlitt Thread No 1036 cream/gold

1 skein Marlitt Thread No 1037 gold/beige

1 skein Marlitt Thread No 1077 gold

1 skein Edmar Glory Thread No 110 variegated green 1 skein Anchor Stranded Cotton No 901 col old gold

Old Ivory and Gold
38cm x 30cm
(15" x 12")

Helen Eriksson

1 skein Anchor Stranded Cotton No 926 cream

1 packet Delica Beads copper gold

milliners needles Nos 3 and 8

fabric pen

1 packet Delica Beads bright gold

chenille needles Nos 16, 18, 20, 24

crewel needle No 7

large hoop (optional)

Place the pattern on the material and mark the placement of the scrolls and urn using a fabric pen. If you prefer to use a hoop, insert fabric in hoop. Make sure it is large enough to cover the working area, otherwise the hoop can leave marks on the fabric.

Thread a chenille needle No 20 with Madeira Metallic Thread No 5017 black/gold. Stem stitch around the outline of the scrolls, keeping the stitches and tension even as you stitch. Keep the thread on the outside of the curve when stem stitching, not on the inside, for this will define the curve shapes as well. When the first outline is completed, add a second row, stitching it very close to the first row.

When all the scrolls are stitched in, add the trellis. Thread a chenille needle no 24 with the YLI Fine Metallic Thread No 601 gold. Stitch the lines going one way, then add the lines crossing the other way, catching them down in some places.

Peony roses

Thread a chenille needle No 16 with Kacoonda Silk Ribbon 4mm No 4 variegated cream and stitch in the peony roses. Stitch the cream roses in the centre of the urn. There are three at the top, then one on each side, draping outside the urn. Before beginning a rose, take note which direction it is facing.

Thread a chenille needle No 20 with YLI Silk Ribbon 4mm No 54 old gold. Add French knots in the centre, pulling the tension tight and covering the material so it does not show through.

Add the final bowl petals in ribbon stitch with Kacoonda Silk Ribbon 7mm No 4 variegated cream, and shape the rose by adding more petals around the edges. You will need a large needle to cope with the layers of ribbon.

Continue to add the other peony roses.

Thread a chenille needle No 18 with Kacoonda Silk Ribbon 7mm No 307 variegated dark green. Ribbon stitch leaves randomly around each rose in groups of three or five, butting them up close and some slightly underneath.

Thread a crewel needle No 7 with Kacoonda Fine Silk Thread No 104 variegated green and hook each leaf and add a stem in couched thread if it needs it.

1. Draw the shape on with a fabric pen.

2. Ribbon stitch the petals in place, following the position of the numbers.

3. Add the bowl petals. Ribbon stitch them in following the numbers, stitching through the base petals as you go.

Gilda rose sprays

Following the pattern, with a fabric pen mark the placement of the gilda rose sprays and circle the heads. Thread a chenille needle No 20 with Kacoonda Silk Ribbon 4mm No 107 variegated taupe/cream. Starting on one side of the circle, ribbon stitch tiny stitches, forming a small forget-me-not flower. Continue to stitch these in with four to five petals, clustering them together to fill the circle. Helen has used three blending colours in the 4mm ribbon, so use the three in each flower head. Change the proportion of each in the individual flower to add interest. The Kacoonda Silk Ribbons are:

4mm No 4 variegated cream

4mm No 8J variegated pale green

4mm No 107 variegated taupe/cream.

When the flower heads are stitched, thread a crewel needle No 7 with Kacoonda Fine Silk Thread No 104 variegated greens and add a French knot in the centre of each flower.

Using the same needle and thread stem stitch down the stem to the base.

When you have completed all the flower heads and stems, add the fern like leaves. Thread a chenille needle No 20 with Kacoonda Silk Ribbon 4mm No 307 variegated dark green. Ribbon stitch the leaves by making the middle petals longer than the side ones. Alter the shape of each leaf by making some smaller and some larger and wider. Hook each leaf up and attach it to the stem.

Remember to add the three roses down at the base of the urn.

Ribbon stitch leaf and hooking up stitch

1. Pierce the ribbon with the needle at the length you require for the leaf. Pull the needle through to the back and pull the ribbon until the ends roll into a point.

2. Bring the thread up just underneath the leaf and run the back of the needle underneath the ribbon. (This is to prevent piercing the ribbon with the point of the needle.)

3. Pull the thread through and bring up through the loop before pulling the thread into a tight knot.

Bullion roses

Mark the placement of the bullion roses.

Thread a milliners needle No 3 with two strands of Marlitt Thread No 1077 gold. Commence the centre, wrapping the thread around the needle eight times. Stitch three bullions side by side.

Change the thread to two strands of Marlitt Thread No 1037 gold/beige. Starting at the top of the centre bullion and working clockwise, continue adding bullions around the centre three. Because the rose will be increased in size, as you add bullions you must increase the wraps around the needle. Start each bullion half way over the bullion before so that you will give an overlapping effect to the rose.

Change the thread for the third time to two strands of Marlitt Thread No 1036 cream/gold. Commence the second round and add extra wraps. Complete all the bullion roses.

Add tiny leaves around the roses. Thread a chenille needle No 20 with Kacoonda Silk Ribbon 4mm No 307 variegated dark green and in a separate needle 4mm No 104 variegated green. Use both these colours to ribbon stitch the leaves in to give a contrast in greens.

Foxglove sprays

Following the pattern, mark the placement in with a fabric pen.

Thread a chenille needle No 16 with $^7/_{16}$" (10mm) Hanah Silk Ribbon Old Ivory, cream with tan edges. Stitch two ribbon stitches side by side for the base. Add one to two ribbon stitches either side of the base petals, piercing the ribbon on the side, not the middle, so that the ribbon rolls back and leaves a little fold. For example, if you have stitched the ribbon stitch on the left side of the base petals, you should pierce the ribbon on the left side of the ribbon and vice versa for the right side.

Fill the centre of the flower with French knots. Thread a milliners needle No 8 with two strands of Anchor Stranded Cotton No 901 old gold. Wrap twice around the needle for each French knot. Fill the centres, almost covering the base petals.

Add the green base and stems. Thread a crewel needle No 7 with Kacoonda Fine Silk Thread No 104 variegated green and stitch straight stitches across the bottom of the flower, stitching through the Old Ivory ribbon. Continue stem stitching in the stems.

Stitch all the leaves in place in fly stitch. Thread a crewel needle No 7 with Kacoonda Fine Silk Thread No 104 variegated green and make sure to keep all the fly stitches compact.

Hand made folded roses

Thread a milliners needle No 8 with one strand of Anchor Stranded Cotton No 926 cream. Make twelve folded roses with the Kacoonda Silk Ribbon 13mm No 303 variegated cream pink. With the Kacoonda Silk Ribbon 7mm No 303 variegated cream pink make eight small roses.

Following the pattern, stitch the roses onto the fabric, carefully stitching through the folds of the ribbon. Make sure the roses are facing towards you as they usually have a distinct front and back look.

When you are happy with the results, add the leaves around each rose. Thread a chenille needle No 16 with $^7/_{16}$" (10mm) Hanah Ribbon Mossy Rock, yellow green, and ribbon stitch the leaves close to each rose.

Queen Ann's lace

Mark the placement of the Queen Ann's lace and draw the shape of the flowerhead with a fabric pen.

Thread a crewel needle No 7 with one strand of Marlitt Thread No 1140 tan. Stem stitch the curved lines of the flowerhead, then continue to stitch the stem in.

Using a beading needle or a fine milliners needle and Anchor Stranded Cotton No 901 old gold, stitch bright gold metallic beads onto the ends of the flowerheads, scattering them at random.

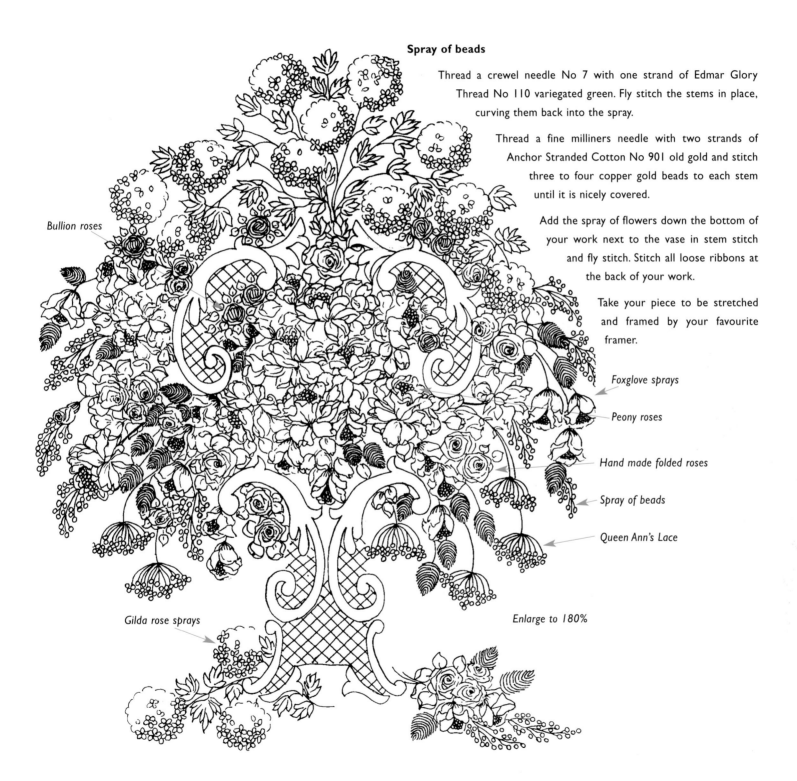

Spray of beads

Thread a crewel needle No 7 with one strand of Edmar Glory Thread No 110 variegated green. Fly stitch the stems in place, curving them back into the spray.

Thread a fine milliners needle with two strands of Anchor Stranded Cotton No 901 old gold and stitch three to four copper gold beads to each stem until it is nicely covered.

Add the spray of flowers down the bottom of your work next to the vase in stem stitch and fly stitch. Stitch all loose ribbons at the back of your work.

Take your piece to be stretched and framed by your favourite framer.

Bullion roses

Foxglove sprays

Peony roses

Hand made folded roses

Spray of beads

Queen Ann's Lace

Gilda rose sprays

Enlarge to 180%

Sumptuous Embroidery

Kaye Pyke

A woman who has inspired countless numbers to take up embroidery, Kaye Pyke is one of the most innovative and original embroiderers working today. Through her books and classes she has introduced women around the world to the joys of working with beautiful and fine fabrics, silken threads, cords and ribbons, all decorated with jewel-like beads, tassels and other embellishments. Kaye has used her great sense of style and design in a range of work, from interiors, through to furniture coverings, her classic cushions and fine elegant embroidery.

Perhaps best known for her three dimensional ribbon embroidery on cushions and her lavish and luxurious settings, Kaye is always looking to develop different ways of working. Here she has produced a beautiful print of a Spode jug on silk, and embellished it with ribbon silk, beads and silver threads.

Spode jug embellished
17cm x 14cm (6³/4" x 5¹/2")

Kaye Pyke

Goldwork

June Fiford

Precious metal is used by June Fiford to give importance and emphasis to the traditional art of embroidery – to give it the value it deserves. In White Cloth 11 for example, she has taken a piece of her grandmother's traditional whitework from a tablecloth and reinterpreted it in gold, capturing the memory of a valued object and creating from it another precious object. Interested in her family's history, skills and traditions, she enjoys the time-consuming medium of embroidery as it allows her to slow down and appreciate the richness of family experience.

All of June's work, however, is not focussed on the past, nor is it soft in design and hue. Falling Colours is based on a kaleidoscope, using bright colours with gold.

An accomplished embroiderer and teacher, June attended the Royal School of Needlework in England in 1989, and there her eyes were opened to the beauty of goldwork. Her works are embroidered on silk using metal thread embroidery (goldwork) techniques of couching and purlwork with coloured stitchery in silk. They contain 2 per cent gold twist thread and Japanese gold substitute thread which is a plated alloy bonded to rice paper and twisted around a silk core. The gold threads are attached by a fine silk couching thread, or, in purlwork, a fine wire is coiled into a spring and cut and sewn on as in beading.

Coastal Book
18cm x 15cm (7" x 6")

White Cloth II
18cm x 20cm (7" x 8")

Falling Colours
5.5cm (2 1/8") each side

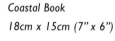

Embellishments

Susan Dickens

One of the most creative embroiderers, Susan Dickens has become best known for her tassels, which she first worked when she was unable to find suitable embellishments for her embroidery. Almost 10 years ago she was searching for tassels to hang from her lovely embroidered cushions and began to experiment with making them herself, playing with colours, textures and sizes to suit her other work.

Her much sought after books offer large numbers of suggestions for combining the shapes and designs of her tassels, allowing others to make their work individual. She explains that making a tassel is like making a new dress, fitting together all the elements to make one cohesive and attractive whole, while adding personal touches to make it unique.

Meanwhile, surrounded by tassels, Susan still enjoys working her beautiful embroideries, and other embellished objects such as the needlecase described here

Needlecase

Requirements

1 brass needlecase made up of one short and one long tube
2 metres (80") strip 1.5cm (^{1}/2") wide light weight wadding

NYMO thread	2 dacron circles
4cm (1^1/2") masking tape	2.5 metres (2^3/4 yards) 12mm (^{1}/2") ribbon
Madeira silk floss	selection of embroidery threads
3 metres (4 yards) gold thread	Madeira Metallic Spiral
19 small gold beads	1 larger gold bead
pins	No 10 milliners needle or bead needle
No 7 chenille needle or wool needle	spray glue

Embellished needlecase
11cm x 2cm (4^1/4 x ^{3}/4")

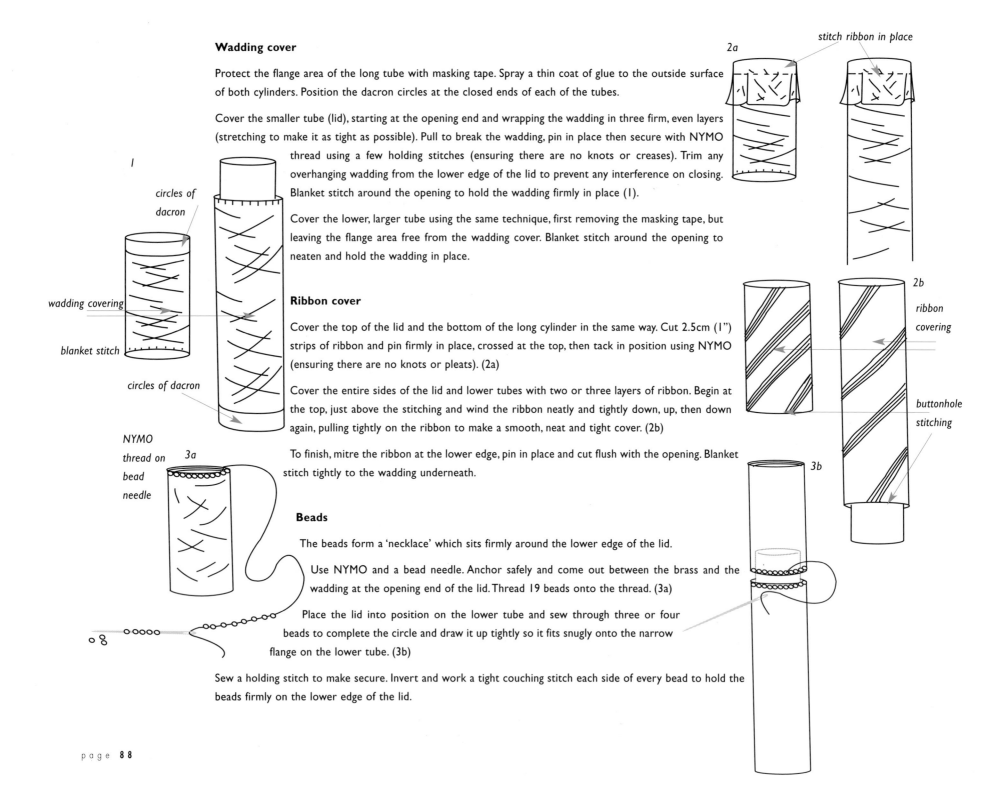

Wadding cover

Protect the flange area of the long tube with masking tape. Spray a thin coat of glue to the outside surface of both cylinders. Position the dacron circles at the closed ends of each of the tubes.

Cover the smaller tube (lid), starting at the opening end and wrapping the wadding in three firm, even layers (stretching to make it as tight as possible). Pull to break the wadding, pin in place then secure with NYMO thread using a few holding stitches (ensuring there are no knots or creases). Trim any overhanging wadding from the lower edge of the lid to prevent any interference on closing. Blanket stitch around the opening to hold the wadding firmly in place (1).

Cover the lower, larger tube using the same technique, first removing the masking tape, but leaving the flange area free from the wadding cover. Blanket stitch around the opening to neaten and hold the wadding in place.

Ribbon cover

Cover the top of the lid and the bottom of the long cylinder in the same way. Cut 2.5cm (1") strips of ribbon and pin firmly in place, crossed at the top, then tack in position using NYMO (ensuring there are no knots or pleats). (2a)

Cover the entire sides of the lid and lower tubes with two or three layers of ribbon. Begin at the top, just above the stitching and wind the ribbon neatly and tightly down, up, then down again, pulling tightly on the ribbon to make a smooth, neat and tight cover. (2b)

To finish, mitre the ribbon at the lower edge, pin in place and cut flush with the opening. Blanket stitch tightly to the wadding underneath.

Beads

The beads form a 'necklace' which sits firmly around the lower edge of the lid.

Use NYMO and a bead needle. Anchor safely and come out between the brass and the wadding at the opening end of the lid. Thread 19 beads onto the thread. (3a)

Place the lid into position on the lower tube and sew through three or four beads to complete the circle and draw it up tightly so it fits snugly onto the narrow flange on the lower tube. (3b)

Sew a holding stitch to make secure. Invert and work a tight couching stitch each side of every bead to hold the beads firmly on the lower edge of the lid.

circles of dacron

wadding covering

blanket stitch

circles of dacron

NYMO thread on bead needle

stitch ribbon in place

2a

2b

ribbon covering

buttonhole stitching

3a

3b

Embellishments

On the lower cylinder work a row of chain stitch around the top edge and whip.

Wrap silk floss tightly around the cylinder to form a barber shop pole stripe. Anchor at the bottom in line with the starting point at the top. Wind back up tightly to make the lattice pattern and anchor at the top. Make sure the cross overs at the back are even.

Border each side of the floss with gold thread.

Sew a large bead in place at the top anchor point, knotting the thread twice either side of the bead..

On the lid, work a row of chain stitch at the top edge and whip.

Either embellish the lid in the same way as the long cylinder or work detached buttonhole stitch to cover the top.

Work a detached buttonhole stitch loop on the lower edge close to the beaded rim, to fit over the large bead on the lower cylinder.

Embellish the top and bottom ends of the needlecase with embroidery.

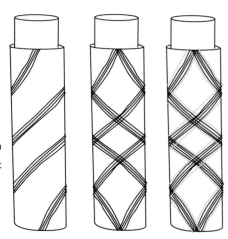

Embellished tassel
28cm (11") including fringe

Nostalgia

Judith Coombe and Kathryn Thompson

Victorian parlour dolls –
Henrietta and
Alexandra
Judith Coombe

South Australian artists Judith Coombe and Kathryn Thompson have a unique partnership. They work closely together and travel on business together, but do not have a joint retail shop, studio or workshop. They create their nostalgic pieces individually, in their own homes. Yet together they have created a range of commercial products which others can buy to emulate their work, or to use in quite different designs. These are sold under the label of Judith & Kathryn Designs.

Judith and Kathryn studied together at the South Australian School of Art. Ten years later they began making and selling bread dough Christmas decorations. These inspired brooches, with themes to suit Easter, Valentine's Day, Mother's Day, proved a commercial success. The simple bread dough designs were the beginning of a thriving business, with products ranging from decorative pieces to wear, to handmade and handpainted items for crafts and embroidery. They produce silk prints of elegant Victorian ladies, cottages and flower baskets, hand dyed laces in a range of colours, hand dyed ribbons, roses, fabrics and tassels.

Judith and Kathryn have produced everything from silk dolls, painted porcelain and plaster ornaments, doll jewellery, designed framed pieces, cushions, small quilts and exquisite miniatures. They have worked with other artists such as Jenny Haskins, Helen Eriksson, Nerida Singleton and Ruth Stoneley, to name only a few, to create interpretations of their ideas and designs.

While their work reflects nostalgic and floral themes, they are boundlessly creative and open to new ideas and influences.

Victorian Parlour Dolls – Henrietta and Alexandra

Judith Coombe

These silk faced dolls have been completely stitched by hand and all the materials used have been hand dyed to suit Judith's love of subtle yet rich colours. She has indulged her everlasting love of things from the past by incorporating precious pieces of antique jewellery with new fabrics and laces especially coloured to look like aged and faded garments, all glowing with the richness of beads and jewellery.

Layer upon layer of texture and colour and intricate contrasts bring to life the tiny form of Judith's parlour dolls, evoking memories of the past with all their richness and warmth.

Requirements

silk print of a Victorian lady

2 or 3 pieces of hand coloured lace

35cm x 15cm (14" x 6") dyed fringing

neutral coloured sewing cotton

pins

lead pencil

assorted small beads in greens, purples and neutral colours

15cm x 10cm (6" x 4") piece of fine fabric in a neutral colour

1 or 2 pieces of tea dyed lace

polyester filling

beading needle and thread

sharp scissors

ribbons and trims in matching colours

favourite pieces of old jewellery – brooches or earrings are suitable

Tape the silk print onto a window and with the lead pencil trace around the outline on the back of the print. Allow at least 1mm ($^1/_{16}$") around the outside edge of the print, curving in near the waistline of the doll.

Place the silk picture face down onto the piece of fine fabric, pinning in several places to hold it in place. Don't trim the fabric at this stage.

Starting at point 1 and using neutral coloured sewing cotton, stitch all the way around with a small backstitch until you reach point 2. (Refer to the diagram.) Backstitch several times at the beginning and the end to secure the thread.

Carefully cut around the figure 5mm ($^1/_5$") away from the stitched edge, and cut straight down to the bottom edge of the print at both sides (point 3 and 4) as shown in the diagram.

Starting at point 1, cut tiny slits into the seam allowance all the way around, until you reach point 2. Carefully turn the figure right side out, using the blunt end of the pencil to help manipulate the shape from inside.

Insert the polyester filling a little at a time through the bottom opening, using the end of the pencil to push it right up to the top of the head. When the whole figure is filled to the point of being quite firm pin across the bottom to close the opening between points 1 and 2. Stitch this area firmly shut. Fold up the rest of the fabric between the area of points 1 to 4 and stitch together to create a small tab.

Using the beading needle and neutral coloured thread, quilt through the figure over the bodice area and add a few stitches in the hair. Start the thread in the seam, backstitch several times and bring the thread out somewhere in the front of the dress. Take the thread back in again, very close to where it came out, and, keep doing this while controlling where you want the needle to come out. You will find it easier to decide where to bring the needle out by pressing down with your thumb to see how the figure will look when being pulled in by the next stitch.

Wrap the fringing around the bottom of the tab at points 3 and 4, wrapping three to four times in the same place and then moving slightly higher each time until you have reached the waistline. Pin the fringing into place. (Practise doing this several times so that you don't end up with too much fringing at the waist.) Secure the fringing into position by stitching straight through from the back to the front from the lower edge of the tab up to the waist area, until all the fringing is stitched into place.

Drape, wrap, fold, pleat, tuck, turn and manipulate the hand coloured lace around the doll shape, pinning it into position as you go. Create shawls, capes, bustles or cloaks, simply pinning the lace down as you place and shape the garment for your doll. If

Birds in my garden lace cushion – Judith Coombe

necessary the lace can also be cut and replaced or rearranged as necessary and then pinned into place.

Drape a piece of coloured netting or some beautiful tea dyed lace across the top half of the fringing to help form a skirt, pinning the edges underneath the coloured lace at each side.

At this stage take some neutral coloured cotton and stitch all of the lace firmly onto the doll, stitching straight through from back to front until everything is secure. Remove each pin as you stitch the garments on.

Now is the time to embellish your parlour doll. Pin on brooches or earrings and stitch into place. Add beads, following the lines and curves of the lace and linking the jewellery to the rest of the doll by stitching beads around and through the jewellery. Add velvet or silk ribbons and stitch onto your doll.

No two of these dolls will ever be alike, as laces and trim will vary, as will the special treasures which are added to each one according to the whims of their creator. You might even consider stitching a twisted cord to the top of your parlour doll and suddenly you have turned it into a most elegant Victorian tassel lady.

Birds in My Garden Lace Cushion

The lace cushion has been constructed by layering pieces of hand dyed lace over velvet, allowing the rich purples and golds to glow through the lace. Forest green hand dyed silk has been scrunched (twisted tightly while wet and allowed to dry while twisted), then layered under and over the lace pieces, giving added texture and dimension to the cushion.

Delicate lace birds perch on their branches among softly coloured roses. Glowing with a silken sheen, dainty tendrils and leaves are cut from fine lace netting and hand stitched down – companions to the silk ribbon, softly shaded violets and leaves meandering gently across the centre of the cushion. Beads and crystals in varying shades of green glisten and weave their patterns and rhythms.

The antique brooch and old mauve flowers are sentimental additions to this little scented cushion (lavender filled).

Romantic Violet

Kathryn Thompson

Requirements

hand dyed lace, V-shaped collar motif	silk print of lady with violets, 9cm x 13cm (3^1/2" x 5")
2 large bread dough pansies	1 tiny bread dough pansy
24cm x 26cm (9^1/2" x 10^1/2") plain fabric	2 packets 30mm (1") Vintage Silk Ribbon, old violet
white embroidery thread	foam-core board 18cm x 19cm (7" x 7^1/2")
polyester wadding	tacky craft glue
pins	embroidery scissors
matching sewing thread	chenille needle No 24
sharp needle No 8	

2m (80") 13mm (^{1}/2") hand dyed silk ribbon, mauve, for ruffle effect

15cm (6") 13mm (^{1}/2") hand dyed variegated purple silk ribbon, for large pansy

1m (40") 4mm (^{1}/8") hand dyed silk ribbon, dark purple, for violets

2m (80") 4mm (^{1}/8") hand dyed silk ribbon variegated purples, for ruched braids

1m (40") 4mm (^{1}/8") hand dyed silk ribbon, pale lavender, for tiny violets

1m (40") 4mm (^{1}/8") hand dyed silk ribbon, for leaves

50cm (20") 4mm (^{1}/8") hand dyed silk ribbon, golden, for pansy centre

DMC Stranded Cotton No 729 yellow, for bullion centres

Place silk print into the centre of the plain fabric and, using matching sewing thread and the sharp No 8 needle, stitch small tacking stitches around the edge of the print. Carefully press all ribbons, with iron on silk setting, before beginning embroidery.

Romantic Violet

Kathryn Thompson

The violets

Begin by stitching the surface flowers on the silk print. The violets are created with the 4mm (^{1}/8") silk ribbon in dark purple and pale lavender, with five petals in ribbon stitch using the No 24 chenille needle. They are placed randomly in a sweeping movement along the right hand side and around the body of the lady to enhance printed violets which are not stitched over. The small leaves are worked in ribbon stitch with the 4mm (^{1}/8") hand dyed green silk ribbon, while the larger leaves around the ribbon pansies are formed by a loose lazy daisy stitch infilled with a ribbon stitch.

Scatter french knots using 4mm (^{1}/8") hand dyed silk ribbon in dark purple and pale lavender for tiny buds and to create a filled in effect. Work out the placement of the bread dough pansies and leave free of embroidery so the pieces can be glued flat against the silk when the piece is finished.

Silk ribbon frame

Take the 30mm (1") Vintage Silk Ribbon, old violet and join into position along the left hand side of the print, across the top and down the right hand side, gently mitring the corners. Use pins again to hold the ribbon in place on the right hand side to create the ruched effect. Then stitch down with tiny stab stitches using a matching sewing thread and a No 8 sharp needle. Repeat the process with strips of the 30mm (1") Vintage Silk Ribbon right around the picture, this time to achieve a random frame, butting joins at the corners and loosely gathering on the bottom left hand corner.

The lace

Place the coloured lace around the print so as to enhance the picture and your embroidery. Using the photograph as a guide, carefully snip away joining threads of any pieces that interrupt the flow of your design and replace in any areas that need filling in. Pin into position. Using tiny invisible stitches on the front and large stitches on the back, secure all the lace to your work with matching sewing thread.

With the 13mm ('/2") hand dyed silk ribbon in mauve, loosely tuck, drape and twist it around the lace across the bottom and up the left hand side, covering the joins in the ribbon and filling in spaces with a textural effect. Pin in place as you go, then return and secure with tiny stab stitches.

4   5

bullion centre

Pansies

1

2cm

pull

For the two lower pansies, choose the appropriate colours from your ribbon and cut two x 2cm (⁴/₅") sections, placing them at right angles to each other. Using a matching sewing thread and No 8 sharp needle, stitch around the edges as shown in the diagram and gather up as tightly as possible to form the top two petals.

2.5cm

6

From a slightly contrasting coloured section of the ribbon, cut an 8cm (3") piece and fold into a U-shape. Stitch, as before, according to the diagram and gather up to form the lower three petals.

pull

2

3

3cm

2.5cm   2.5cm

Join the five petals carefully to form the pansy and then add white French knots and, using two strands of DMC Stranded Cotton No 729 Col Yellow in the No 8 sharp needle, work an eight wrap bullion for the centres.

For the larger pansy, cut 2.5cm (1") lengths of 13mm ('/2") hand dyed silk ribbon. Fold in thirds lengthwise and place the two pieces at right angles. This fold will give a double petal effect. Stitch according to diagram. Gather and secure. This forms two double petals for the top.

For the lower petal, take 3cm (1¹/₅") of the 13mm ('/2") hand dyed silk ribbon, fold in half and gather from the folded edge along the raw edges and back to the folded edge. Pull up firmly to form one petal. Stitch this to the top petals with matching sewing thread and work one ribbon stitch

fold in thirds

7

8

9

10

pull   3cm

11

folded edge

ribbon stitch centre

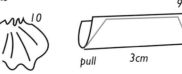

Crazy patchwork –
Trailing roses
Kathryn Thompson

with the chenille needle and 4mm ($^1/_8$") golden hand dyed silk ribbon for the centre. Attach the three pansies to the print with tiny stab stitches.

Narrow ruched ribbon

This effect is created by taking little stitches along the length of the ribbon for about 2cm ($^4/_5$") and then gathering up and stitching back down into the fabric in almost the same place, creating little rosette effects. Move along 3 – 4mm ($^1/_8$") and repeat the process, creating an interesting little 'braid' effect. Use this technique to fill in areas, and hide joins in the ribbon down the right hand side, and to follow movements on the left hand side. Decide for yourself when to place the ribbon as by this stage each piece of work is individual.

Finishing

Cut thin wadding to fit the piece of foam-core board and stretch the underlying fabric over by lacing the back firmly. Attach the bread dough pansies with tacky craft glue. Your embroidery is now ready to be taken to the framer.

Crazy Patchwork – Trailing Roses

This piece was inspired by a workshop with Judith Baker Montano. The crazy patchwork is created using the techniques which Judith uses by building outward from a five-sided picture as the starting point. Various related colour fabrics (satins, silks, laces and damasks) are used to create an interesting textured crazy patchwork for over-working with old laces, braids and hand-dyed laces. Silk ribbons and embroidery threads have been used to richly embellish the joins with a variety of stitches and techniques.

Experiment with:

twisted ribbon roses – concertina roses – French knot ribbon roses – spider web roses – grub roses

Use lazy daisy ribbon buds and ribbon stitch leaves and lots of silk ribbon French knots to fill in spaces and create tails. Chain stitch, looped chain stitch and feather stitch are used along the ditches and whatever other decorative stitches you can create or invent.

Interesting effects can be created with 4mm ($^1/_8$") ribbon by gathering and stitching or by creating a flower braid by gathering and leaving a 1cm ($^2/_5$") gap, then gathering, then a gap, and so on. Gathered Mokuba ribbon creates interesting little flowers. Seal one end with a flame, gather up with the inbuilt gathering thread, then pull as tightly as possible before sealing off the other end with the flame. Last, add charms, tiny buttons or any other appropriate memorabilia. A piece like this is lots of fun as it just grows and is limited only by your imagination.

Needlelace

Christine Bishop

Christine Bishop is well known for her interest in fine embroidery and laces of the past, the re-creation of original patterns and designs; and for her skill in passing on her passion to others through her regular classes and workshops. In 1971 she purchased a copy of Frederick Vinciolo's book *Renaissance Patterns for Lace, Embroidery and Needlepoint*, first published in 1587, and it sparked a desire to embroider an example of punto in aria, a lace originating in Italy. It took her twenty years to fulfil this desire. In the meantime she studied further and worked other embroideries which included needlelace, but it wasn't until recent years that she began working in the areas of pure lace, culminating in this example of punto in aria.

Punto in aria translates as 'stitches in the air', and the term was used originally to describe raised embroideries. In the sixteenth century it was used to describe embroidery worked over a cut work grid and later the name was transferred to the needlelace worked free of the grid. Punto in aria was at its peak in the late sixteenth and early seventeenth century when millstone ruffs would take up to 21.6 metres (24 yards) of lace. (The distance around this mat is a mere 60cm (24").) Embroiderers in the sixteenth century worked with fine 200+ linen thread, under appallingly damp conditions, with poor light for up to eighteen hours per day, six and a half days per week. As the linen thread had to be worked while damp, many died of what was then known as 'consumption'.

Requirements

14cm x 20cm (5¹/₂" x 8") fine linen (Kingston, church linen or heavy handkerchief linen) for the centre

ball of ecru No 100 Cordonnet Special DMC thread

ball of ecru No 10 Cordonnet Special DMC thread (for the foundation cord)

2 x No 7 crewel needles

No 24 Piecemaker tapestry needle

ecru tacking thread

A4 sheet of light card

blue or pink 'contact' adhesive film

dry stick glue

Punto in aria cloth
27cm x 21cm (10³/₄" x 8¹/₂")

Photocopy the design from the photograph and trim the paper back to the design edge. Cut the adhesive film slightly larger than the design sheet. Using the glue fasten the centre of the design sheet to the card. Sandwich the design sheet between the film and the card. To prepare the linen, mark with the tacking thread a rectangle 11.5cm x 18cm (4³/₄" x 7"). Fold the edge under once only and work buttonhole stitch, vertically over three fabric threads in from the hem, and horizontally into every fabric thread, using the No 100 Cordonnet thread and a No 7 crewel needle.

Special note: Keep in mind that tension is the most important factor with needlelace, closely followed by the correct thread and needle for the particular project.

To begin the needlelace, first lay foundation threads marked by the curved 'train tracks'. With a sharp needle secure the end of the No 10 Cordonnet thread into the hem. Thread up a length of ecru tacking thread in a sharp needle. Use this thread to couch down the No 10 Cordonnet on the inside of the curve, beginning at A, working to B, through the buttonhole stitch hem to C and back to D. Secure into hem. Lay these foundation threads for all 10 curves. The entire embroidery is now worked with No 100 Cordonnet and the tacking thread.

Diagram 1

With the finer No 100 thread begin buttonhole stitch over the foundation thread from A to B. Note: Where the two couched threads are linked, take the thread across under the second foundation thread and whip back to complete the buttonhole stitch. The buttonhole stitch from C to D on diagram 1 is worked in reverse buttonhole stitch.

The needlelace edge to the curve is worked next. Secure the thread in the buttonhole stitch hem at 1, then into the purl edge of the buttonhole stitch at 2, back to 1. To maintain the curved shape, couch these two threads in place with tacking thread. The tacking thread is used to hold the needlelace in place and is worked from the back of the embroidery with a separate needle. When all the embroidery is completed, these tacking threads are carefully cut and the needlelace lifted off the card.

Diagram 2

Buttonhole stitch from 1 to 2, working a picot half way along (see 'picot' instructions), travel to the next loop along the edge of the buttonhole stitch to 3. Take the thread from 3 to 4, then to 5, back to 4 and 3 (couching these threads in place with the tacking thread). Buttonhole stitch from 3 to 4 and only half way along 5.

Diagram 3

To lay the threads for the next loop, take the thread from the centre of 5 back to the centre of 4 into the edge of the buttonhole stitch and buttonhole at back along all of this loop and complete back to 5.

Diagram 4

Travel to 6, and take the thread to the centre of the third loop to 7 and buttonhole stitch to 8, working picots where indicated.

Diagram 5

Picots

Complete the appropriate number of buttonhole stitches up to the designated picot. Instead of working the next buttonhole stitch, place the needle back to the purl edge loop and work a buttonhole stitch. Next wrap under the needle and around it three times and draw up the bullion stitch. (Diagram 5)

Diagram 6

To complete the bullion stitch picot, take the needle into the base buttonhole stitch. Hold the picot in place while you work the next buttonhole stitch.

Continue working from 8 back to 6, working the picots evenly.

Repeat the above steps four times for each curve. To bring in a new thread, secure it under the couching and into a buttonhole stitch loop and work buttonhole stitch back over this thread. Begin each repeat with a new thread.

Diagram 7

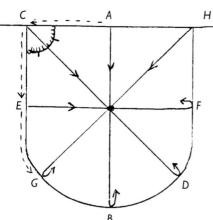

Needlelace Pyramid Fillings

Fillings 1, 2 and 3 as shown in the photograph, are repeated as indicated on the design sheet. The corners are the same and hold the sides together.

The foundation threads are laid and couched in the centre only. Begin at A, take the thread to B, back to A and to B, and then wrap back to A. Travel under the edge buttonhole stitch to C and lay the thread from C to D, back to C and to D, then wrap back to C. Work the buttonhole stitch loop at C. Continue until all four foundation threads are completed. Remember to work the loop at H with a separate thread which can then be used to work the loop between this and the next curve.

Diagram 8

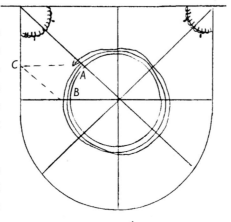

Filling No 1

Work the pyramids first by laying a foundation thread twice around the design line by piercing the wrapped bars with the needle. Work approximately twelve buttonhole stitches from A to B, take the thread back to the left side into the first buttonhole stitch and work eleven buttonhole stitches in the next row, then ten, nine, eight, seven, six, five, four, three, two, and one buttonhole stitch. At the last buttonhole stitch, take the thread to C and wrap back to the buttonhole stitch. Then whip stitch back along the side of the pyramid to B ready to begin the next pyramid. To bring in a new thread, lay it along with the foundation threads.

The picots are worked after completing all the pyramids. To work them, whip half way down the side of the pyramid, then work a picot, whip to the point and half way up the opposite side. Continue until all picots are completed – secure the thread ends in the foundation buttonhole stitch row.

The centre 'wheel' is now worked. Lay two foundation threads and work buttonhole stitch over these threads, working a picot as indicated.

Diagram 10

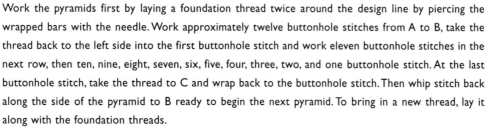

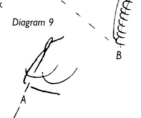

Diagram 9

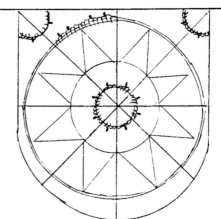

Diagram 11

Filling No 2

Lay the threads the same as in Filling No 1.

Note these pyramids do not have picots on the side and have seven buttonhole stitches in the foundation row. It is easier to work the pyramids first and place a pin in the last buttonhole stitch to hold it in place until all pyramids are completed. Then lay the outer ring foundation threads. Buttonhole stitch over these foundation threads working picots as indicated. Attach the point of the pyramids with the buttonhole stitch as you work around the circle. The centre ring is worked the same as with Filling No 1.

Diagram 12

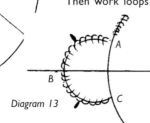

Filling No 3

Lay the threads the same as in Filling No 1. Note the pyramids have picots on one side only. The other side is attached to the outside and the next pyramid with a wrapped bar. The picots and bars are worked after completing all the pyramids.

The centre filling is different from Nos 1 and 2. Lay the foundation ring and wrap all the way around. Then work loops in the same manner as the other needlelace. Lay the thread from A, piercing the wrapped bar at B, then to C and return to A. Buttonhole stitch from A to B, working a picot half way and continue buttonhole stitches, taking the thread over the wrapped bar at B to C. Continue working all eight loops.

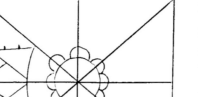

Diagram 13

Filling No 4 - The Corners

The corners are embroidered working back from the first needlelace group on the second side.

Diagram 14

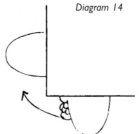

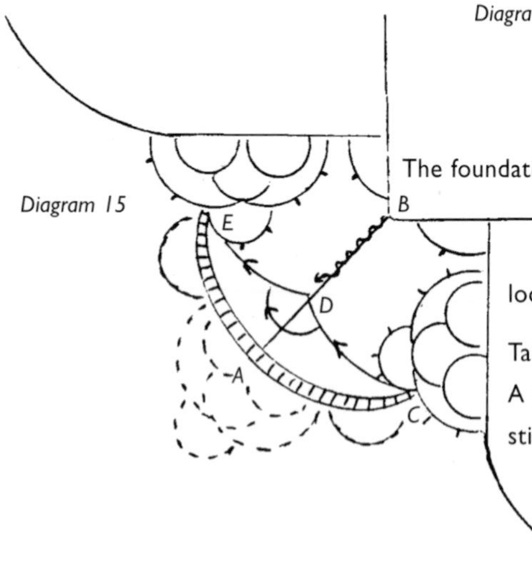

The foundation curve at A is worked in the same manner as the 'train tracks' you have already worked (i.e. couched foundation thread, buttonhole stitch over the foundation thread) only this time you will have to secure the thread ends into the buttonhole stitch loops instead of the buttonhole stitched fabric hem.

Take the thread from B to the centre of A, back to B and wrap back to A. Whip the foundation A row to C and take this thread to D, (piercing the wrapped bar) and then to E. Buttonhole stitch from E to D plus a picot, and half way to C. Work the loop indicated (plus picots) and back to C (plus picots).

The needlelace outside the A foundation row is a repeat of the basic needlelace.

Diagram 15

Illuminated Letter

Although Christine teaches mainly whitework techniques, needlelace and other lesser known forms of embroidery, she has a keen interest in metal thread embroidery and gold work. She has worked this illuminated letter on Olympia linen backed with cotton fabric. Cobalt blue fabric has been couched first to the background linen within the letter outline. The body of the letter is worked in gold kid padded with string over the blue fabric and stippled with red and blue thread. The centre embroidery is split stitch in a single strand of stranded cotton DMC Nos 680, 991, 498 and ecru. The Celtic knot feature is worked in imitation Jap Gold metal thread. The figure head is worked in a single strand of black stranded cotton. Satin stitch is worked in cobalt blue No 796 stranded cotton beneath the Celtic knot work. All embroidered areas and gold kid is edged with DMC antique gold thread, using only a single strand to edge the split stitch.

This is the initial B of the first verse of the Harley Psalter fol 4B Psalm 1...'Beatus Vi...' Blessed is the man. Written at the Winchester Cathedral Priory c. 980. Initial drawings by Jim Billingsley, design further simplified and adapted for embroidery by Christine Bishop.

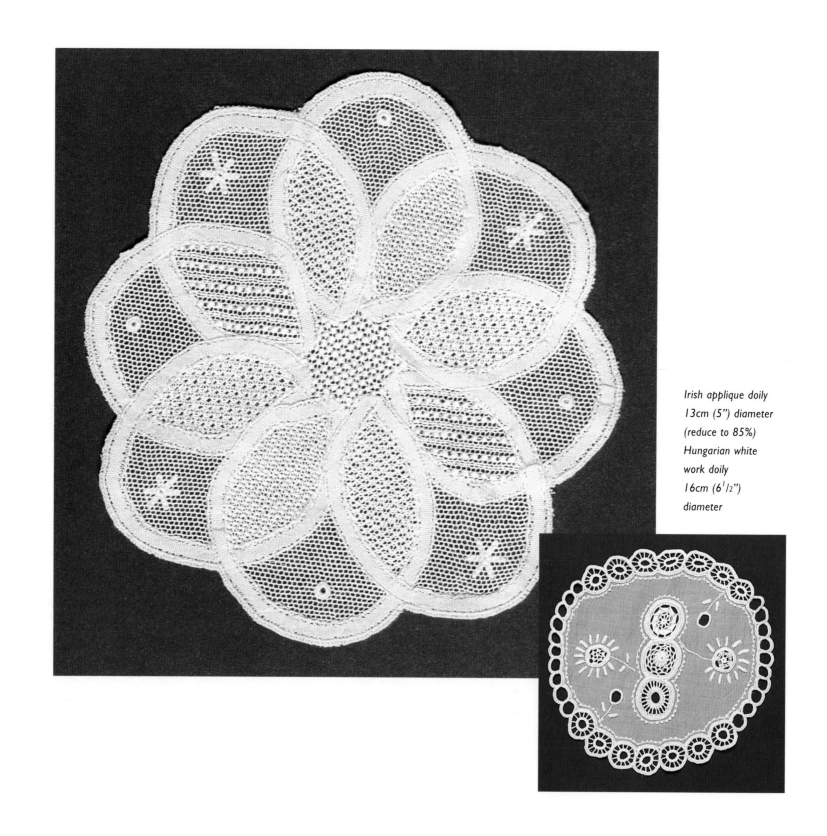

*Irish applique doily
13cm (5") diameter
(reduce to 85%)
Hungarian white
work doily
16cm (6^1/$_2$")
diameter*

Traditional Needlepoint Lace

Marie Laurie

Lace was once more highly valued than gold, with import restrictions, tariffs and quotas applied in Britain. Now a small but dedicated and highly skilled number of devotees work to retain the traditional skills of lacemaking while translating them into more contemporary designs.

While travelling overseas in 1982 Marie Laurie was introduced to needlelace and has since returned on a regular basis, learning the traditional techniques from England, Ireland, Belgium and Hungary. She has studied overseas, where the individual laces originated, and subsequently she has taught the following: Branscombe tape lace, Hollie Point, Limerick, Carrickmacross, Youghal, Halas, as well as others.

Marie modestly claims to have little artistic ability yet her work is detailed, fine and truly beautiful.

Irish applique doily

Marie has called this Irish applique although the Irish do not claim it as their own. She was shown a doily which was worked about 1900 and was told it was Irish applique. The original net was of the old type but she works the same stitches now. The braid or tape is the same as used for Branscombe and Borris lace. Marie has made many enquiries in Ireland regarding this lace but they do not believe it is one of their traditional laces. Is it an Australian adaptation to which the name Irish applique was given because Limerick stitches have been used?

This Irish applique is the application of a narrow cotton embroidery braid or tape to a fine cotton net, with needlerun filling stitches to complete the chosen field.

Requirements

cotton net 20cm x 20cm (8" x 8")	2 metres (80") fine cotton embroidery tape or braid
No 26 petit point tapestry needle	DMC No 30 sewing thread or skein stranded cotton
blue tissue paper 20cm x 20cm (8" x 8")	tracing paper 20cm x 20cm (8" x 8")
felt tip pen Artline 210 (not biro)	embroidery scissors
embroidery hoop 15cm (6")	pins
basting thread	calico 30cm x 30cm (12" x 12")

Marie Laurie

Trace pattern from the photograph onto the blue tissue paper using the felt tip pen. Working on an even surface, place down the tracing paper then the blue tissue paper. On top of this align the net to the pattern and pin. Baste or tack the three layers together about 2cm (^{4}/$_5$") from the edge of the pattern design. Turn back the cut end of the tape 5mm (^{1}/$_4$") with the fold end uppermost. Start attaching the tape to the pattern by tacking with small running stitches, sewing in the centre of the tape in a continuous outline. Make sure the outer curved edge of the tape is flat when tacking, but you will find that the inner edge has a gathered appearance. This should press out on completion. It is important to keep the outline of tape continuous so bend over on itself at meeting curves. To complete the tape attachment, cut and fold the end under about 5mm (^{1}/$_4$"). Place on top of the starting point fold and this conceals the cut ends of the tape, thus showing no raw edges.

Cobweb stitch.

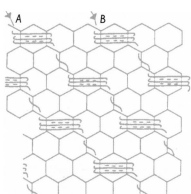

With the finishing embroidery thread in the needle, oversew around all edges of the tape to the net (except do not sew the outside edge until all the filling stitches are complete).

Cut a hole in the calico smaller than your hoop. Place the calico with the cut window over the design part and then mount all the layers into the hoop. The calico prevents the hoop stretching the net and also helps to keep the work clean.

Embroidery

Needlerun Filling Stitches are worked in the spaces to complement the chosen design. Many different techniques have been used here but it would look just as interesting with only one or two filling stitches. Choose from: darning, repeat darning, cobweb, spot and darn, diagonal spot and darn, oversewing and pickup. (See page 109).

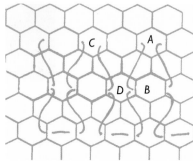

Oversewing stitch.

Filling stitches

Cobweb stitch. Start by attaching your thread into outlining couching on the right of the area to be decorated. Pass the needle and thread under the bar into the space marked A. Miss one row. To the right of B take the needle and thread under two bars from right to left into space D. Pass needle into space A under two bars to space C again,

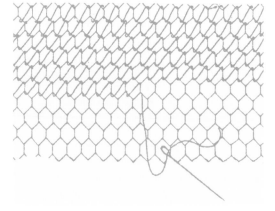

Diagonal spot and darn

right to left. Then take down to space D again. Continue in this manner.

Diagonal spot and darn. This is worked on the diagonal of the spaces of the net. Start at A, work over and under two bars or one space of net three times.

Carry the thread under, over and under the bars in a diagonal, as illustrated. Continue.

Oversewing stitch. This stitch has many variations. Oversew each space by making sure the needle is placed directly under each bar of the net for every stitch. It can be worked in both directions. As illustrated it is worked in every row but for a variation miss a row of spaces. It may also be worked on a diagonal of spaces.

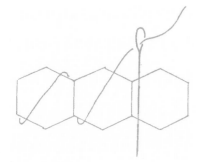

Diamond stitch

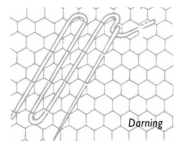

Darning

Dot stitch

diagram

Diamond stitch. This stitch is worked on two parts of the mesh. The first part resembles a figure of eight and then the second part is worked underneath.

Dot stitch. Start at 2. Go to 1 with needle directly under the upright bar, then right over to 4, again with needle under bar, back to 3 and repeat. Almost like one step forward and one step back.

Darning. This is an in and out movement through the net holes once.

Repeat darning. Repeat the in and out movement as for the previous stitch and on the return alternate the stitch.

Pickup. A very dainty stitch worked on every row. Pickup two bars and then in the row below pickup the next two bars and repeat. Turn work and repeat for the next row.

Finishing

Decorate the unworked areas with the traditional 'pops' and florets. (See page 119).

The outside edge of the article is worked in buttonhole stitch over the tape and net, again two or three stitches for each hole in the net. The number of stitches to be worked depends upon the size of the net as this varies often from order to order.

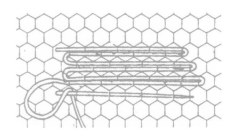

Repeat darning

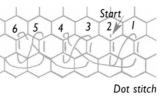

Dot stitch

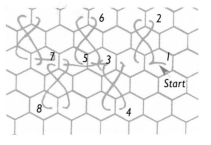

Remove the completed work from the embroidery hoop, then all the basting stitches. Wash, and press the finished piece on the wrong side. Cut the net close to the buttonhole stitch edge.

Hungarian white work embroidery

Requirements

20cm x 20cm (8" x 8") cotton organdie
DMC Broder Special No 25 shade B5200
No 7 or 8 sharp needle
embroidery hoop about 15cm (6")
HB pencil for tracing design to material

20cm x 20cm (8" x 8") calico
DMC Special Dentelles No 80 shade B5200
sharp pointed embroidery scissors
thimble (if preferred)

Trace off design to organdie with the HB pencil from photograph and enlarge 260 per cent. Cut a window in the calico about 2cm ($^3/_4$") smaller than the embroidery ring. Not only does the calico prevent the organdie from stretching but it also helps to keep the work clean.

Put down the inner embroidery ring. On top of this place the design part of the organdie, then the calico with the window circle cut out. Make the working assembly with the outer ring of the embroidery hoop.

When overcasting or buttonholing the circular patterns, always take the needle down through the centre of the hole, working from left to right. The raw edges of the material should fold under as you work around the hole. The small design circles or eyelets are to be worked first.

Thread the needle with the DMC Broder 25 and work a continuous line of small running stitches in a figure of eight pattern for the full length of the design. (Detail 1)

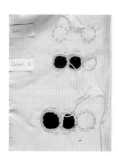

Repeat so that there are two rows of running stitches around the circles. Try and have as much thread as possible remaining on top of the work to give an extra padding to the finishing stitches. Cut a small circle of material from the inside of one of these eyelets, but not too close to the running stitches (leave about 2mm, $^1/_{10}$"). Work around the hole covering the running stitches with overcasting on the inside edge of the pattern design and on the outside edge finish with buttonhole stitch. Link the touching points of the eyelet circles with about three overcasting stitches only. This should make a bar between each eyelet. (Detail 2)

To finish a thread, pass the needle through a few stitches on the back of the work. Cut off close to embroidery.

Large wheel eyelets are the next technique to work using the Broder No 25. Outline the design in small running stitches using the same figure of eight method. Work twice around and set the second row close to the first. Cut away material to 3mm ($^1/_8$") from running stitches then overcast and buttonhole stitch the same as the small eyelets or circles. Work another circle and link the touching points neatly. With the fine thread, Dentelles Special No 80 in needle, return to the first completed outlined circle and work 13 twisted buttonhole stitches evenly around the circle.

For the twisted buttonhole stitch, work an extended length buttonhole stitch into the overcasting, then at the base pick up the thread with the point of the needle from underneath up (detail 3). This gives an extra twist on the stitch. Pull up until about 4mm ($^1/_8$") long. Repeat twelve times and join into the top of the first stitch. (Detail 4)

To complete the wheel weave over and under the stitches alternately, pulling up the centre in a neat circle. Weave around for about eight times more before taking the thread to outside edge on the first buttonhole stitch. Continue to work the large eyelets around doily. (Detail 5)

Large circles in the central motif are worked with the Broder No 25 for the outlining and finer thread to decorate. Work running stitches, cut and overcast around circles as detailed for outside embroidery, although all outlining should be worked in continuous overcasting.

The inner embroidery is worked with the fine thread, Dentelles No 80. To work the Loop Stitch Circle strengthen the inner edge by working two rows of buttonhole stitches, but not too close together. The first row of buttonhole stitches are worked over the overcasting. On completion of the second row, work a whip stitch into every loop of the buttonhole stitches, in an anti-clockwise direction. Pull up slightly to give a firm edge to attach the next round.

Divide the circular space to be filled either by marking with a pencil, or by eye, into ten portions. Work buttonhole stitches firmly, returning to starting stitch point. Next round, work buttonhole stitch over each loop of previous round. Continue to work over all loops of all rounds until a firm centre is worked, about nine rounds.

The whole area need not be filled although the example worked has a centre filling of twisted buttonhole stitches worked over two base threads of the round. To make a neat centre, whip around centre threads. This gives a firm outline to work a row of buttonhole stitches. Finish the thread by working into back of stitches just worked. (Detail 6)

Spider Centre Wheel is worked by following details as given for Loop Stitch Circle to completion of whipped second row of buttonhole stitches. Work twelve buttonhole stitches evenly around the centre, but make sure the loops betweeen the stitches are firm. Work another round in the same place. Into spaces or loops work another two rounds of buttonhole stitches. From these stitch spaces hang twisted buttonhole stitches, but make these long to almost reach the centre. Darn around to give a firm centre before working a spider to fill up the space. Fasten the thread off by carefully running it through the back of the loops along a ray to the centre. (Detail 7)

Knotted Centre Wheel is worked the same as the Spider Centre Wheel and Loop Stitch Circle until the completion of two rows of buttonhole stitches and the whipping to strengthen. Work long twisted buttonhole stitches with spaces of two missed stitches in between. Continue around full circle, joining up to the first stitch worked. Darn around the centre, pulling the centre into a firm circle. To make the knotted effect, work four buttonhole stitches on the shafts of the long twisted buttonhole stitches. The circle is completed by working a row of buttonhole stitches around the centre. (Detail 8)

Flower. As previously described, work the overcasting and space out groups of five buttonhole stitches five times. Hang another five buttonholes on bar between the groups. Complete the circle by working five twisted buttonhole stitches and weaving over and under the threads to pull in the centre neatly.

Petals and Leaves. Work these with the Broder No 25 thread by commencing with a few little running stitches to cover the pattern line. Pick up one or two threads of material then return to the other end and repeat. Repeat again so that you have four parallel threads for the length of the petal. (Detail 9)

Cover with small satin stitches taking up the padding and ground material. All the padding is on the surface. (Detail 10)

The continuous satin stitch dots are worked with the Broder No 25 thread by picking up about 2mm ($^1/_{10}$") of material three times. Continue around all embroidery as shown in sample. (Detail 11)

To eliminate the small holes left by the needle and threads opening the organdie fibres, work a line of chain stitch around all embroidered sections as shown above. Complete by working stems in outlining or stem stitch.

Remove embroidery from assembly, wash and press on wrong side. Cut around the outside to remove the foundation material.

Lace Knitting

Furze Hewitt

A small but dedicated band of women, led and inspired by Furze Hewitt, has been collecting and working knitting patterns from the nineteenth century. They have also used these as the basis for many new designs. The Victorian era in Britain, in particular, saw a rapid rise in the popularity of 'knitted lace', as a substitute for the expensive and often imported laces on which high tariffs and quotas had been imposed, and as a result of the availability of inexpensive knitting cotton from the industrial mills. The new women's magazines spread the message, reproducing patterns containing intricate combinations of plain and purl and requiring the tiniest of metal needles. White cotton knitting swept the land and yards of finely knitted lace were added to pillow shams, bedspreads, sheets, valances, petticoats and outer garments.

Unfortunately, by the mid twentieth century, the vogue had passed and much of this beautiful work has disappeared. Furze, combining her love of antiques with her love of white cotton knitting, has tried to find as much of this work as possible, while also searching for the original patterns and adapting them for present day use.

Miniature colonial four poster, hand crafted in Australian cedar by Flick Evans of Somers, Victoria. Original c. 1835.
Bedcover hemstitched and embroidered by Joan Jackson
Knitted edgings and valance by Furze Hewitt
17cm x 13cm x 20cm high (6³/₄" x 5" x 8")

The Wrexham

Bedcover hemstitched and embroidered by Joan Jackson

Knitted edgings and valance by Furze Hewitt

Requirements
2 x 20g (1 oz) balls DMC 100 Cordonnet 2500
pair of 1mm (20) needles
fine fabric for bedlinen
sewing needle and cotton for attaching lace
filling for pillows

Bedcover – lace edging
Special abbreviation: K.P.K. knit, purl, knit
Cast on 15 sts.
Row 1. K2, m1, k3, m1, k2tog, k3, k2tog, m1, k3
Row 2. Sl1, k15
Row 3. K2, m1, k5, m1, k2tog, k1, k2tog, m1, k4
Row 4. Sl1, k16
Row 5. K2, m1, k1, k2tog, m2, sl1, k2tog, psso, k1, m1, sl1, k2tog, psso, m1, k5
Row 6. Sl1, k9, (K.P.K) in m2 of previous row, k5

Row 7. K1, k2tog, m1, k2tog, k3, k2tog, m1, k3, m1, k2tog, k3

Row 8. Sl1, k16

Row 9. K1, k2tog, m1, k2tog, k1, k2tog, m1, k5, m1, k2tog, k2

Row 10. Sl1, k15

Row 11. K1, k2tog, m1, sl1, k2tog, psso, m1, k1, k2tog, m2, sl1, k2tog, psso, k1, m1, k2tog, k1

Row 12. Sl1, k4, (K.P.K) in m2 of previous row, k7

Repeat rows 1 – 12 until length desired.

Pillows – lace edging

Special Abbreviation: K in F.B.F. Knit in front, back and front

Cast on 5 sts

Row 1. Sl1, k1, m1, k2tog, k1

Row 2. As row 1

Row 3. As row 1 to last st. K in F.B.F

Row 4. Sl1, k1, psso, k1. Pass first st over, k1, m1, k2tog, k1

Repeat rows 1 – 4 until length desired.

Valance

Special abbreviation: K.P.K. knit, purl, knit

Cast on 14 sts.

Row 1. K2, m1, k3, m1, k2tog, k2, k2tog, m2, k2tog, k1

Row 2. Sl1, k2, p1, k11

Row 3. K2, m1, k5, m1, k2tog, k6

Row 4. Sl1, k15

Row 5. K2, m1, k1, k2tog, m3, sl1, k2tog, psso, k1, m1, (k2tog) twice, m2, k2tog, k1

Row 6. Sl1, k2, p1, k5, (K.P.K) in m2 of previous row, k5

Row 7. K1, k2tog, m1, k2tog, k3, k2tog, m1, k7

Row 8. Sl1, k15

Row 9. K1, k2tog, m1, k2tog, k1, k2tog, m1, k3, k2tog, m2, k2tog, k1

Row 10. Sl1, k2, p1, k11

Row 11. Sl1, k2tog, m1, sl1, k2tog, psso, m1, k9

Row 12. Sl1, k13

Repeat rows 1 – 12 until length desired

Lace-edged aromatic cushion

Knitting by Furze Hewitt
Embroidery by Joan Jackson
'Lafrowda' – a pattern from c. 1848
26cm x 26cm (10" x 10") including
lace, 3cm ('/s") wide

Requirements

1 x 50g (2oz)ball DMC 40 cotton
pair 1.25mm (18) needles
cushion of choice   DMC
embroidery thread shade 25
sewing needle and thread for
attaching lace

Cushion edging

Cast on 16 sts
Row 1. Knit
Row 2. K3, m1, k2tog, (m2, k2tog) 5 times, k1
Row 3. K3, (p1, k2) 5 times, m1, k2tog, k1
Row 4. K3, m1, k2tog, k16
Row 5. K18, m1, k2tog, k1
Row 6. K3, m1, k2tog, m2, k2tog. Cast off 9 sts, thus: k1. Return the k1 to left hand needle, drawing 9 sts over without knitting them. Cast on 7 sts on right hand needle, k2tog, m2, k2tog, k1
Row 7. K3, p10, k1, p1, k2, m1, k2tog, k1
Row 8. K3, m1, k2tog, k15
Row 9. Cast off 4sts. K12, m1, k2tog, k1
Repeat rows 2 – 9 until length desired. Press the lace. Join the ends and sew to cushion.

Braid

Cast on 8 sts
Row 2. M1, k2tog, k1, k2tog, m2, k2tog, k1
Repeat rows 1 – 3 until length desired.

Row 1. M1, k2tog, k6
Row 3. M1, k2tog, k1, p1, k4
Using DMC stranded cotton, shade 25, thread cotton through holes in braid. Attach to cushion with small stitches.

Dahlia
A doily by Edna Lomas
20cm (8") diameter

Dahlia

A doily by Edna Lomas

Requirements

1 x 20g (1oz) ball DMC 20 cotton set of 4 double pointed size 2mm (14) needles

Cast on 8 sts, 3sts on each of 2 needles, 2 sts on 3rd needle. Knit with 4th needle.

Round 1. Knit

Round 2. (M1, k1) to end of round (16 sts) Knit 3 rounds

Round 6. As round 2 (32 sts) Knit 3 rounds

Round 10. K1, (m1, k2) to last st, m1, k1, (48 sts)

Round 11. K1, [(k1, p1) into m1 of previous round, k2)] to last 2 sts, (k1, p1) into m1 of previous round, k1, (64sts)

Round 12. (K2tog, m1, sl1, k1, psso) to end of round (48 sts). Repeat rounds 11 and 12, 4 times

Round 21. K1, [(k1, p1, k1) in m1 of previous round, k2)] to last 2 sts, (k1, p1, k1) in m1 of previous round, k1, (80 sts)

Knit 3 rounds

Round 25. (M1, k5) to end of round (96 sts)

Round 26. And alternate rounds. Knit

Round 27. (K1, m1, sl1, k1, psso, k1, k2tog, m1) to end of round

Round 29. (M1, k2tog, m1, sl1, k2tog, psso, m1, k1) to end of round

Round 31. (Sl1, k1, psso, m1) to end of round

Round 33. (M1, k2tog) to end of round

Round 34. Knit

Round 35. K1, (sl st from R.H. needle onto L.H. needle. Insert needle into this st. Cast on 2 sts. Cast off 5 sts). Repeat until all sts have been cast off.

Lace knitting general instructions

Invisible cast-on method

1. Using contrasting thread, cast on the number of stitches required, work two rows in stocking stitch.

2. With main thread, continue work until length required.

3. When work is completed, remove contrasting thread. Either graft or sew together open stitches from both ends of work.

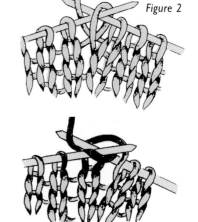

Invisible casting-on

Figure 1

Increasing in lace knitting

There are three methods of increasing the number of stitches in a row, or in a round. One way is to knit twice into a stitch (see Fig. 1). This increase can be worked k-wise or p-wise. Read your pattern carefully and work as directed.

A second method is is to pick up a loop between two sts, and knit into that loop (see Fig. 2). This prevents a hole forming in the knitting.

The third method (see Fig. 3), make one (or m1), produces the holes in lace knitting. The way it is worked depends on whether the extra stitch is to be made between two knit stitches, a knit and a purl, or two purl stitches. For example, between knit sts the yarn is brought forward, and over the needle as you knit the next stitch, thus forming a new stitch. Once again, read your pattern carefully.

Figure 2

Figure 4(a)

Decreasing in lace knitting

Again there are several methods. One method is to knit or purl two stitches together (see Fig. 4a and 4b). A second method is to pass the second last stitch previously worked over the last one (Fig. 4c and d).

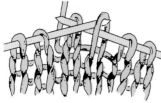

Figure 4(b)

Fig. 3a. Make one between two knit stitches

Knitting picot cast-off

Knit 1st st. *Sl st from RH needle onto LH needle. Insert needle into this st, cast on 2 sts, then cast off 5 sts. Repeat from * until all sts have been cast off.

Knitting off your stitches if you can't crochet

K1, *k2tog, m1, k2tog, turn. P1, [(k1, p1) twice, k1] in next stitch.

P1, sl1 p-wise, turn. Cast off 7 sts (1st left on RH needle)*.

Repeat from * – * to last 5 sts. K3tog, m1, k2tog, turn, p1, (k1, p1) twice, k1, in next st, p1, sl 1 p-wise, turn.

Cast off remaining stitches.

For a larger loop on your edging, make 9 sts instead of the 5 sts just described.

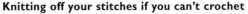
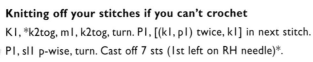

Figure 4(c)

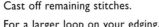

Figure 4(d)

Fig. 3b. Make one between two purl stitches

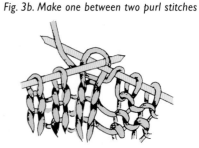

Fig. 3c. Make one between a knit and a purl stitch

Jenny Rees

I n 1982 Jenny Rees had a few lessons in bobbin lacemaking from a cousin who was learning herself. Since then she has taught herself from books. Perhaps her background as a scientist with mathematical ability has helped her to work out patterns from photographs or lace pieces and translate them into modern designs.

Left:

Carrickmacross gum leaf mat 19cm x 19cm (7¹/₂" x 7¹/₂")

Bedfordshire lace collar 52cm long x 83cm wide (20 ¹/₂" x 32")

Now Jenny teaches and makes a range of bobbin laces. Torchon, which is usually worked on a 45° grid and is geometric and logical (although the piece shown here is rather floral), was a peasant-style lace, rather than a very expensive lace. Bedfordshire (as shown here in the collar) which developed in England in the 1850s after the Great Exhibition, is similar to Maltese. Cluny is the French version of Bedfordshire. Buck's Point lace is worked with a traditional net background and a finer thread. Honiton (British) and Withof (Dutch) are non-continuous laces which are made up of motifs and are very fine.

Jenny also teaches and works the needlelaces of Carrickmacross and Limerick, both Irish.

The laces shown here have taken hours of work. The collar took approximately 150 hours, the handkerchief about 60 hours and the mat about 30 hours. Jenny is able to take some of her work with her wherever she goes although care needs to be taken with humidity to prevent the threads drying out.

Carrickmacross gum leaf mat

Carrickmacross lace is an Irish needlelace. It developed during the 1820s and 30s and came to prominence during the potato famine, giving many otherwise destitute families an income and employment.

It is traditionally made by appliqueing cotton organdie onto net by couching and then the excess organdie is cut away. Originally cotton net was used, but as today's cotton net is much coarser than the old net, nylon net or tulle is used now. The original net had square holes whereas today's net has hexagonal holes. Cotton organdie is used as it does not fray as easily as organza.

Requirements

nylon tulle 23cm x 23cm (9" x9") with approx 1mm holes

cotton organdie 23cm x 23cm (9" x 9")

coloured transparent contact film – a large enough piece to cover the pattern

threads:	thick thread or padding cord – white Cordonnet Special 60
	fine thread – white Mettler 60/2 or
	white Tanne 80 or
	white Brok 100/2
	tacking thread – white sewing thread
needles:	large crewel for Cordonnet
	fine sharps 10 or similar
scissors:	blunt nosed scissors to cut away the organdie safely –
	proper Carrickmacross scissors, suture scissors or baby nail scissors

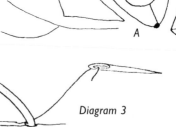

Increase size to 200%

Photocopy and enlarge the pattern and cut it out leaving a 2cm – 3cm ($^1/_8$") border around the pattern and cover with contact.

Diagram 1

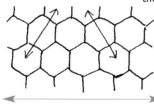

horizontal

As the net is hexagonal there is a horizontal row and two diagonal rows. Find the horizontal row and align this with the pattern and carefully pin to the pattern. *Diagram 1*

Place the organdie over this and pin it down.

Now tack all three layers together, placing the tacking knots at the back of the pattern. Tack about 1cm ($^2/_5$") away from all the couching lines where the organdie will be cut away. It is also worth oversewing the edges to prevent them catching the thread as you go.

Thread the large needle with the Cordonnet Special 60. Leave the thread attached to the ball. Take this through the pattern at A from the front to the back of the pattern. *Diagram 2*. Unthread the needle and tie a knot in the thread at the back to prevent it pulling back through the pattern.

Diagram 2

Thread the fine needle with a standard embroidery length of fine thread. Work two small running stitches along the outline towards A from left to right – to where the padding cord comes through the pattern. *Diagram 3*

Diagram 4

Lay the thick thread down along the outline towards the left and hold it down with your left thumb. Work three tight, close stitches over the padding cord where it comes through the pattern to secure both threads. *Diagram 4*

Diagram 3

Diagram 5

The couching stitches are worked close together, approximately 2mm ($^1/_{10}$") apart, going in where the organdie will be cut away and out where it will be left behind. The stitches are worked at right angles over the padding cord and diagonally underneath – to be more certain of catching the net. *Diagram 5*

Couch around the leaf working a buttonhole or anchor stitch at B. At C work a vein. *Diagram 6*

B

Diagram 6

Work an anchor stitch at the base of the vein. Leave the padding cord and take the fine thread up to the top of the vein. Take a small stitch with the top of the needle facing towards the vein wrapping the needle around the thread, catching a couple of threads of organdie as it goes under the thread to hold the vein in place. The needle would probably go under the thread four or five times. *Diagram 7*. When the padding cord is reached continue as normal.

C

D *E*

Diagram 7

Work up the stem of the gumnut and around the base, past E and around the top to D. At D work a division back to E across the middle of the gumnut. *Diagram 8*

Diagram 8

E

Diagram 9

D

Leave the padding cord at D. Take the fine thread over the organdie to E, pass the needle under the padding cord at E, return to D and go under the cord again and return to E. Go under the cord once more and then couch back over three threads to D. *Diagram 9*. Continue normally. Finish working round the gumnut. When the stem is reached couch the padding cords together and continue.

When the section is nearly finished cut the padding cord and thread it through to the back of the pattern and leave. Continue couching to the end adding a few tight close stitches over the 'end' of the thread where it goes through the pattern.

To finish the thread make three small loops along the padding cord. Lay the needle in the loops and pull the loops down onto the needle. Pull the needle through and tighten the loops onto the thread. Cut off the end.

Work the inside edge next, starting and finishing as necessary.

Traditionally Carrickmacross lace has picots or twirls on the outside edge. These are decorative loops of the padding cord that are worked as the edge is couched. The thread is started as usual. They are evenly spaced and should be of even size.

Loop the padding cord around to form a circle where the threads overlap on the outline and work three close stitches to anchor it. Work two stitches after the loop, just over the single cord and gently pull the picot down to the required size. Make another loop and continue. *Diagram 10*

Diagram 10

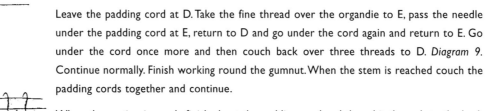

When all the couching is finished remove all the internal tacking stitches, leaving those outside the pattern, and carefully cut away the excess organdie inside the pattern. Use blunt nosed scissors as it is very easy to cut the net with pointy nosed scissors.

Work the pops. These are the small circles of buttonhole stitches that are often scattered throughout the unadorned net. Anchor the thread by weaving a circle of thread around the hole to be the centre of the pop. Insert the needle into the centre hole and stitch around the bar of the net. Continue working two or three buttonhole stitches into each box around the central hole until a dense pop has been worked. *Diagram 11*

Carefully remove the rest of the tacking stitches and lift the lace off the pattern. Cut away the rest of the organdie, being careful not to cut any of the picots.

Diagram 11

Sturt's desert pea handkerchief

Torchon lace for advanced lacemakers

Requirements

threads: Tanne 50

                   Coton Perle 12

bobbins: approximately 146 pairs

                   9 pairs gimps

The handkerchief is worked diagonally across from one corner to the opposite corner with pairs added and discarded as shown.

Worker through the gimp

Rather than taking a passive pair out through the gimp, working the pinhole, and bringing a ground pair back through the gimp where a diagonal row of ground stops and another starts, the worker inside the gimp travels out through the gimp to work the outside pinhole in the ground and then goes back through the gimp and continues normally.

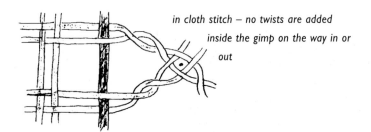

in cloth stitch – no twists are added inside the gimp on the way in or out

in half stitch — one twist is added on the way out of the gimp and two on the way back in

Gimp loop

Sometimes a gimp works back 'up' a pattern. To avoid adding extra gimps and finishing off gimps a loop can be worked so that the gimp can continue on in the pattern.

This is used with a number of leaves in the edging.

1. Make a large loop with the gimp and hold it out with a berry pin. Take the gimp back up to follow the pattern markings and hold it with another berry pin before it turns to the left and works through the pairs going to A and B.

2. Work the gimp through the four pairs coming in from the right hand side. Pinholes A, B and C cannot be worked until the gimp swings around and is worked through the pairs above them

3. Now work the feature inside the gimp as normal, carefully passing the pairs over and under the gimp as usual as needed. When the section inside the loop is finished, carefully pull the loop up into place using the first berry pin to stop it twisting.

Similarly, the following can be used to finish off a gimp pair where there are not many pairs available to wrap the gimps back through.

This works for the small, lower petals of the middle flower.

When there are about six pinholes left, make a gimp loop of both gimps by hooking them around a ber down the pattern and then taking them back up and laying them to the back of the pillow.

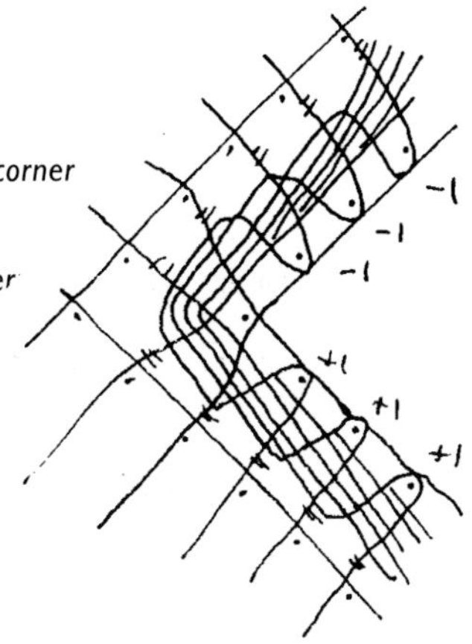

● **Pattern Diagrams**

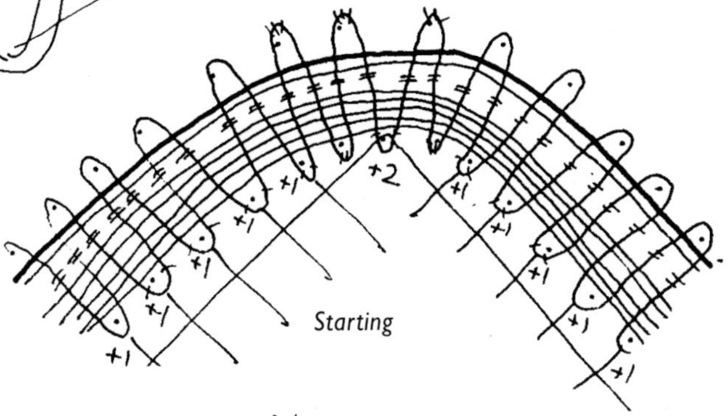

Starting

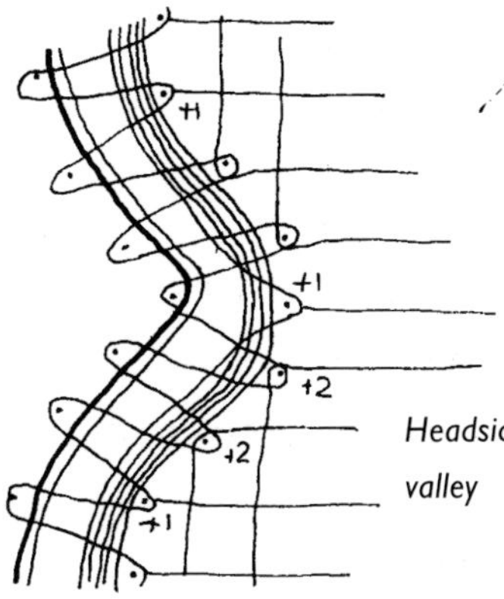

Inside corner

Headside valley

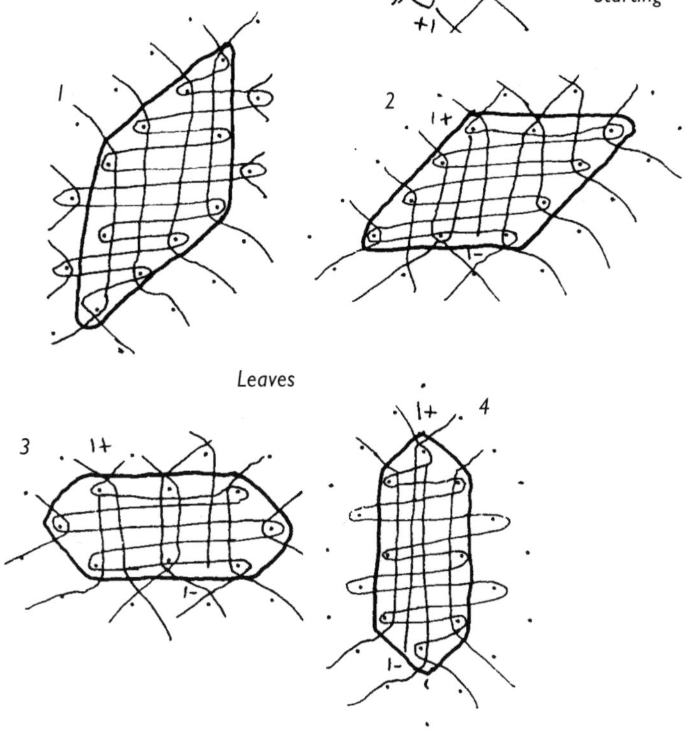

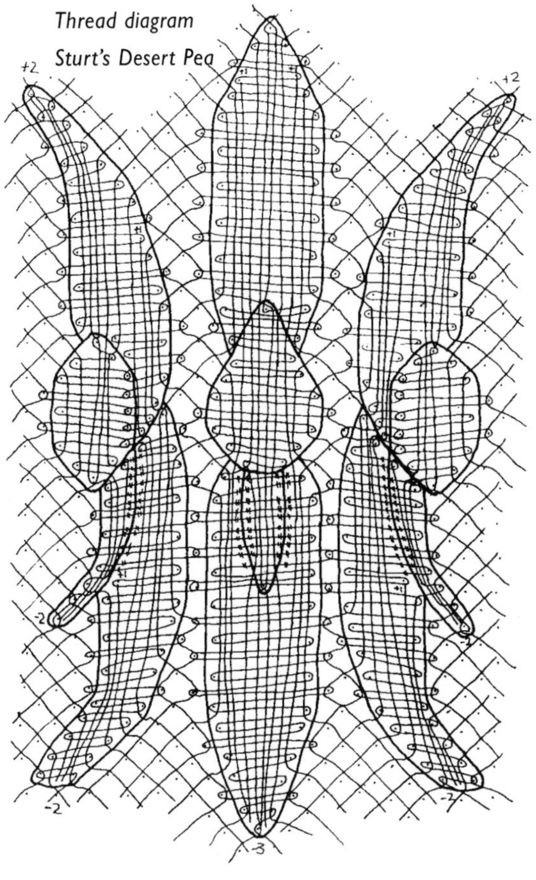

Gimp diagram

1

2

Leaves

3

4

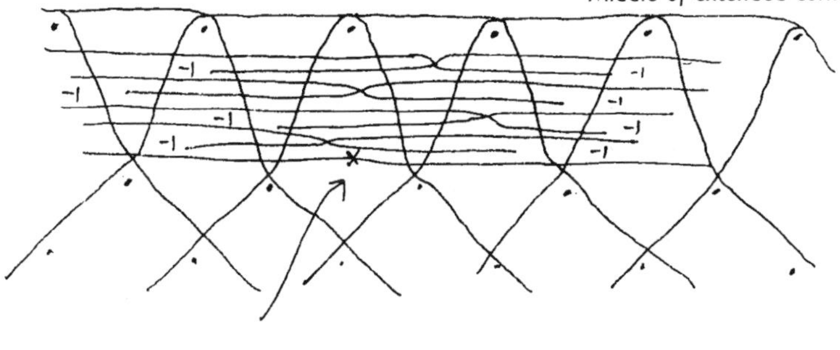

Thread diagram
Sturt's Desert Pea

Middle of extended corner

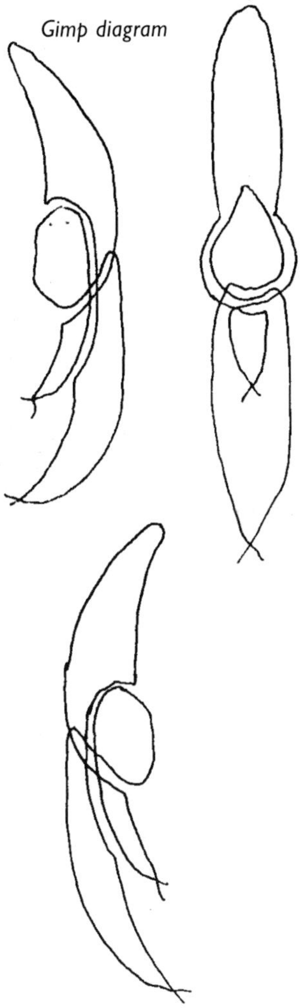

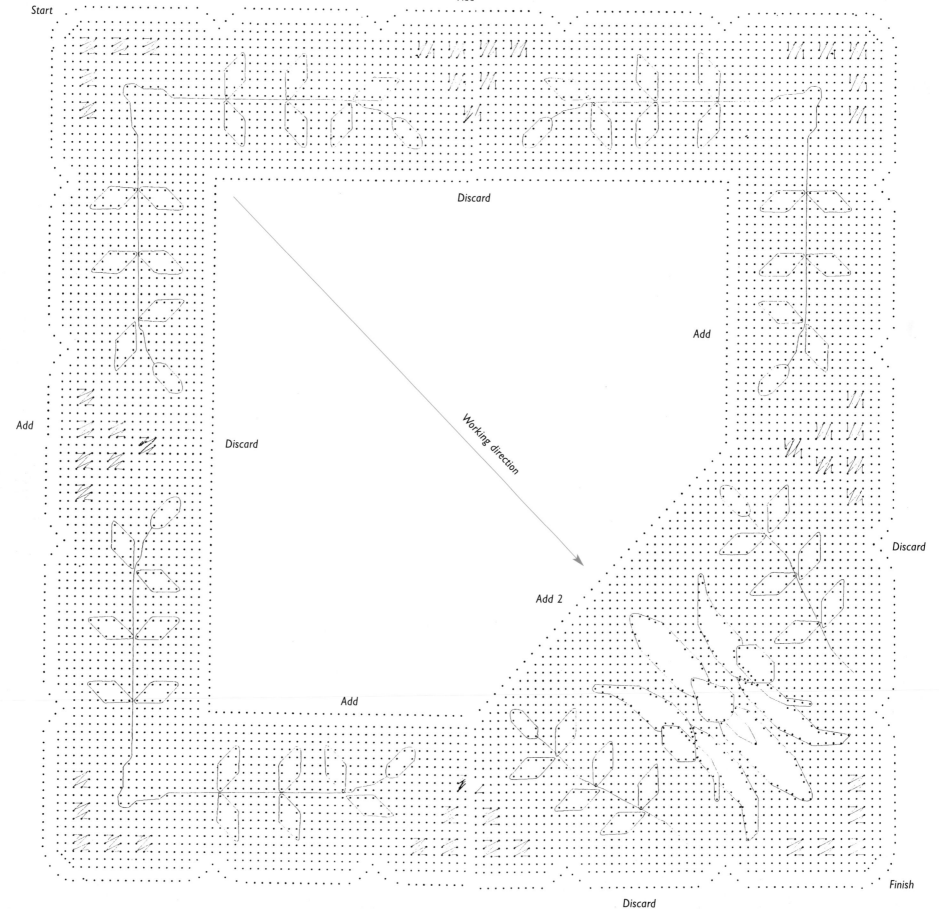

Sturt's desert pea
handkerchief edging
Torchon lace
24cm x 24cm
(9^1/$_2$" x 9^1/$_2$")

Above: Christening robe edging and insertion

Left: Chatelaine in presentation box

Tatted Lace

Stephaney Packham

Tatted lace is created using a minimum of equipment: a shuttle (sometimes two), a fine crochet hook and suitable thread. The lace is very strong, consisting of a series of knots made with a shuttle over a core thread. Lengths of this knotting are formed into rings and connecting chains which combine to make up the basic structure of the lace. Picots are used as an aid to join parts of the lace. They are also used as a decorative element.

During the Victorian era, 'upper class' women liked to tat as a means of showing off their lovely hands as their fingers flew with the shuttle. Many had their portraits painted with shuttle in hand and tatting bag swinging from wrist.

Tatting has evolved over centuries, almost certainly from knotting and macrame and continues to do so today as practitioners experiment and discover more ways to exploit the 'knot'

Stephaney Packham has always had a love of fine linen, embroidery and lace but it was not until she retired that she was taught to tat by her husband's aunt. By this time in her mid 40s, she was dubious about attempting such a manipulative craft but was assured that the aunt had been 60 when she had learned, so it would be simple. This proved to be true and now, with many projects behind her, and at 60 herself, she is teaching others older than herself the craft. Stephaney's craft time is now shared between tatting and bobbin lace which she began learning about nine years ago.

Abbreviations used:

ds = double stitch or stitches, p = picot, ps = picots, – = picot in diagram 3, 4, & 5 and in Christening robe edging, daisy = traditional four ring motif which has the appearance of a daisy.

Chatelaine

Requirements

quantity of cereal box weight cardboard

a minimum of 35cm x 45cm (13³/₄" x 17³/₄") each of linen (or other suitable fabric) and felt to match

2 balls No 20 mercerised crochet thread

2 tatting shuttles

fine crochet hook

2 metres ribbon, 1cm (²/₅") wide

packet small beads to tone or contrast with fabric and ribbon

sufficient stuffing to fill pincushion

small quantity baby flannel to use in needle case

small press stud (to close needle case)

small amount craft glue

Diagram 1

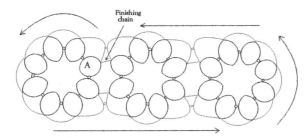

Finishing chain

A

Make 42 motifs. This number may be increased or decreased by two as required, to allow for ribbon threading. All rings and chains consist of three picots separated by 3ds with the exception of the connecting chain which has 4ds. Begin with Ring A following arrows for 42 motifs then finish at base of ring A with connecting chain of 4ds. Thread with ribbon ensuring tails at each end are at back of the work.

First make tatted braid as per instructions in diagram 1. Thread with ribbon.

Cut out cardboard, linen and felt following instructions on diagram.

Lightly glue felt to both sides of cardboard as padding. Make up pin-cushion including ribbon ends of braid in seam. Stuff and close with slip stitches. Buttonhole stitch right around pin-cushion ensuring stitching is in front of ribbon joined into seam. Cover three oval pieces with fabric and finish with buttonhole stitch around edges. Cover the two parts of the scissors case with fabric. Buttonhole stitch across the top of the smaller piece (Shape D).

With shuttle only, tat a series of rings across this section (three picots separated by 3ds) with spaces of approximately 2mm ($^1/_{10}$") between, joining rings to each other as you tat. In the spaces, join with shuttle thread to buttonhole stitches. Now buttonhole stitch the two pieces of the scissor case together, tat around as before, joining to side picots of rings at end of previous tatting across top of smaller piece. In a similar manner, tat around the oval pieces, joining the buttonhole stitching around each one as you tat. Hinge two of these together across one end by approximately five or six rings as you tat.

Insert baby flannel between these for needles and sew on a press stud to hold closed.

Make three beaded circular motifs as shown in Diagram 3.

Hand sew these motifs in place on pincushion, needle case and scissors case.

For the pincushion, make a string of tatted rings as before, long enough to go around the cushion. Measure as you tat and join to braid ends as you reach position of each ribbon. Stop when you are three rings short of length required to go right around. Without cutting from the shuttle, slip stitch the tatting to buttonhole stitching on the cushion and then complete the last few rings, joining up to the first ring to finish. Sew ends away into cushion. (By doing it this way you avoid the difficulty of tatting to the edge of the stuffed cushion.)

Diagram 2

Shape A

Back – Shape C

Front – Shape D

Shape B

Here to show position only

Enlarge pattern by 200%
From fabric: cut two shape A, six shape B, two shape C and two Shape D, allowing for seams on all pieces
From felt: cut six shape B, two shape C and two shape D. No allowances necessary
From cardboard: cut three of shape B, one Shape C and one Shape D.

Diagram 3

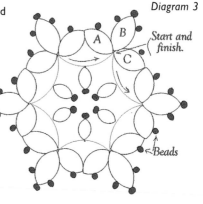

A B
C

Start and finish.

Beads

Thread 36 beads onto ball. (Stiffen end of thread with a little glue.) Wind 2 shuttles keeping thread continuous between them. Arrange beads so that Shuttle A has 30 beads and Shuttle B has six beads. Begin with ring A. Rings A and C have 4 picots separated by 3ds. Ring B is 3ds – 4ds bead 4ds bead 4ds bead 4ds – 3ds. The chain has 6ds then a ring made with shuttle B of 6ds then finish chain with 6ds.

Diagram 4

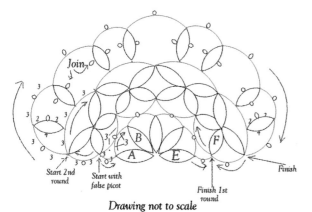

Drawing not to scale

Now make the body and lid of the thimble case as shown in diagrams 4 and 5.

Sew these in place on the third oval piece. Make two small (3cm and 5cm, $^1/8$" and $^1/4$") tassels, with beads on them. Sew the smaller to the bottom of the thimble holder. Sew a bead to the centre of each 'daisy' on the body and two or three to the centre of the lid. Make up a button from three or four beads to close the thimble holder.

Attach the second tassel to your scissors. Use doubled ribbon (shaped where necessary) and hand sew pieces to the pincushion as shown in the photograph.

Use two shuttles. Start diagram 4 with a false picot, ch, 3ds – 3ds, change to 2nd shuttle, don't reverse and carry on as diagram. Don't reverse after Ring E. Join all 2nd round rings together by side picots.

Start diagram 5 at Ring A and follow illustration using second shuttle to make eight rings of 5ps separated by 4ds, one large ring of 5ps sep by 4ds then complete 4 more rings as before.

Diagram 5

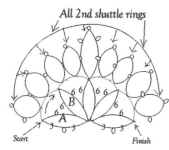

Christening robe edging and insertion

This edging can be used on its own or doubled up as an insertion. The work as illustrated was done using Coats No. 60 crochet cotton. When used alone it is slip stitched to the robe where required, catching the picots on the chains.

When used as an insertion, the two edges are joined at the chain picots as the second one is made then joined to the robe through the picots and base of each ring on the lines shown on the diagram. Thread the ribbon under the joined extended clovers and over the smaller joined clovers

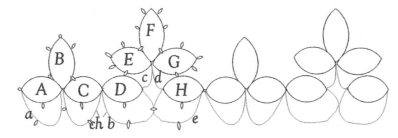

Christening robe edging and insertion

ch a false p4 – 4 – 4
ch b 4 – 4 – 4 join to middle picot ring C 4 – 4 – 4
rings A, C, D & H s ps sep 3ds
ch c & 3ds
ring B 3 – 3 – 2 – 2 – 3 – 3
ring F 3 – 3 – 2 – 2 – 2 – 3 – 3
ring E & G 5 ps sep 3ds
ch e as ch b joining to middle p
Ring H

Collectables

Jan Hanlon, Susie McMahon, Linda Benson

H andmade bears and dolls are never simply toys. Individually designed and stitched, they might be beloved playthings, but, if well cared for, they will be treasured by their owners for life.

Collectors, too, search out finely made dolls and bears, always looking for new designs, unusual colours, individual detail and individual character. Some search for lifelike recreations in dolls, others search for personality, themes and character dressing. In bears, some want perfect replicas of the original 'teddy' bear, while others want creative designs, shapes, even clothing. All want exquisite workmanship and quality of design and materials.

The three artists featured on these pages are all award winners in their fields. All Tasmanians, and sisters, they have developed their bears and dolls from a love of needlework and other crafts. Each now runs a successful business making and selling their dolls and bears.

Far left: Penny – Farthing
pair of mohair bears
40cm (16") and 20cm (8") high
Jan Hanlon

Left: Clown doll – detail of face
Susie McMahon

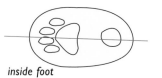

inside foot

Reverse for pairs

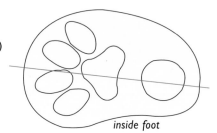

inside foot

Penny – Farthing by Jan Hanlon

Pair of bears – 40cm (16") and 20cm (8") in height, with applique pads

Requirements

tipped mohair fur fabric with 1.6cm ($^5/_8$") pile, 140cm x 33cm (56" x 13")

ultrasuede or good quality wool felt to match background colour of mohair, 16cm x 25cm ($6^1/_2$" x 10")

ultrasuede or good quality wool felt to match the tips of the mohair, 12cm x 9cm (5" x $3^1/_2$")

fusible webbing for the applique, 12cm x 9cm (5" x $3^1/_2$")

		Penny	Farthing
Eyes		10mm ($^3/_8$") glass	6mm ($^1/_4$") glass
Joints:			
Head		2 x 45mm wooden discs	2 x 25mm wooden discs
		1 x $^3/_{16}$" x $1^1/_4$" bolt	1 x M3 x 25mm bolt
		2 x $^3/_{16}$" x $^1/_2$" washers	2 x $^1/_8$" x $^5/_{16}$" washers
		1 x $^3/_{16}$" Nyloc nut	1 x M3 Nyloc nut
Shoulders		4 x 40mm wooden discs	4 x 20mm wooden discs
		2 x $^3/_{16}$" x $^3/_4$" bolts	2 x M3 x 16mm bolts
		4 x $^3/_{16}$" x $^1/_2$" washers	4 x $^1/_8$" x $^5/_{16}$" washers
		2 x $^3/_{16}$" Nyloc nuts	2 x $^3/_{16}$" Nyloc nuts
Hips		4 x 55mm wooden discs	4 x 25mm wooden discs
		2 x $^3/_{16}$" x $^3/_4$" bolts	2 x M3 x 16mm bolts
		4 x $^3/_{16}$" x $^1/_2$" washers	4 x $^1/_8$" x $^5/_{16}$" washers
		2 x $^3/_{16}$" Nyloc nuts	2 x M3 Nyloc nuts

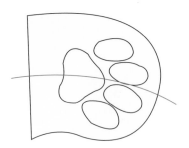

Enlarge to 200%

Guide to placement of applique
for both bears

perle No 5 thread, black, for nose, mouth and claws (No 8 for Farthing)

wax, black and masking tape to wax nose (optional)

extra strong thread for ears and closures

good quality polyester sewing thread in two colours to match background and tips of mohair

fibrefill stuffing

thin cardboard or template plastic to make pattern

fine felt-tipped permanent marker

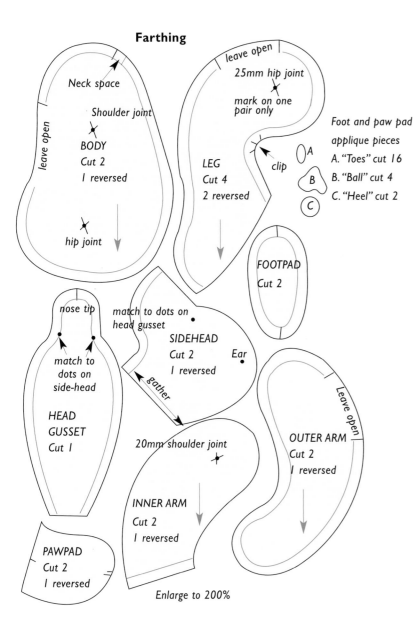

Farthing

leave open

Neck space

Shoulder joint
✕

BODY
Cut 2
1 reversed

leave open

hip joint
✕

leave open

25mm hip joint
✕

mark on one pair only

LEG
Cut 4
2 reversed

clip

Foot and paw pad applique pieces
A. *"Toes" cut 16*
B. *"Ball" cut 4*
C. *"Heel" cut 2*

Ⓐ
Ⓑ
Ⓒ

FOOTPAD
Cut 2

nose tip

match to dots on head gusset

match to dots on side-head

SIDEHEAD
Cut 2
1 reversed

Ear

gather

HEAD GUSSET
Cut 1

20mm shoulder joint
✕

Leave open

OUTER ARM
Cut 2
1 reversed

INNER ARM
Cut 2
1 reversed

PAWPAD
Cut 2
1 reversed

Enlarge to 200%

Jointing tools:

10mm ($^3/_8$") socket tool and spanner (Penny)

No 2 phillips head screwdriver (Penny)

5.5mm ($^7/_{32}$") socket tool and spanner (Farthing)

No 1 phillips head screwdriver (Farthing)

long nose pliers (both bears)

doll needles	stuffing stick
awl	tweezers
small sharp scissors	long pins
general sewing equipment	

Trace pattern pieces onto thin cardboard or templastic, transferring all markings. Stroke the fur pile to find the pile direction and mark with an arrow on the reverse side. Align the arrows on your pattern pieces with this arrow when marking out.

Mark around your pattern piece with a fine permanent marker, reversing pieces where necessary. Mark the openings and joint positions. Cut out your pieces with small sharp scissors, making sure you cut the backing only and not the fur pile. Cut away the pile for 5mm ($^1/_4$", the width of the seam allowance) around each piece.

GUIDE TO PLACEMENT OF APPLIQUE FOR BOTH BEARS

Mark out the paw and foot pads on the right side of the main colour fabric, remembering to reverse each piece before marking the second one so you have pairs. Also, make tiny marks inside the seam allowance on the rounded and straight edges of the paw pads and at each end of the foot pads as shown on the pattern.

At this stage do not cut out the pads. Mark them on the fabric only.

Now take a piece of plain paper and place it on your ironing board to protect it. Place the contrast pad fabric face down on the paper and position the fusible webbing, paper side up, on top. Cover with a cloth and steam iron until the webbing has fused to the fabric.

Peel off the paper and mark out the back of the contrast fabric with the applique design using a fine marking pen. This is not too difficult as the webbing should be slightly tacky which keeps the pieces stable while you

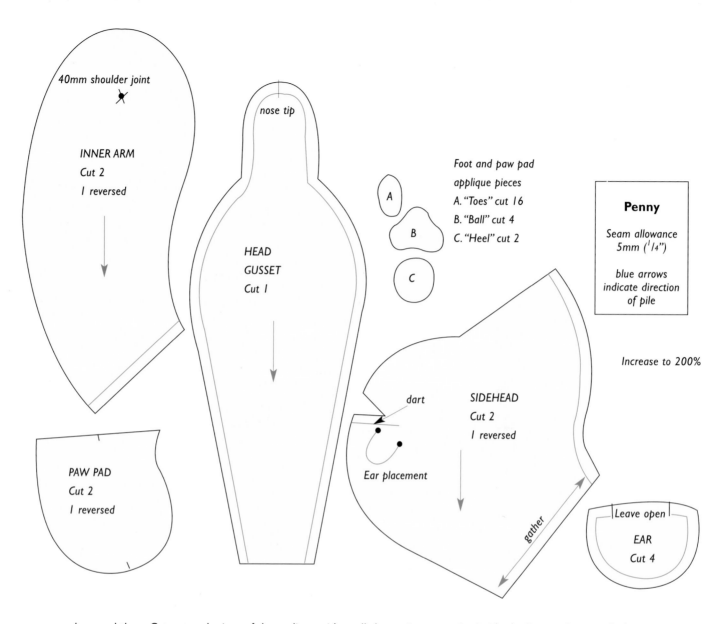

40mm shoulder joint

INNER ARM
Cut 2
1 reversed

nose tip

HEAD
GUSSET
Cut 1

Foot and paw pad
applique pieces
A. "Toes" cut 16
B. "Ball" cut 4
C. "Heel" cut 2

A

B

C

Penny

Seam allowance
5mm ($^1/4$")

blue arrows
indicate direction
of pile

Increase to 200%

dart

SIDEHEAD
Cut 2
1 reversed

Ear placement

PAW PAD
Cut 2
1 reversed

gather

Leave open

EAR
Cut 4

mark around them. Cut out each piece of the applique with small sharp scissors, cutting inside the line you have marked.

Now you must place the applique pieces onto the pads. If you draw an imaginary line between the marks you made in the seam allowance it should help with the placement. Keep in mind that you must maintain a 5mm ($^1/4$") seam allowance around each pad. Tweezers can be a helpful tool when handling the tiny pieces. When you are happy with the applique placement, check each piece to make sure you have maintained the seam allowance. Place your fabric onto the ironing board, cover with a cloth and steam iron to fuse the applique to the pad. Stitch around each piece of applique with matching thread, then cut out the pads.

Sewing 'Penny' together

Sewing can be done on a machine (set at 1.5 stitch length) or by hand. If hand sewing use small, firm backstitch and doubled polyester sewing thread. Make sure you maintain a 5mm ($^1/4$") seam allowance throughout, to avoid bald patches along the seams where you have trimmed the pile. All pieces are sewn with right sides together. They are pinned first, then tacked if necessary, before sewing. After sewing each seam, release any trapped fur using the eye-end of a large needle. This step is particularly important around the muzzle, paw and foot pad areas.

Head: Sew the darts in the side-head pieces, then sew the two side-head pieces together from nose to chin. Insert the head gusset, one side at a time, easing to fit. It is usually better to sew the tip of the nose by hand. Turn right side out.

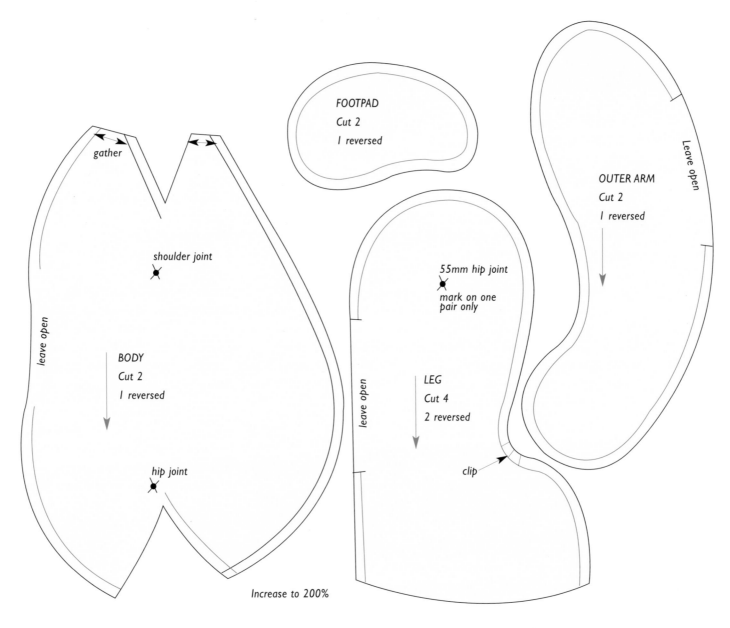

FOOTPAD
Cut 2
1 reversed

gather

shoulder joint

BODY
Cut 2
1 reversed

leave open

hip joint

55mm hip joint

mark on one
pair only

LEG
Cut 4
2 reversed

leave open

clip

OUTER ARM
Cut 2
1 reversed

Leave open

Increase to 200%

Ears: Sew together in pairs. Look at the pattern and note that the seam turns each corner onto the bottom edge, leaving a space in the centre. Clip off the corners carefully, turn the ears making sure the corners are nicely squared. Turn in the raw edges and oversew to close.

Body: Sew the top and bottom darts on each body piece, then sew the two body pieces together, leaving an opening in the neck edge and at the back as shown on the pattern. Gather up the neck hole with extra strong thread and fasten securely. Turn body right side out.

Arms: Sew pawpads to inside arms, making sure you keep the curve correct. Sew inside arms to outside arms, leaving a space at the back as shown on the pattern. Turn paw and arms right side out. Using an awl, pierce holes at the joint marks (do this carefully and spread the fabric threads rather than break them). Insert 40mm joint assemblies ($^3/_4$" bolts through a washer then 40mm disc), then turn tops of arms right side out.

Legs: Sew the legs together in pairs, making sure that each leg has a joint-marked piece, and leaving a space at the back. Sew the foot pads into place, matching the small marks at each end of the pads to the leg seams. Make sure that the inside edge of the paw pads (the concave side) corresponds to the joint-marked side of the leg. It may be easier to sew the pads in by hand. Clip ankle curve. Turn bottom of legs right side out and insert 55mm joint assemblies in the same manner as for the arms. Turn rest of leg.

Completing the head: Stuff the head very firmly, particularly in the muzzle area, keeping the shape even by moulding with your hands as you go. Fill to approximately 1.5cm ($^3/5$") of the neck edge. Run a very strong gathering thread around the neck edge, place the 45mm joint assembly inside the neck hole, with the thread end of the bolt protruding. Pull up the gathering thread tightly around the bolt and fasten off securely. Lose the ends of the thread inside the head. Trim pile on the muzzle — as much or as little as you prefer.

Nose: With perle No 5 cotton, stitch the outline shape of the nose first. The top edge extends from one side of the gusset to the other, about 1cm ($^2/5$") back from the tip. The two sides of the nose meet in the nose-to-chin seam, about 1cm ($^2/5$") down from the tip. Stitch the nose in two layers, starting with a horizontal satin stitch for the underneath layer. If desired, several base layers can be done to give the nose body. The top layer is stitched with vertical satin stitch, one half at a time, starting in the centre and with each stitch becoming shorter as you approach the corner. Neaten the outside edges of the nose with long straight stitches if necessary. Finish off your threads by bringing them out in another area of the head, knotting close to the fabric and then 'popping' the knots to the inside.

Mouth: Thread your longest doll needle with a double thickness of perle No 5 cotton. Pass the needle through the bottom corner of the nose to the back of the head. Remove the needle, make a knot in the thread and 'pop' it inside. Now use pins to determine your mouth (usually an inverted 'Y'). When satisfied, stitch mouth into place then bring thread out and 'pop' another knot to finish off.

Ears: Pin into place, using long pins. Top edge of ear is placed about 1cm ($^2/5$") down from the gusset seam on the side-head dart. The ear is them curled around so that the bottom corner is about 1.5cm ($^3/5$") down from the top corner. Check pinned ears from all angles for evenness before stitching into place with strong thread and ladder stitch. Stitch the back first, then the front – this is a little awkward becuase of the curve – popping in your knots as you did when stitching the nose and mouth.

Eyes: Determine eye positions with glass headed pins and check carefully for evenness. Make a hole with the awl for the first eye. Have extra-strong thread in your long doll needle. Insert needle through eye hole and out just in front of the disc under the bear's chin. Remove needle and rethread it at the other end. Place first eye onto thread. Make a hole at the second eye position and insert needle back into first eye hole and out through the second. Place second eye on thread, then pass needle back into second eye hole and out through the head under the chin about 1 – 2mm away from where the thread starts. Now knot the threads together once, and while pushing the eyes with your thumb and pulling the threads which you have wound around your fingers, indent the eyes. When you are happy with the look, knot the threads off securely, bury the ends inside the head, pulling them sharply so that the knot sinks in.

Jointing

For the head: Push the bolt protruding from the bottom of the head through the gathered-up hole at the top of the body. Place the disc then washer on the bolt. Screw on the locknut until it stops, then grasp the bolt, as close to the disc as possible, with the long nose pliers. Holding the pliers tightly, screw down the locknut as far as possible with the screw tool, then change the plier-grip to above the locknut and finish tightening with the spanner.

For the limbs: Locate joint mark inside body and make a hole with the awl as you did when inserting the joints into the tops of the limbs. Push the bolt that protrudes from the limb through the appropriate joint position in the body. Place correct-sized disc onto the bolt, then a washer, then a locknut. Screw up the locknut with your fingers until it stops, then tighten completely by holding the head of the screw steady with the screwdriver and tightening the locknut with the socket tool. Tighten up the limbs to the point where they can only be moved with difficulty as they will loosen considerably with stuffing and handling.

Stuffing: Fill the limbs first, placing the stuffing in small wads and pushing it down firmly with your stuffing stick. Take your time and make sure there are no empty pockets. Close the openings with ladder stitch using strong thread. Fill the tummy, again with small wads of fill, pushing it in well, and paying particular attention to the areas around the joints to avoid empty pockets. Another area to watch is the curve of the tummy – make sure you don't create wrinkles here. Close back with ladder stitch.

Waxing the nose (optional): Stick masking tape firmly into place along each edge of the nose to protect the mohair from the wax. Rub the nose stitching vigorously with the black wax then polish with a piece of plain paper. Remove the masking tape.

Making up Farthing

You make up Farthing in much the same way as for Penny, with the following variations.

Head: There are no darts in the side-head pieces. Before turning the head, mark the ear positions with threads that hang on the outside. The nose embroidery is positioned 5mm ($^1/_4$") back from the tip for the straight top edge and 5mm ($^1/_4$") down from the top where the two sides meet in a point on the nose-chin seam. Perle No 8 cotton is used for the nose and mouth embroidery. The ears are positioned with the top corner placed where the marker thread emerges from the head. The bottom corner of the ear is curled around until it meets the top corner. The ears are ladder-stitched around the back only, then the marker threads are snipped off.

Legs: The opening is at the front instead of the back.

Joints: Head and hips – 25mm (1") Shoulders 20mm ($^4/_5$")

Body: There are no body darts and the neck space is a small gap in the stitching. There is no gathering.

Yukon by Linda Benson

Yukon is a bear with 11 joints in his body, which gives him many possibilities for posing.

Requirements

50cm (20") fur fabric	pair 6mm (^{1}/$_4$") glass eyes
perle 8 cotton (black)	ultrasuede
calico	8 x 25mm (1") discs
2 x 30mm (1^1/$_5$") discs	8 x 50mm (2") discs
2 x 75mm (3") discs	2 x 85mm (3^2/$_5$") discs
artificial sinew	11 bolts or pins (as preferred) and washers to suit
fibrefill stuffing or similar	strong sewing thread to match fur fabric
general bearmaking tool kit	

Make a copy of the pattern and transfer it to thin card or template plastic, transferring all markings. Using a laundry marker, trace the pattern onto the back of your fur fabric, making sure the arrows are running in the same direction as the fur pile. Reverse pieces where necessary to make pairs, and mark joint holes. Cut out all pieces, taking care to snip only the backing fabric and not the pile, to ensure a good cover of fur over the seams.

The Head

Trim the fur from the shaded areas on the head pieces. Do this before the seams are sewn to avoid obvious seam lines in the face. With strong sewing thread sew the under chin seam using backstitch and then overcast the seam to strengthen (do this on all seams). Fold the head gusset in half and pinch it tightly at 'A' to mark the centre of the nose; match this point with the under chin seam and sew in the gusset, pinning and easing it in place.

Turn the head through and stuff it firmly, using small amounts of stuffing at a time. When you are satisfied with the firmness and shape of the head, embroider the nose and mouth using perle 8 cotton. First outline a basic triangle and fill it in using satin stitch. To create 'nostrils', make some longer stitches at each side. Build up layers of embroidery, laying the stitches in neatly and snugly until you are happy with its shape (use the photo as a guide).

Sew the pairs of ears together and ladder stitch them to the head, pulling the corners in to cup the ears in a natural manner.

Insert a 50mm (2") joint assembly into the bottom of the head; run a gathering thread of sinew around the opening, pull up and secure firmly.

It is best to do a little needle sculpting to bring in the eye 'sockets' before tying in the eyes. Thread a doll needle with a length of sinew. Push the needle through the head under the chin as close to the joint as possible, bringing it out at one eye position and leaving the end hanging. Take a small stitch and pass the needle across the nose to the other eye spot and take a small stitch. Pass the needle through to each eye once more and then down through the head, exiting where the other end of the sinew is hanging. Pull the threads as tightly as possible to indent the eye 'sockets' and tie off securely. Rethread each end of the sinew into the needle and pull tightly to 'pop' the knot in, then trim. Use an awl to make holes for the eyes and, using sinew on a doll

Yukon 38cm (15")

needle, follow the same procedure as with the needle sculpting, this time threading an eye in place; tie off securely and 'pop' the knot into the head.

The neck

Sew the two neck pieces together where indicated on the pattern. Sew in the two discs (top and bottom), easing them in place. Make the joint holes and turn the piece through. Joint onto the head using a 50mm (2") disc, then insert a 75mm (3") joint assembly into the bottom of the neck.

The body

The upper body is constructed in the same way as the neck. Use a 75mm (3") disc in the top and joint to neck, then insert an 85mm ($3^2/_5$") joint assembly into the bottom.

Sew the darts in each lower body piece and then sew the two pieces together as indicated on the pattern. Sew the disc in place, make joint holes and turn through. Joint arm to the upper body using 85mm ($3^2/_5$") disc.

Trapunto for feet and paws

Trace a pair each of paws and feet onto paper and colour in the trapunto pattern with a black felt tip pen (make sure you have a left and a right of each). Take the paper pieces to a window (or light box if available) and trace around them onto the calico, outlining all the shapes inside as well as the whole paw shape. Tack around each calico paw onto ultrasuede and cut out a little larger than the pattern (this makes handling the pieces easier while doing the trapunto and will be trimmed off later). Carefully sew around each of the toes and pads, either using a machine or by hand. If sewing them by hand, sew around each shape using tiny running stitches and then go around again to fill in the gaps. Make a small slit in the calico in the middle of each shape and stuff each one firmly using tweezers. Close the opening using herringbone stitch, taking care not to pull the edges in. Trim the excess fabric away and sew pads into hands and feet.

Arms and hands

Sew the arms together in pairs where indicated on the pattern. Sew in the discs, make joint holes and turn through. Sew the hands together, sew in the paw and the disc, make joint hole and turn through, easing the trapunto through carefully. Joint hands to arms using 25mm (1") joints.

Legs and feet

The legs and feet are constructed in the same manner as the arms and hands. Insert a 50mm (2") joint assembly into each of the limbs. The arms are then jointed onto a 30mm ($1^1/_5$") disc in the body. This allows the arm to ride over the lower joint of the neck which gives the bear a more natural appearance. The legs are jointed onto 50mm (2") discs.

When the jointing is completed, stuff the bear, paying particular attention to the tight areas in the neck, arms, legs and feet. Close over the openings and brush any caught fur out of the seams. Sew the tail pieces together and ladder stitch in place.

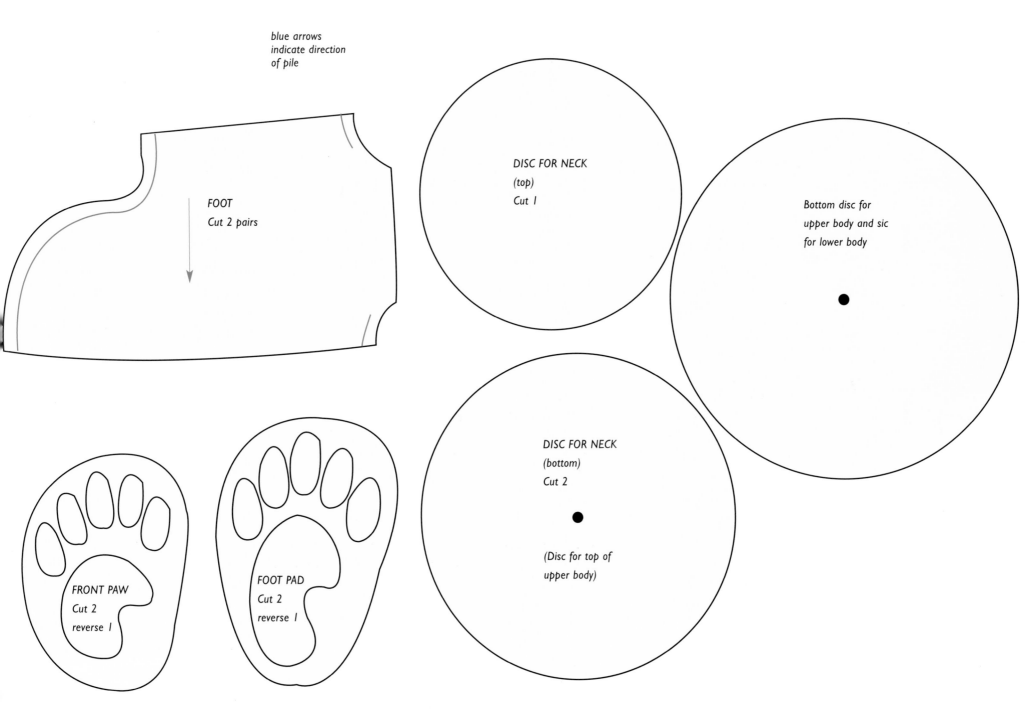

blue arrows
indicate direction
of pile

FOOT
Cut 2 pairs

DISC FOR NECK
(top)
Cut 1

Bottom disc for
upper body and sic
for lower body

FRONT PAW
Cut 2
reverse 1

FOOT PAD
Cut 2
reverse 1

DISC FOR NECK
(bottom)
Cut 2

(Disc for top of
upper body)

Actual size

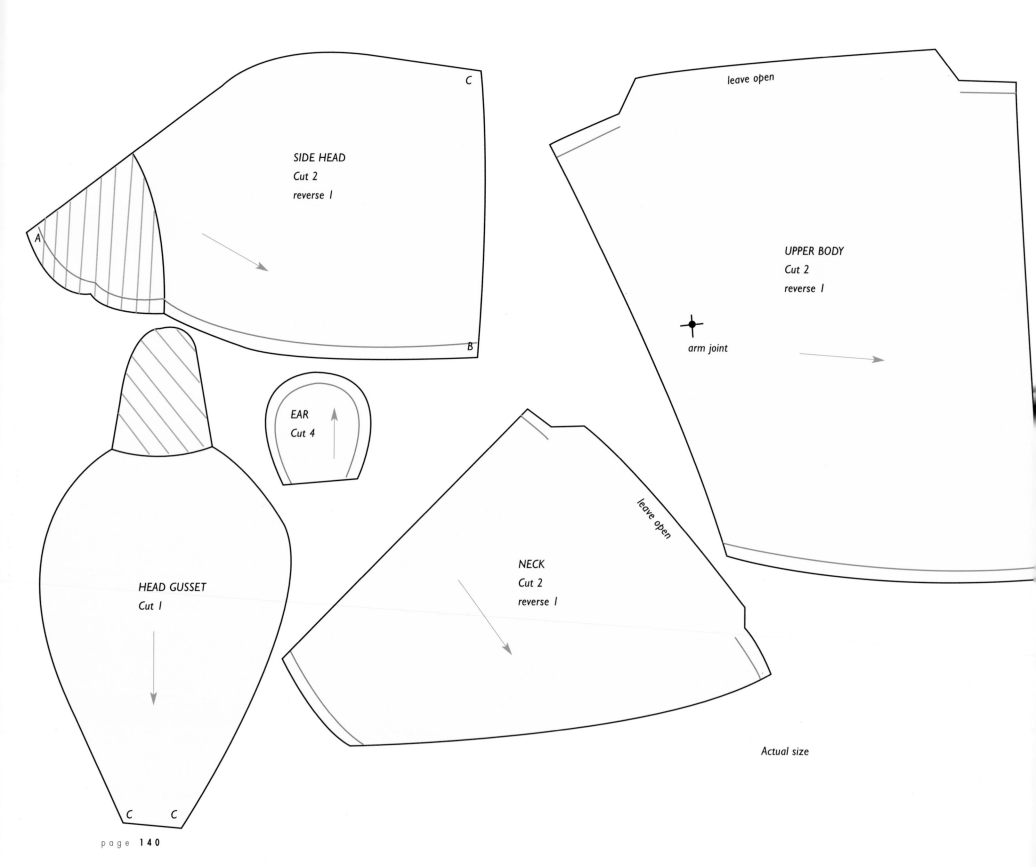

SIDE HEAD
Cut 2
reverse 1

C

A

B

UPPER BODY
Cut 2
reverse 1

leave open

arm joint

EAR
Cut 4

HEAD GUSSET
Cut 1

NECK
Cut 2
reverse 1

leave open

Actual size

C   C

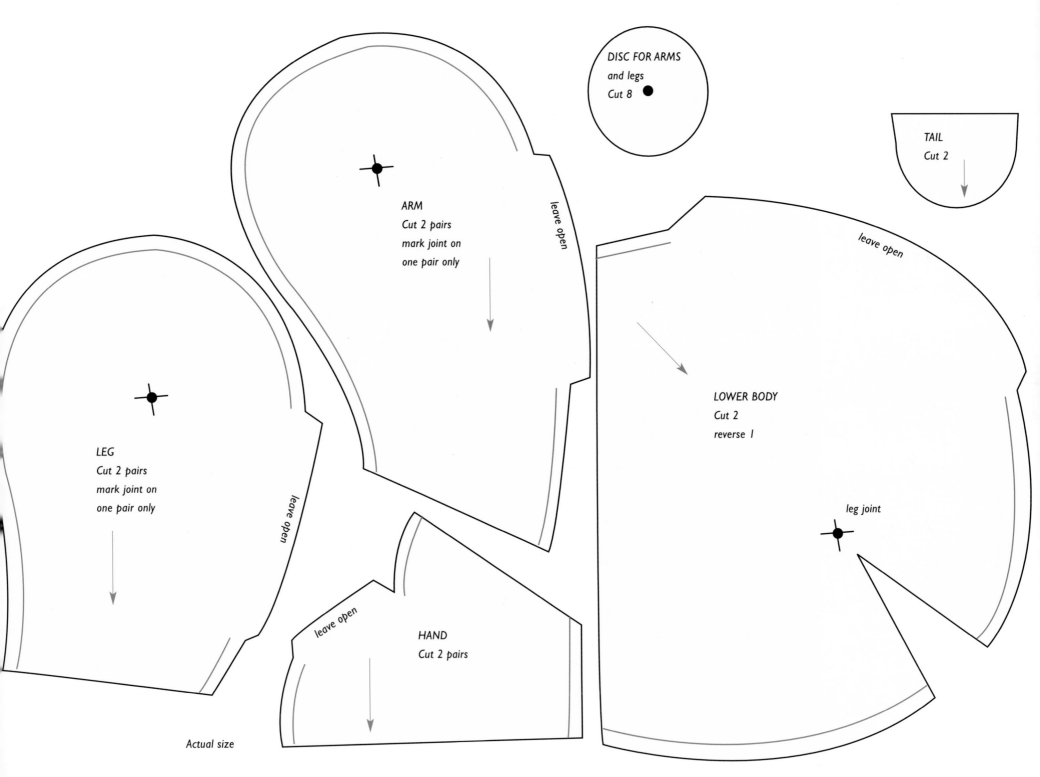

DISC FOR ARMS
and legs
Cut 8

TAIL
Cut 2

ARM
Cut 2 pairs
mark joint on
one pair only

leave open

LEG
Cut 2 pairs
mark joint on
one pair only

leave open

LOWER BODY
Cut 2
reverse 1

leave open

leg joint

leave open

HAND
Cut 2 pairs

Actual size

Elizabeth's Clown by Susie McMahon

Elizabeth is a doll of oil painted cloth approximately 45cm (18") high with moulded cloth head on jointed cloth body.

Requirements

thread to match	30cm x 30cm (12" x 12") stretch knit fabric in stripe or pattern
strong thread or dental floss (for jointing)	small package polymer clay in flesh, or colour of choice, or air-drying clay may be used
small quantity fibrefill stuffing	sculpting tools (nothing special – knitting needles are good)
fine tipped silver paint pen	stuffing tool (a bamboo skewer with rounded tip will do)
acrylic paints in basic colours	fine sable or similar brushes
thin card or plastic to transfer pattern	fine sandpaper
gesso or acrylic undercoat, small quantity	small piece aluminium foil
acrylic varnish	PVA glue
small bell (optional)	embroidery thread, coloured to match or contrast with body fabric

Trace all the pattern pieces onto the card or plastic. Accuracy is very important, especially with such small pattern pieces. Transfer all pattern markings. Cut the pattern pieces out.

Trace around the pattern pieces directly onto the reverse of the fabric (doubled, right sides together) using the silver pen and noting the direction of the stretch.

Note: this silver line is the stitching line. **Do not cut out fabric**.

Body and limbs

Sew around all the pieces, leaving openings where indicated for turning and stuffing. Use a small backstitch and follow the lines as accurately as possible. After sewing, cut the pieces out using small sharp scissors. Clip any inside corners taking care not to snip the thread.

Turn the pieces and stuff without over filling. Close the openings using ladder stitch.

Bind with doubled thread around the wrists, ankles and neck, drawing it up quite tightly and finishing off securely.

Using strong thread, joint through the body, attaching the limbs in the positions marked. The thread can be hidden by not stitching right through but simply catching the fabric on the inside of the limb in the marked spot.

Face

The face is made separately from polymer or air drying clay, and glues onto the head later.

Make a small mound out of crushed foil to correspond with the size and shape of the head. Form the face over this mound, using a flattened piece of the clay. Any excess can be trimmed from around the edges using a sharp knife. The drawing on the next page shows the approximate face size.

Elizabeth and her clown doll 45cm (18") high

Make small indentations halfway up for the eyes. Add small pads for the cheeks, chin and forehead and blend in.

The nose is added next. It is a small ball with two tiny balls each side for nostril flares. Make nostrils with a knitting needle. Add a small wedge to form the upper lip and a tiny roll for the lower lip. Use a knitting needle to refine the mouth shape. Sculpt eye definition using a needle.

If using polymer clay, follow the manufacturer's instructions to bake the clay. Remove the foil support after it has cooled. If using the air drying clay allow it to dry thoroughly in a warm place before removing the foil support. In both cases, when baked or dry, trim carefully with a trimming knife. Make sure the edge which will contact the head is smooth and bump free.

Smooth with sandpaper. Coat with several coats of gesso or acrylic undercoat.

Paint as desired, with acrylics, and seal with acrylic varnish when thoroughly dry.

Glue face directly onto the head.

Finish off your clown in any way you fancy. Susie likes to use tiny bells and a piece of silk ribbon gathered into a ruff for around the neck. She also likes to gesso the hands and feet a couple of times and then paint them to match the face.

Face approximate size

Make some hair from coloured embroidery thread, or something similar, and then sew the hat, turn and attach to the head, securing the hair firmly at the top front. You can add a little stuffing inside the hat, or leave it floppy according to your own preference. A small bell on top of the hat will finish it off!

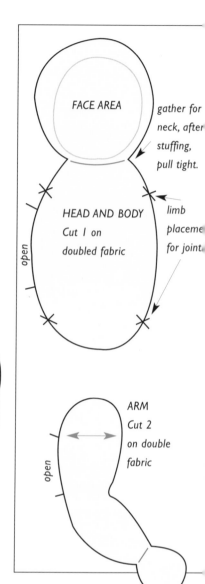

FACE AREA

gather for neck, after stuffing, pull tight.

HEAD AND BODY
Cut 1 on doubled fabric

limb placement for joint

open

ARM
Cut 2 on double fabric

open

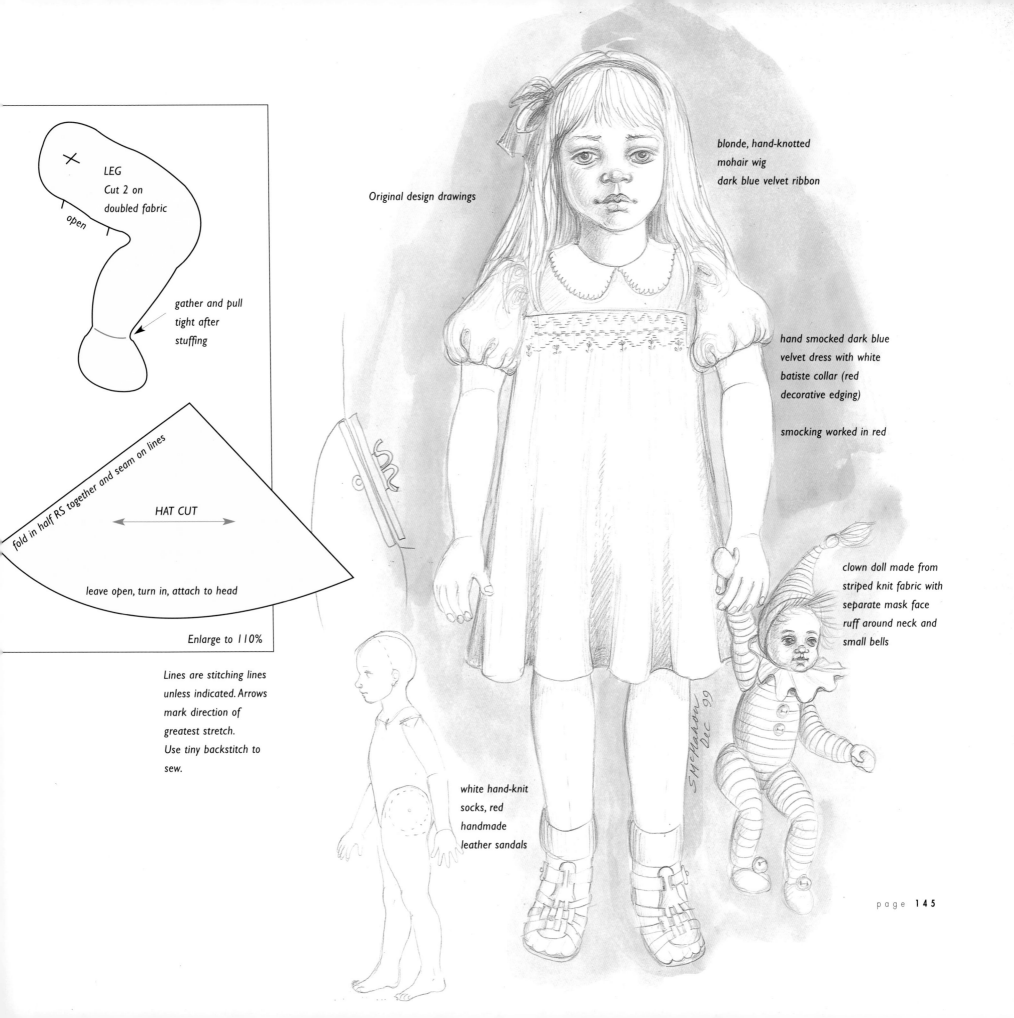

LEG
Cut 2 on
doubled fabric

open

gather and pull
tight after
stuffing

fold in half RS together and seam on lines

HAT CUT

leave open, turn in, attach to head

Enlarge to 110%

Lines are stitching lines
unless indicated. Arrows
mark direction of
greatest stretch.
Use tiny backstitch to
sew.

Original design drawings

blonde, hand-knotted
mohair wig
dark blue velvet ribbon

hand smocked dark blue
velvet dress with white
batiste collar (red
decorative edging)

smocking worked in red

clown doll made from
striped knit fabric with
separate mask face
ruff around neck and
small bells

white hand-knit
socks, red
handmade
leather sandals

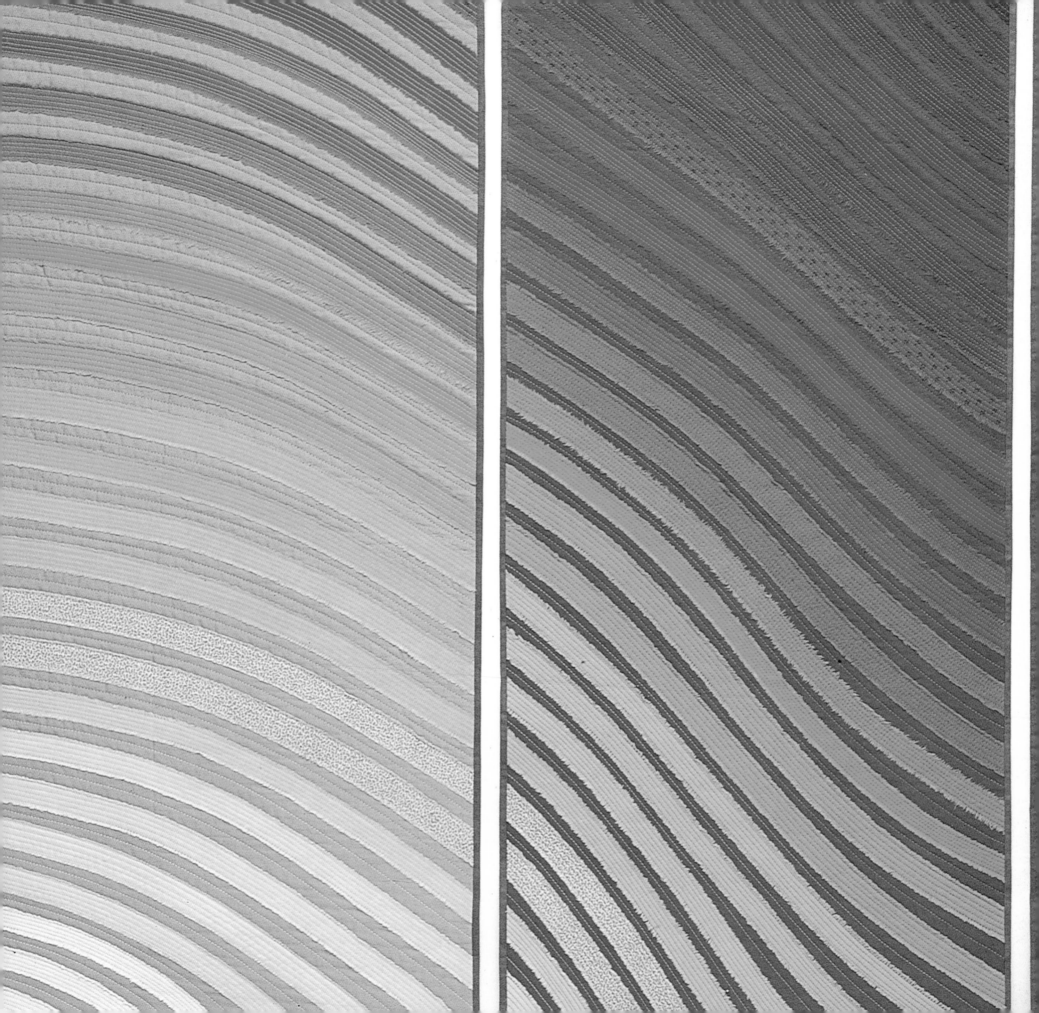

Landscape Quilts

Dianne Firth

The Australian landscape is Dianne Firth's inspiration. Its distinctive forms, patterns and colours of earth, rock, water and vegetation are a continual source of ideas for her quilts and she has developed a technique to capture these special qualities of landscape. These exquisitely finished works reflect her training as a landscape architect and her passion for environmental issues.

Quilting as an interest started in 1982 for Dianne and she has progressed from making practical quilts for family, friends and community projects to making the art quilts shown on these pages. She is basically self-taught but enjoys attending workshops by visiting quilters when she has the time in her heavy academic schedule.

In Black and White, 1998, Dianne, influenced by tyre tracks on wet roads, attempted to break from rigid geometrical forms and develop her own voice. In order to provide the freedom of expression required, she developed for this quilt the technique of torn strips machine-appliqued onto a base. Other quilts worked since then have continued to explore this technique.

The quilts are made by arranging the torn strips (with their frayed edges) onto a background fabric. This surface is sandwiched with backing and batting and the whole piece is applique-quilted together.

The first requirement for the fabric is that it should tear easily. Then Dianne looks for a range of tones from light, through medium, to dark. Plains are usually best, but small patterned tone-on-tones also work. Only a light-weight batting is needed.

Desert Contours Continue
85cm x 126cm (33^1/$_2$" x 122")
Cotton

In *Desert Contours II* the inspiration came from patterns in sand and the way sand moves. A simple abstracted line sketch was made. Seven fabrics in graded earth tones were selected. The darkest was used for the square background and cut slightly larger than the required finished size. The other fabrics were torn into strips of approximately 1.5cm to 2.5 cm ($^5/_8$" – 1") width. The torn strips were gently steam-pressed to form a smooth curve (the more open the weave, the easier this happens). Strips were assembled and tacked onto the base in a tonal progression with the mid-tone of the seven fabrics placed towards the centre of the composition. The three layers of backing, batting and tacked applique were assembled and pinned in readiness for machine applique-quilting. A thin batting was used and a plain fabric was chosen for the backing so that the stitching would enhance the back of the quilt as well.

Starting at the centre, and with a matching thread, machine stitching commenced at the centre of each strip, then about 3mm ($^1/_8$") in from the raw edge using the machine foot as a guide, and then at uniform spacing in between. Once all the strips were applique-quilted, the background was quilted with a single stitching line down the centre of the space using a lighter coloured thread.

To finish the piece, threads outside the stitching lines along the raw edges were pulled out, the piece was lightly pressed and trimmed square and a 5mm ($^1/_4$") binding of the background colour was added.

Desert Contours II (above)

51cm x 51cm (20" x 20")

Cotton

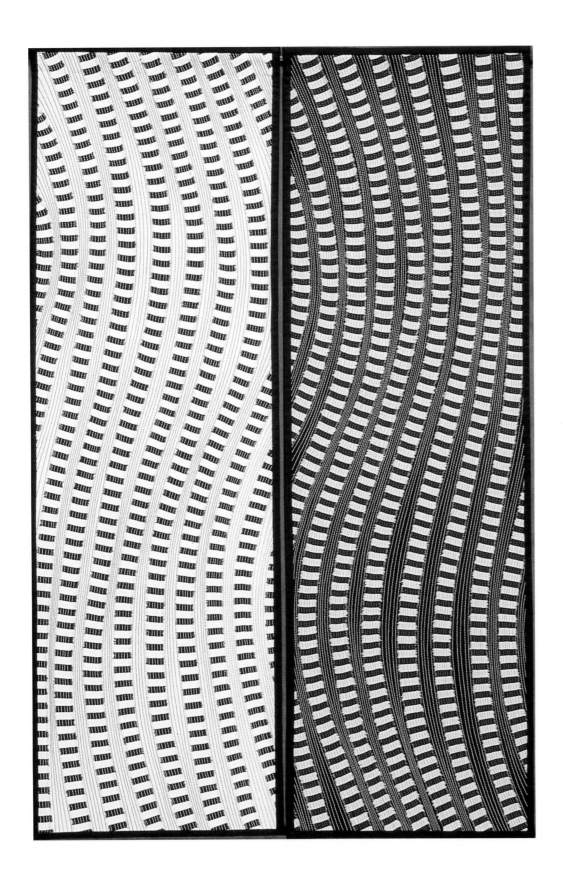

Black and White

89cm x 58cm (35" x 23")

Cotton

Pieced Colour

Beryl Hodges

A patchworker since 1980, Beryl Hodges, well-known teacher and regular exhibitor, is inspired by colour and colour combinations which 'bounce'. Her works have always been rich in colour although earlier works were more restrained. Recent designs are vibrant and exuberant. Unlike many quilters, it is not landscape which gives her ideas, but colours which 'zing' and her desire to combine these colours. She has always been an advocate of the use of black in quilts, because black heightens the colours which it borders, while white, on the other hand, subdues other colours. Her earlier quilts featured little or no yellow however, which is surprising when one sees her current work. There were, quite simply, few yellow fabrics around in the 1980s.

Beryl sews by machine because 'life is too short' and her main aim is to create an impact with colour in her quilts, not show off her hand work. However, she is a patient 'unpicker' and will remove any pieces which jar in her arrangements. Working vertically on a design wall in her studio/workshop, she stands back and critically eyes all stages of her arrangements. A favourite trick is to use a pair of binoculars reversed. These draw the pattern in and allow her to see any flaws in her design or colour combinations.

The work shown on these pages feature triangles which Beryl has individually custom-made from strips of different coloured fabric in order to create the correct colour shading. In *The Fourth Day* the design appears to feature rectangles because of the flow of colour. Similarly, the changing angles of the triangles create movement. It almost seems as if curved pieces of fabric have been used, when all are straight-edged.

Another hallmark of Beryl's work is her use of borders. She believes that all quilts need a border, just as a painting needs a frame. The quilts shown here have different types of borders – an applique border on *The Fourth Day*, and, in *The Gift of Prometheus*, the quilt has been cut and a border inserted.

Beryl's quilting is simple and almost purely practical although in *The Gift of Prometheus*, the upwardly slanting yet random quilting makes the triangles of the work appear curved.

Above: Grid I: The Gift of Prometheus 130cm x 145cm (52" x 58")

Left: Grid V: The Fourth Day 121cm x 112cm (48 1/2" x 49")

Hand Quilting

Kerry Gavin

Another of the Canberra quilters, Kerry Gavin began patchworking more than 17 years ago, taking it up with enthusiasm and dedication. Already a keen sewer she honed her skills as a patchworker in numerous classes and workshops, and was always prepared to put in the long hours of work required to complete the quilts and to experiment with new ideas and colour patterns.

Although working in a wide range of styles, from traditional through contemporary to experimental, Kerry is best known for her white quilts which have appeared in numerous books and magazines, but her greatest passion is hand quilting, laborious work which others are often unprepared to undertake. One quilt may take up to three months, eight hours a day, every day, to hand quilt. However, the results speak for themselves as her quilts have a wonderful, soft quality, and she enjoys the time to reflect, and plan other projects

Kerry's quilts are snapped up by collectors and, working everyday in her workroom, her output is prodigious. Even when she reaches a particularly tight deadline and is apparently exhausted, she will be at work within a few hours, trying out new ideas and fabrics.

The quilt shown here was made for her son, Bradley, who died before it was completed. It is made in colours deliberately chosen for their timeless quality and will remain a lasting memento for the family.

Twenty treasured years – for the love of a son
249cm x 204cm (8' x 6')
appliqued oak leaf pattern, hand quilted, using fabric from secondhand shirts

Kerry Gavin

Woollen Strands

Judy Turner

Well known for her colourwash quilts which blended strips of printed fabrics, Judy Turner has, in recent years, been working with dyed woollen yarn whose saturated colour has always fascinated her. She has switched the medium she was working with from strips of printed fabric to strands of woollen yarn to create work which is truly original. Yet still her focus is the subtle blending of colour to create impressions of places, moods, and natural themes such as the changing seasons.

These days Judy sits surrounded by hundreds of ball of wool, making decisions as she goes. The work is labour intensive with many technical difficulties to overcome. As the quilts are stiff, they are constructed with satin stitch. The fabric shrinks because of the intense machine couching, for example, some quilts a metre square (40" square) have used approximately 5000 metres of thread. It took Judy about five weeks to source the yarn and make the fabric for *Colour Me Crazy* shown here. The fabric was made by machine couching hundreds of strands of woollen yarn to a black chintz background. Because of the gentle gradation of colour, the quilt has the appearance of silk.

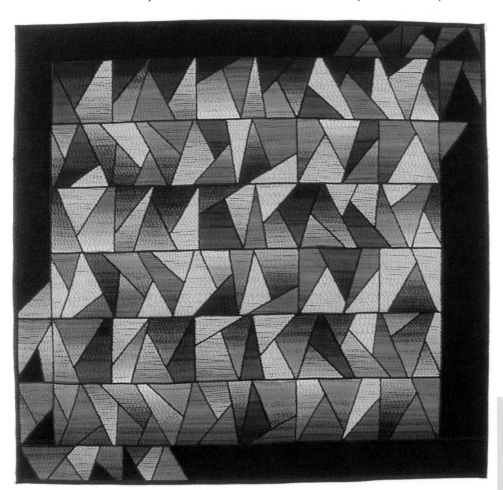

Colour Me Crazy
90cm x 85cm (36" x 34")

Bears in the Smoky Mountains

Margaret Rolfe

It might be trite to describe someone as 'one of Australia's leading quilters', but in Margaret Rolfe's case this is undeniably true. And she has had an enormous influence on the popularity of patchwork and quilting in her own country, encouraging hundreds if not thousands of others to take up this absorbing activity. Her willingness to pass on her knowledge and ideas is refreshing and her enthusiasm is definitely catching, as hundreds of quilters in the region of Canberra, where she is based, will confirm. Other quilters represented in this book would acknowledge the role Margaret has played in their development, as well.

Margaret is perhaps even better known in the United States of America, the 'home' of patchwork, than she is in Australia. She is a highly successful author in the United States and travels there regularly for teaching, exhibitions and events. It is perhaps only natural she should have chosen to work a quilt with an 'American' theme. However, the bears and trees can always be replaced with other motifs.

The blocks were largely made while Margaret and her husband were on a trip to the United States in 1996 when they made a visit to the Smoky Mountains. They saw a small black bear while walking on one of the trails in the National Park, hence the name of the quilt. The bear was small enough not to be very frightening, but not large enough to be away from its mother, who must have been nearby. They remained a safe distance from the bear and, when it saw them, it ran off into the woods.

The quilt blocks were hand pieced as Margaret's 'travelling sewing'. Margaret says, 'I like to have some piecing to do when I am travelling as I find it very relaxing. Often I prepare the blocks before I leave, or else pack templates and pick up fabrics on my travels. For this quilt I did both, and many of the trees are made of fabrics which I bought on the trip.'

Margaret completed the quilt at home when she finished the borders and machine quilting. The background was free machine quilted.

Bears in the Smoky Mountains 152cm x 184cm (60" x 72¹/₂")

Margaret Rolfe

Requirements

3.2 metres (3$^{1}/_{2}$ yards) total assorted beige prints for background

2.3 metres (2$^{1}/_{2}$ yards) total assorted prints in red, green, golden yellow and orange for trees and pieced border

10 cm (4") black print for bears

Small piece of brown print for bear noses

60cm (24") autumn-toned print for binding

3.5 metres (3$^{3}/_{4}$ yards) backing fabric

165cm x 195cm (64" x 77") piece of batting

Brown stranded embroidery floss

Finished quilt size: 152 cm x 184 cm (60" x 72$^{1}/_{2}$")

Hand pieced blocks, machine pieced top and borders, machine quilted

Quilt assembly

1. Make three Bear blocks, using the full size pattern given. Make one of the bears as given, and two in reverse. Use either template method or foundation piecing to construct the bears, making each bear in two sections. Within each section, follow the order of the numbers to sew the pieces together. Applique a circle of black print for ears. Use two strands of brown embroidery floss to embroider a small circle of chain stitch to make eyes. Trim blocks to exactly 4 $^{1}/_{2}$" x 6$^{1}/_{2}$". Make the blocks up to the 9" block size by adding quarter-square triangles. Each block will need two triangles cut from a 10$^{1}/_{4}$" square and two triangles cut from an 8$^{1}/_{4}$" square. Trim finished blocks to exactly 9$^{1}/_{2}$" x 9$^{1}/_{2}$".

2. Make 29 Tree blocks. Draw block to full size from pattern given, and use either foundation piecing or template method to construct block. Trim finished blocks to exactly 9$^{1}/_{2}$" x 9$^{1}/_{2}$".

3. From beige prints, cut seven squares, each 9$^{7}/_{8}$" x 9$^{7}/_{8}$". Cut squares in half across the diagonal to make 14 half-square triangles for sides of quilt centre. Cut one square, 10$^{1}/_{4}$" x 10$^{1}/_{4}$". Cut square across both diagonals to make four quarter-square triangles for the corners of the quilt centre.

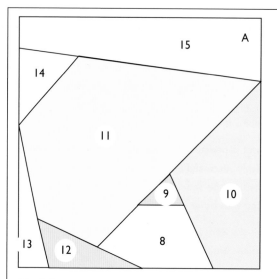

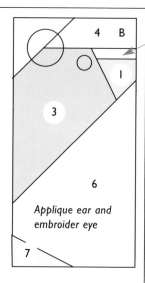

Black bear

Full size pattern for 6" x 4" Bear

Note that the Bear is made in two sections (Section A and Section B), then the sections are joined together to complete the block. The Bear may be constructed by foundation piecing or made with templates. Follow order of the numbers to piece each section.

Colour:
Bear body – black
Nose – brown

Finishing:
Ear – applique circle of black
Eye – embroider circle, using two strands of brown floss and chain stitch.

4. Arrange the Bear blocks, Tree blocks, side and corner triangles to make quilt centre, as shown in quilt diagram. Sew blocks and triangles together by first sewing the blocks into rows on the diagonal and then sewing the rows of blocks together.

Pieced border

1. From assorted beige prints, cut 18 squares, each $5^3/8$" x $5^3/8$". Cut squares in half across the diagonal to make 36 half-square triangles. Cut 36 squares, each $2^3/4$" x $2^3/4$". Cut one square, $10^1/4$" x $10^1/4$". Cut square across both diagonals to make four quarter-square triangles for the corners.

2. From assorted prints for trees, cut 20 squares, each $5^3/8$" x $5^3/8$". Cut squares in half across the diagonal to make 40 half-square triangles. Cut 36 squares, each $2^3/4$" x $2^3/4$".

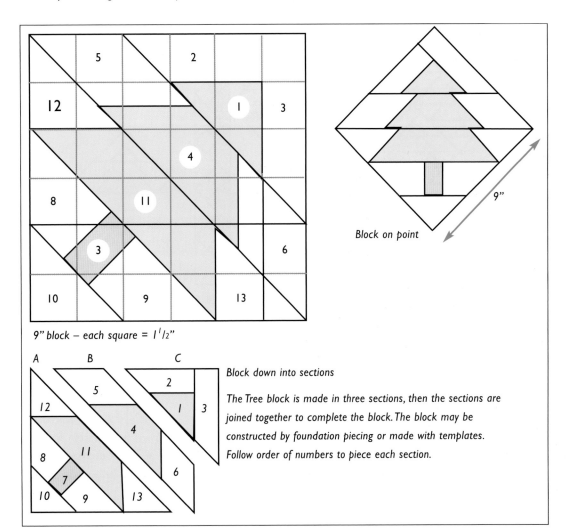

9" block – each square = $1^1/2$"

Block down into sections

The Tree block is made in three sections, then the sections are joined together to complete the block. The block may be constructed by foundation piecing or made with templates. Follow order of numbers to piece each section.

Block on point
9"

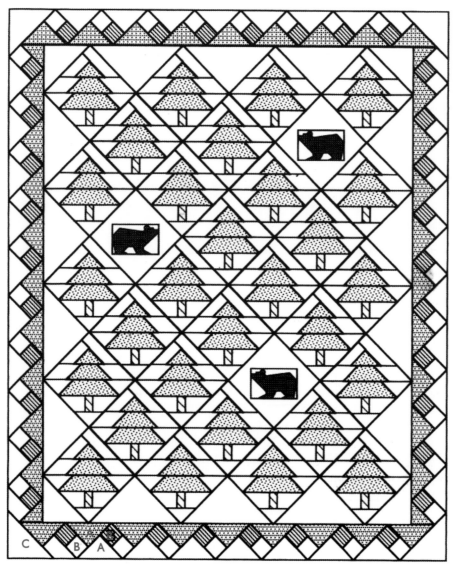

6" (f/s)

Quilt centre

6" x 4" (f/s) Bear block. Make one block, and two reverse blocks.

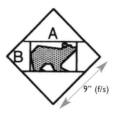

A

B

9" (f/s)

Make Bear blocks up to 9" (f/s) with quarter-square triangles (cut A from $10^{1}/4$" square and B from $8^{1}/4$" square); sew triangles to Bear then trim to make block $9^{1}/2$" x $9^{1}/2$")

9" (f/s) Tree block. Make 29.

Note: quilt has bias edges.

A

$4^{1}/2$" (f/s) half-square triangles (cut from $5^{3}/8$" square).
Cut 20 print and 18 background squares (to make 40 print and 36 background triangles).
Note: trim triangles as required to complete the corners.

B

$2^{1}/4$" (f/s) square (cut $2\ ^{3}/4$" square).
Cut 36 print and 36 background squares.

C

9" (f/s) quarter-square triangles (cut from $10^{1}/4$" square)
Cut one square (to make 4 corner triangles).

Side triangles –
9" (f/s) half sq. triangles (cut from $9^{7}/8$" square).
Cut 7 squares (to make 14 triangles)

Corner triangles –
9" (f/s) quarter sq. triangles (cut from $10^{1}/4$" square).
Cut 1 square (to make 4 triangles)

page **158**

3. Arrange squares and triangles to make border strips, as shown in quilt diagram. Piece border strips together. Note that the triangles will need to be trimmed back to make a right-angle at each end of the side border strips.

4. Sew side borders to quilt centre, then add top and bottom borders. Add corner triangles, trimming away excess of border strips after stitching.

5. Stay stitch around the edge of the quilt, being careful not to stretch the bias edges while sewing.

Finishing

1. Trim away the selvages from the backing fabric, then cut into two equal lengths. Stitch the lengths together side by side. Press this seam open.

2. Layer backing, batting and quilt top. Baste or safety pin layers together.

3. Machine or hand quilt. Outline quilt the bears, the trees, and the print shapes in the border. Free quilt meandering lines into the background.

4. From fabric for binding, cut seven strips, each $2^{1}/_{2}$" wide. Piece the strips together to make the lengths required (measure quilt through the centre to find the exact measurements). Press strips in half lengthwise.

Bind quilt.

Note: measurements for quilt assembly are in inches as this is still the international standard. Black Bear block design from Go Wild with Quilts, *published by That Patchwork Place.*

Enriched Quilting

Ruth Stoneley

For the main work displayed here, Ruth Stoneley has reached back into the past, but the majority of her quilts are highly contemporary. She moves beyond the norms of quilting in her other recent work, using material and techniques from the tradition to create panels of intense colour and texture, employing varied and often unorthodox materials, and decorating with beads and other glittering objects, including the tawdry and the brilliant. And through her use of colour and materials, she is able to develop her emotional themes, reflecting feelings from tumultuous anger to calm and serenity. She has a sure eye and is able to balance finely all the elements of her work to create a controlled and sustained masterpiece.

Ruth has been quilting for more than 20 and has an established international reputation. She acknowledges the example of Miriam Shapiro from the United States and the expanded understanding she gained on a study tour scholarship awarded by the Churchill Fellowship. All her trips overseas to teach, whether it be to the United States of America or Abu Dhabi, generate new ideas as well as adding to her store of fabrics and embellishments.

The Memory Quilt

This quilt, like many of her others, is a work with great personal resonance for Ruth Stoneley, as she explains. 'The bride in the photograph is my grandmother Georgina, who died when my mother was fourteen, her husband Philip, seated, her attendants and her mother, my great grandmother Minnie, seated to the right. I was recently given this photograph and had a fragment of velvet from a dress of my great grandmother's so I decided to incorporate these into a "memory piece".'

The photograph was transferred to a base cloth of cotton fabric by a commercial photo transfer process.

The construction technique is similar to crazy patchwork. Ruth has started with the photograph placed onto a base cloth and then has placed complimentary fabrics around until satisfied with the composition. The theatrical backdrop used by the photographic studio also influenced the choice and placement of fabrics. As the velvet fragment also needed to be incorporated, soft faded tones have been used in parts instead of the whole quilt being made in the grey tones of the photographic print.

Pieces of fabric were laid down, pinned, then attached with small, unobtrusive stitches in matching thread in the following sequence, onto a base measuring 60cm x 75cm (24" x 30").

1. Photograph 42cm x 26cm (16^1/$_2$" x 10^1/$_4$") was placed 15cm (6") from top, 15cm (6") from right hand side.
2. 10cm (4") square of velvet was placed on point at lower right hand corner of photograph.
3. Metallic grey dupion silk 10cm x 36cm (4" x 14") was placed at top of photograph.
4. Grey lace 38cm x 5cm (15" x 2") was then placed over edge where silk (see above) meets photograph.
5. Bronze ribbon 38cm x 5cm (15" x 2") was placed above grey lace.
6. Metallic grey silk dupion 15cm x 8cm (6" x 2") was placed with the selvage to the edge of the photograph and the lower edge tucked under the velvet square.

From the ashes
90cm x 75cm
(36" x 30")

Memory quilt 60cm x 75cm (24" x 30")

7. Metallic silk/metal mesh fabric 31cm x 16cm (12$^{1}/_{4}$" x 6$^{1}/_{4}$") was placed on a sloping angle to emulate the style of the theatrical drapes in the background of the photograph. This was then edged with dull gold braid and embroidery added – herringbone in beige plus straight stitch crosses in dusty pink.

8. Metallic mesh fabric 35cm x 14cm (13$^{3}/_{4}$" x 5$^{1}/_{2}$") was placed on right hand side.

9. Hand-dyed silk ribbon 50cm x 12cm (20" x 4$^{3}/_{4}$") was placed along lower edge of photograph.

10. & 11. Tissue ribbon 55cm (22") was attached along lower and upper edges where silk and photograph meet, using small careful stitches. Right ends of both were left free to continue over the border which was attached later.

12. Place braid 13cm x 4.5cm (5$^{1}/_{4}$" x 1$^{3}/_{4}$") on diagonal across lower edge of velvet square.

13. & 14. Two strips of floral border fabric were cut 55cm x 12cm (22" x 4$^{3}/_{4}$"). Left hand corner was mitred to match the print and then set into position and secured. This forms the left and lower border.

15. Old lace fragments were placed on lower right side at end of print piece.

16. Fine antique braid was couched along top edge of lower print border.

17. Bronze dupion silk 34cm x 8cm (13$^{1}/_{2}$" x 3") was sewed to right edge to form the right border. When sewn, it was flipped over and pressed into place.

18. Lace hearts aged by dying in coffee or Condy's crystals were placed on lower right with

19. Circle of antique lace.

20. Bronze ribbon length 75cm x 3.5cm (30" x 1$^{3}/_{8}$") was placed along the top. Lower edge was secured with erringbone.

21. Coffee dyed lace fragments were attached to the top left corner and arranged down the side.

22. Hanah silk ribbon (Ivory) was casually folded down left hand side to cover the raw edges of the print border.

23. A length of the same Hanah silk was attached at the top left hand corner and secured casually along top, folded back and forth, until approximately 8cm (3") from the right edge. Then it was brought down so that it covered the join between the mesh silk and the right border and fastened carefully with invisible stitches.

24. Tassel was secured.

25. Old gold braid was attached around velvet square.

26. Metal heart with lily motif was attached.

27. French knots in various coordinating threads, such as beiges, greys and dusty pinks, were trailed around heart motifs and velvet square.

To finish, the worked piece was layered together with backing and lightweight batting and then quilted through all three layers to hold where appropriate. The edge was bound with a dark cotton binding and a rod pocket made on the top back edge to hang the finished work. Finally a novelty beige thread was couched around the inner edge of binding.

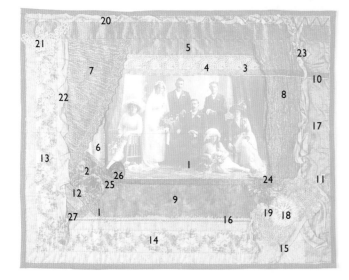

Sculptured Forms

Annemieke Mein

All Annemieke's textiles, whether freestanding sculptures, wall panels or wearables, portray the endless diversity of Australian flora, fauna and landscape, both climatically and seasonally. Occasionally, she has depicted human involvement related to environmental or historical events. Annemieke explains: 'Each individual work is a statement of respect and love for my environment and it is through this work that I hope to make people more aware of the importance of preserving our natural heritage.

'I prefer to portray my subjects in larger-than-life dimensions. This size scale enables me to enhance their visual impact through varying relief angles and sculptural levels. As well, it allows me to introduce detailed textural variations and subtle colour combinations. Minute details, such as the inside of a bird's beak, the interplay of light on an insect's wing venation, or the glisten of fish scales underwater, are deliberately accentuated to capture an event or experience and the mood or emotion that the subject has aroused in me.'

Each of Annemieke's works is preceded by hours of research, observations and documentation. Whether it be insect, reptile, bird or human, countless sketches and cartoons are made before the full size layout is designed. Only then are paints, fibres, fabrics and threads selected. Finally, the sewing can begin.

For Annemieke, fibre manipulation and embellishment has become a delightful tactile and sculptural medium.

Annemieke Mein lives at Sale in Victoria, Australia. The surrounding district has an abundance of magnificent wetlands. Many major rivers and hundreds of creeks wind through Gippsland on their way to the sea, while huge inland lakes with their associated flood-prone grasslands are dotted all over the region. Bass Strait, at the edge of the Pacific Ocean, washes the coastline, which includes the spectacular Ninety Mile Beach.

An astonishing array of Australian flora and fauna make this area their temporary or permanent home. There are countless representatives from most families found on earth (such as birds, fish, insects, spiders, reptiles, marsupials and other mammals, amphibians and crustaceans, and a wondrous array of plants).

The Wetlands of Gippsland have been a source of endless fascination and inspiration for Annemieke over the past 25 years. These 'Water and Wetlands' textile works are a direct response to her personal experiences.

Annemieke Mein

De Lapjes

This fanciful interpretation of two butterflies, five cocoons, a branch and a gum leaf was made just for the joy of creating. To Annemieke, this sculpture says 'I love embroidery!' She goes on to explain its name:

'In the construction stages of all my works, there are many tedious and rather boring hours spent doing nitty-gritty jobs like tying off loose threads, sorting cottons and winding bobbins. At these times, my mind has often turned back to my childhood in Holland, when I first encountered embroideries.

'My maternal grandfather enjoyed smoking cigars in the 1930s and 40s. His favourite brand of boxed cigars contained a machine-worked embroidery in each box. He had a wondrous collection of dozens of these little treasures which he kept in empty cigar boxes. My favourite 'game' was to have him recline on a couch while I covered every square inch of his body with these embroideries. He nicknamed them 'lapjes' meaning 'little rags' in Dutch. Hence the title of this work is in honour of that gentle grandfather who introduced me to the beauty of machine embroidery.'

Requirements

dyed wool and mohair (combed, spun and plied)	crystal organza
dyed silk organza	satin
felt (recycled and new)	covered wire
beads	dacron filler (quilters' wadding)
machine threads (cotton, polyester, silk)	embroidery cotton.

Techniques

machine embroidery	hand embroidery
collage of wool and mohair under organza	padding
quilting	stuffing
pleating	shaping
dyeing	plying
wiring	lining

Both butterflies, the five cocoons and the branch are made of two layers of black crystal organza with various tones of combed wool, spun wool and plied wool between the two layers. (Black crystal organza mutes or tones down the underlying brighter colours and so gives a softer appearance, emulating a dark rich Persian carpet). The layers were then stitched together with a tight bobbin tension on the machine to achieve a low-relief quilted look. This stitching, using the free-sewing technique, follows the patterns created by the underlying wool colours glowing through the silk.

The cocoons were hand sculpted into domes, with pleats and puckers hand stitched together to hold form to their designed shape. Finally they were lined with quilted satin so they appear to glow from within.

For each butterfly, the wings were pleated into shape and stitched together at the point where the four wings meet. Their bodies were made of old yellow and green recycled felt hats, and wrap over the wing junction points.

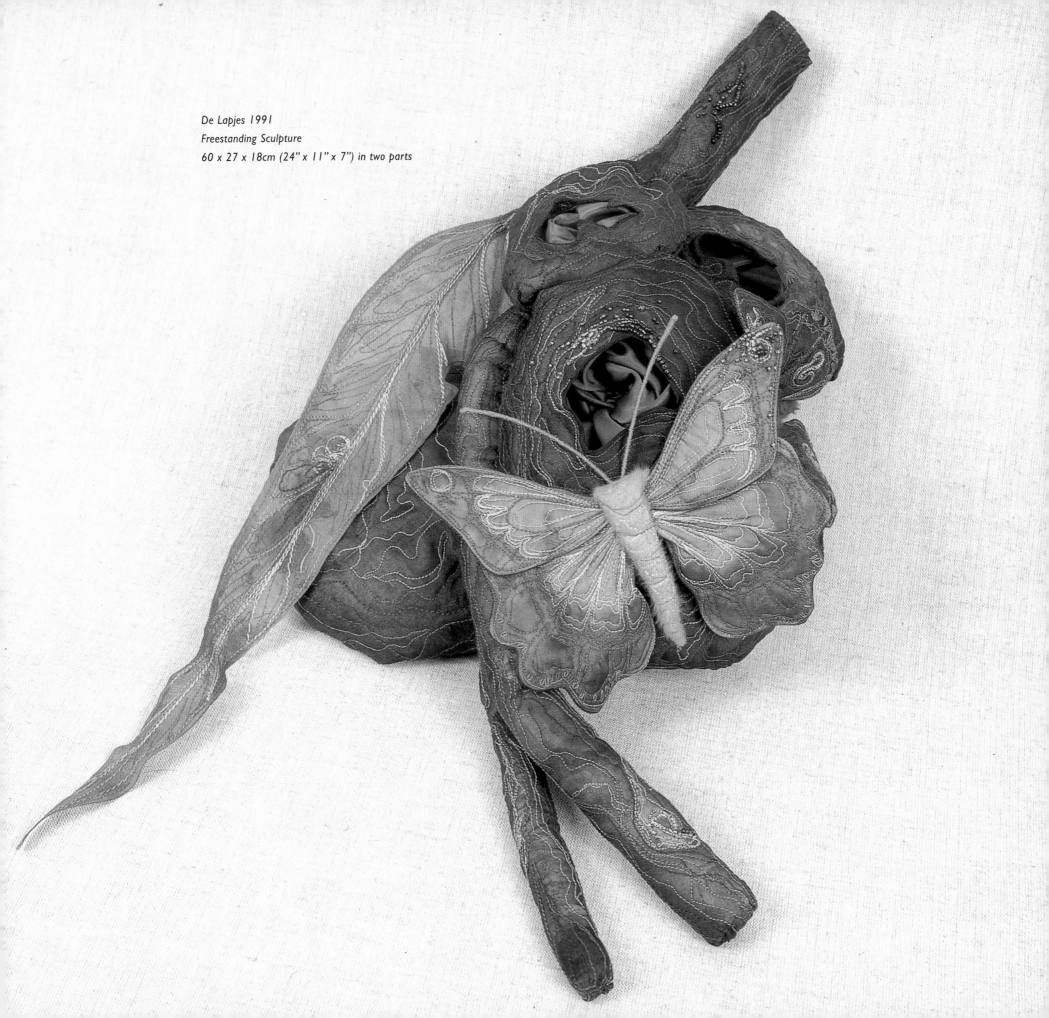

De Lapjes 1991
Freestanding Sculpture
60 x 27 x 18cm (24" x 11" x 7") in two parts

The antennae of the yellow butterfly are of thread-covered wire while the antennae of the green butterfly are plied embroidery cottons. The branch was initially stitched in the shape of a long thin rectangle. It was then tightly stuffed with dacron filler to hold its shape.

The eucalypt leaf is of two layers of organza, dyed to be blotchy in tones of green and wired down the central vein before being machine embroidered. All parts of the sculpture are beaded at points designed to catch the light.

The two parts of this freestanding sculpture can be arranged in a variety of ways to suit the display area available.

Splash! 1994

Splash! depicts a frog that has just hit the water. Its eyes and head are protectively held upward while its partially-webbed hind feet, are splayed out to break the fall. Annemieke has captured the action and frozen this moment of time, showing the ease and elegance of the frog hitting the water while surrounded by airborne spray and splash. The frog portrayed is loosely based on a species of leaf-green tree frog (*Litoria phyllochroa*) whose numbers are sadly declining in their natural habitats.

The distinctive mauve-coloured flesh of the frog at its inner joints were a concern to Annemieke. She wanted to portray them credibly and with some flair, as the colours of yellow-green and pinkish-mauve are not a comfortable colour combination for her. It became apparent that the colour-balancing and colour-uniting factor would be the colour tones chosen for the painted water on the canvas. She has kept the mauve tones in the water below the frog's mauve legs.

The underwater movement and flow in *Splash!* has been greatly accentuated to try to get a graceful yet dramatic effect of water pushing upward, downward and sideways with the impact of the frog's entry. Deliberate painterly bleeding areas enhance the watery appearance on the canvas. The machine-stitched lines all follow the painted flow of water, both in the upward splash and underwater flow. Some fluffy tailor-tacking stitches in white, cream, aqua and green, help give texture to the splash. The dark lower area of the canvas alludes to deep water beyond the canvas.

Splash!
Low relief wall panel
83 x 94cm
(33" x 37½")

Requirements

cotton canvas	fabric paints
silk organza	fluorescent organza
satin	felt
iron-on interfacing	machine threads (cotton, silk, synthetic and metallic)
dacron filler	

Techniques

painting (silk organza and canvas)	machine embroidery
tailor-tacking	quilting
padding	stuffing
moulding	fabric layering

Against the Tide (King George Whiting) 1992
Low relief wall panel
72 x 100cm
(29" x 40")

The frog's body was initially painted on one piece of silk organza. Then eight different coloured fabrics were cut in precise shapes to use as 'underlays' for their colours to glow through the painted silk. For example, slivers of yellow fluorescent crystal organza lie under the painted silk of the jaw line, the padded elbow, the raised kneecap and the splash-pointing two toes. These areas will glitter when the work is lit by a spotlight. Also, cream satin, together with blue and pink crystal organza pieces lie under the frog's breast, with mauve, green, aqua and blue satin under the legs and feet. Supporting all these little bits of fabric is a thin layer of cream felt, backed with iron-on interfacing.

With everything pinned and tacked together, the machine embroidery began. Annemieke used stitches that emulate the warty knobbly shapes on the frog's flesh, free-sewing them in roughly circular shapes.

The frog's jaw line, throat, belly and a foreleg were moulded, padded and quilted into low-relief. The partial webbing between the toes was not attached to the canvas so the toes would also stand out in low-relief.

Quilted and Printed Fragments

Wendy Holland

Trained in art and a teacher for several years, Wendy Holland switched to working full time with fabrics in 1978. She lived and worked in England, studying costume and textiles, before starting to make quilts in 1980. Wendy is recognised nationally and internationally for her lively, detailed, complex works, incorporating many different techniques from stitching, applique, quilt making, as well as printing. Much of the fabric she incorporates into her designs are old, scavenged and collected pieces or samples.

In *Ontological connotations*, the main piece shown here, Wendy played with very basic printing techniques using blocks and stencils. She built a surface suggesting trapped layers, was pleased with the arrangements of the old pieces of fabric and the variations of colour and texture of weave, but, as she says, she 'just wanted to see what happened' when she added all of the printing.

In this work, Wendy has used old woollen blanketing, fragments of old cream kimono silks – a few with a bit of pattern or embroidery, gold-painted lace curtain samples, a couple of scraps of old furnishing fabric and strips of old cotton lace. She also needed printing ink, acrylic paint and gold powder mixed with glue.

Ontological connotations 123cm x 99cm (48" x 36")

All the pieces of fabric were stamped and printed several times over, starting with simple polystyrene blocks for the palest colours, then various combinations of foam roller through to cut stencils – board, old Indian carved wood blocks, simple lino blocks, photographic screen prints, for example the fish, and finally paper and plastic flop stencils under a silk screen such as the gold spirals which went on last

Exotic Textures

Glenys Gudgeon

An experienced embroiderer, Glenys Gudgeon completed the course in machine embroidery with the Embroiderers' Guild of New South Wales in 1993 and has never looked back. While still working in other areas of needlecraft, she enjoys the freedom of machine embroidery and is keen to pass on her skills to those many others who participate in her private classes on the north coast of new South Wales.

Glenys has undertaken many commissions, including the ceremonial gowns for the Chancellor and Deputy Chancellor of the Southern Cross University on which she worked the machine embroidery and some of the gold work.

The bag, *Turkish delight*, inspired by a card sent from friends in Turkey and featuring a tile, was made using several machine embroidery techniques. All threads used were machine embroidery rayon threads. The fabric was black lycra (which was also used plain for the lining) painted with gold paint. When the paint was dry Glenys stitched onto the fabric using free machine embroidery techniques with a metallic thread in the bobbin and a dark thread on the top. This gave the fabric the textured effect.

The star shaped design was made separately and stitched onto the bag. The same fabric, not textured, was used as a background, and the flowers, leaves and cord were stitched onto this. The flowers were made by stitching with two threads through the needle (sometimes one being a metallic thread) onto organza fabric and cut out. Two or three of these flowers were placed one on top of the other. The flowers were sewn onto the bag and decorated with gold beads. The leaves were made in the same way as the flowers but sewn onto pantyhose so the fabric curled. These flowers and leaves were then linked with machine made cords.

Again the machine was used to make the fringe, which was placed between the star design and the background fabric. The handle was made with eight machine cords twisted together and was stitched to the bag with machine made tassels at the base for decoration.

Above left: Turkish delight 22cm x 22cm ($8^3/_4$" x $8^3/_4$")
three dimensional cords, tassels, fringes, flowers

Left: Soft wall hanging 20cm x 15cm (8" x 6")
brass stitched on painted fabric using metal threads

Above right: Glenys Gudgeon pictured with mantel ruby lustre stand.
Collection of Embroiders' Guild of NSW.

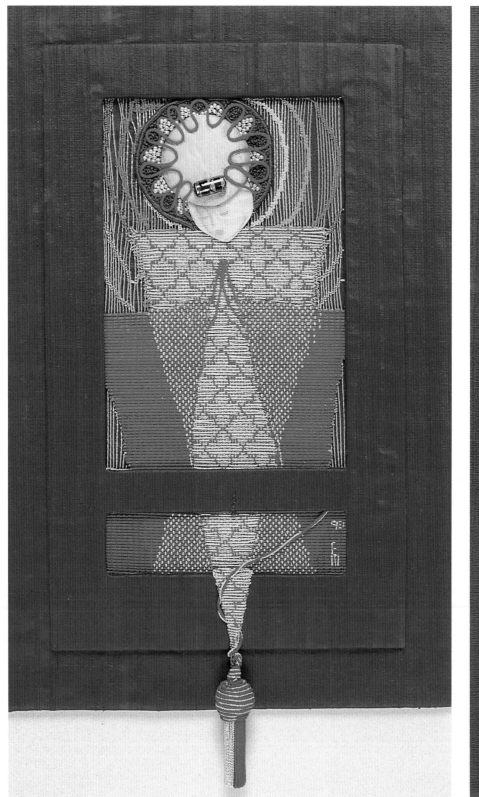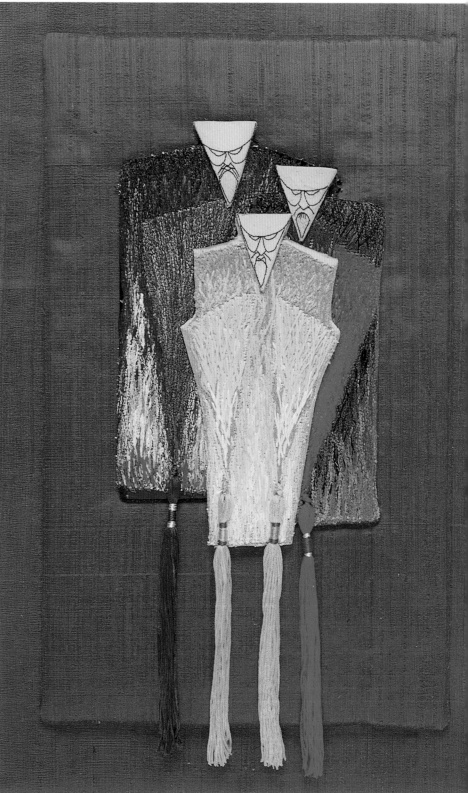

Iconography

Effie Mitrofanis

E ffie Mitrofanis has spent many years not only studying to perfect her own techniques, but to place her work, and the work of others, into its rich context. She has a passionate interest in the art, the pattern and texture of embroidery, its history, its makers and techniques and she researches, studies, writes and teaches about creative hand embroidery. She teaches and exhibits throughout Australia and New Zealand, including Textile Fibre forums. Her work has been exhibited in France and Japan and is in many Guild and private collections. Effie has studied lace and embroidery not only in Australia but in Italy and the United Kingdom.

Effie designs by two methods, one a pre-planned design where the images and elements to be included are drawn on paper to define the size, proportions and division of space. These elements are inspired by a theme or subject matter, often a narrative or story.

Effie became passionate about the theme Icons while studying the evolution of lace for her Masters Degree, over a period of three years. Lace developed in Venice in the sixteenth century and a study of Venetian history revealed its close ties with the Byzantine Empire, established in 330 A.D. by the Emperor Constantine. Constantine also established a new religion for his empire, Christianity, and the art of Byzantium focused around its religion until 1453 when the Turks took over Constantinople and renamed it Istanbul. Venice's impressive St Mark's Cathedral houses many art treasures which have survived from the Fourth Crusade in 1204 when the French and Flemish Crusaders, joined and led by the Venetians, stormed Constantinople's previously safe defence and raped, sacked and pillaged the city. A visit to Venice, its beautiful Cathedral and Treasury in 1998 gave Effie the opportunity to see first hand the wonderful icons but in particular the Pala d'Oro or Golden Altarpiece which contains the Archangel Michael, taken to Venice from Byzantium in 1204.

Effie is inspired not only by the icon images, but the vibrant colours, rich jewels, and the way the space is divided, particularly the borders surrounding the images. She is also interested in the way the icons are mounted and framed, sometimes as holy pictures, other times in boxes or reliquaries, the small boxes in which relics are kept and shown.

The presentation of her piece *Triptych – Reliquary – Beginnings* of a Legend, the story of Medusa, is inspired by the reliquaries, while the format of the *Elephant and Angel* icons are inspired by the borders and space divisions.

The other method of designing which Effie likes to use is what she calls 'intuitive', where she gathers together materials and threads in rich, vibrant colours and starts stitching onto silk fabric, allowing the piece to develop as she keeps on adding stitches, beads and applique. Such a method was used in Byzantine Angel. She first started couching the gold thread freely to create a free-flowing, curving frame for the image of the Angel. Stitches and rich beads were added to the frame for a 'feeling' of rich jewels, though not in the structured, geometric order that characterises the Byzantine focus. At this stage gold paint was sponged onto the background fabric of the inner space and open buttonhole stitches worked randomly to create a background

Left:
See how long are the
tassels on their clothes
58cm x 43cm (23" x 17")

Far left:
The Messenger
58cm x 43cm (23" x 17")

surface of crackling and ageing. Finally the angel was stitched into place, a misty image intended to blend into the background.

 Further details of how Effie has worked her pieces, and some of her inspiration, are given below.

Triptych – Reliquary – Beginnings of a Legend

Inspired by the ancient Greek mythological story of the Gorgon Medusa, the triptych tells the story in three parts. Paint, hand and machine embroidery, padded and raised work, stumpwork, applique, needlelace, wrapping, couched gold and metallic.

Part One: Medusa. Snakes curling and writhing around her head. Look in her yes and turn to stone.

Part Two: Perseus. Borrowed a magic helmet to make him invisible and, while looking at Medusa's reflection in his shield, beheaded her with one stroke and placed the head in a magic wallet. The winged horse Pegasus arose from the trunk of Medusa and flew away with Perseus to slay the dragon of Andromeda.

Part Three: Disintegration and release… and, too late, Medusa's two sisters awoke, screaming with horror at the sight of her corpse and staring everywhere after their invisible enemy.

Elephant

Padded and raised work, applique, hand embroidery, beading.

Angel

Padded and raised work, applique, hand embroidery, beading.

See how long are the tassels on their clothes

The Old Testament of the Bible refers to the time when God instructed the Jewish people to make cloaks to wear in the temple. The cloaks were to have tassels hanging from the base as a sign of devotion to him. The work depicts three hypocrites in the temple wearing their cloaks with very long tassels as a sign of their extreme devotion to God. The Bible refers to the hypocrites as follows: 'See how long are the tassels on their clothes'.

The Messenger

Gold work, hand embroidery and beading on painted canvas.

Byzantine Angel

Gold work, hand embroidery, beading on painted silk.

Byzantine Angel
36cm x 28cm (14" x 11")

Elephant
30cm x 25cm (12" x 9³/₄")

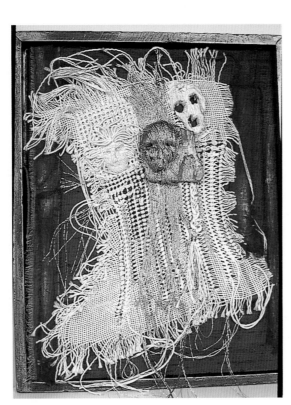

Detail: Triptych - Reliquary - Beginnings of a Legend

Angel
30cm x 25cm
(12" x 9³/₄")

Triptych - Reliquary - Beginnings of a Legend
3 panels, each 32cm x 26cm (12¹/₂" x 10")

Gabriella Verstraeten

The embroidery of Gabriella Verstraeten follows the traditions and quality of the past yet it is new, exciting and contemporary. The colours and fabrics are deliberately vivid, bold, busy and metallic. Gabriella's work reflects her love of fabric and patterns. She combines embroidery techniques with fabric manipulation, such as applique, layering, cutback, padding and sculpting, to create her designs. She employs shapes, patterns and repetitive motifs to create a sense of movement and visually rich and exciting surfaces.

Working at her machine embroidery since 1982, Gabriella has achieved international recognition with her huge range of machine embroidered pieces which include hats, bags, shoes, jewellery as well as household items such as chairs, cushions, wallhangings and curtains. Cushions are one of her favourite canvases because they are a good size, do not need framing and hanging, but can be scattered about.

Regency cushions

Requirements

50cm (20") mustard coloured satin for base cloth

50cm (20") black organza for fabric overlay

50cm light weight wadding – as thick as you would like your cushion cover to be

1 metre (40") Vliesofix fusible webbing, 90cm (36") wide

50cm (20") lining silk for interlining – colour does not matter

50cm (20") backing fabric for reverse side of cushion – colour of your choice

18cm (7^1/$_2$") each deep teal and wine burgundy fabrics for appliques

2 metres (80") flanged decorative piped cushion cord trim to suit fabrics

4 reels black rayon machine embroidery thread, No 30/40, 1000 metres (1110 yards)

1 reel each of teal and burgundy rayon machine embroidery thread No 30/40, 250 metres (277 yards)

2 reels metallic gold machine embroidery thread, No 30/40, 500 metres (555 yards)

1 reel slightly heavier textured gold thread, e.g. Madeira FS12 or FS15

packet gold and blue small round sequins

4 small gold tassels

selection of seed beads colour coordinated to fabrics

handsewing needles for beading

spare bobbin case for machine

small pair sharp pointed embroidery scissors

machine needles 130N size 90

grey lead pencil HB/2B

tailor's chalk

dressmaker's square or long ruler

Regency cushions
each 36cm x 36cm
(14" x 14")

Fabric preparation

From the base cloth fabric, interlining fabric, organza and padding, cut a square approximately 45cm x 45cm (19" x 18")

From the Vliesofix cut two squares approximately 43cm x 43cm (17" x 17")

From the remaining Vliesofix cut two pieces 15cm x 48cm (6" x 19").

From your backing fabric cut two rectangles of fabric to measure 45cm x 30cm (18" x 12"). Neaten the hem edges as follows. On one long side of each of these pieces, fold over 5mm ($^{1}/_{4}$") to the wrong side of the fabric and press. Repeat this procedure again on top of the previous fold. Straight stitch the folded edges down using normal machine settings. Keep backing pieces to one side.

Applique design

Note: You will want to lay your applique design out on the cushion top in one go. The width of a normal ironing board will not be enough. Lay out several old towels on a table and use this as your extended ironing board surface.

Using the template given here, trace the diamond shape only of the applique onto the paper side of the two long skinny pieces of Vliesofix using a lead pencil. Try to be as economical as you can. You will be folding the strip of fabric for the diamonds up concertina style so you can cut out several full and half diamond shapes at one time. Trace out five full diamond shapes starting from one short end and arranging them as shown.

Using two applique mats, one to protect the ironing board surface and one to place between your fabrics and the hot plate of the iron, fuse the length of the Vliesofix to the wrong side of one of your applique fabrics. Repeat with the other piece of Vliesofix and your other applique fabric.

1. Vliesofix on applique fabric with diamond patterns marked out and folds for concertina.

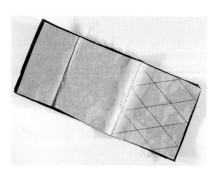

Concertina up the fabric strip by folding where the edge of your pencil tracings come to. Refer to photograph No 1. You should have two folds.

Cut out at least 15 full diamonds and as many half diamonds lengthwise and width wise. Repeat with the other applique fabric.

Now take your base cloth fabric. Using tailor's chalk and a long dressmaking ruler mark in a border 3cm (1 1/5") on all sides.

Fold the front cushion base in half and in half again lengthwise. Lightly press the folded fabric to create creases you will use as applique placement guidelines. Repeat the process in the opposite direction.

Flatten the base fabric out again and lay it right side up on the ironing surface. The creases should be visible but still allow the fabric to sit flat.

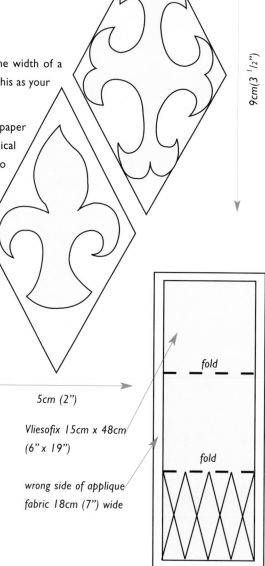

9cm(3 $^{1}/_{2}$")

5cm (2")

fold

fold

Vliesofix 15cm x 48cm (6" x 19")

wrong side of applique fabric 18cm (7") wide

2. Diamond appliques fused into position on base fabric.

Choose one of your applique colour fabrics. It doesn't matter which one. Peel away its paper backing. Beginning at the centre point of the base cloth, lay the diamond in the centre, matching up the points of the diamond with the centre of the creases of the base cloth square.

You now continue to complete that row of diamonds by lining up their side points next to and touching each other whilst also lining up the top and bottom points of the vertical of the diamonds along the vertical crease line. You may decide to alternate colours as you go or you may decide to have the colours the same on each row. Refer to photograph 2.

The colour sequence of the diamonds is a matter of personal choice. The main photograph shows that Gabriella has varied her pattern or sequence on each cushion. Remember to use the half diamond pieces as well. The 3cm (1 1/5") chalk border is a guide line. You may decide to take the applique right up to this line or you may decide to leave a border where you may freehand stitch a decorative edge. Whichever, be sure to leave a 2cm (4/") seam allowance all around.

Once you are happy with the arrangement of the diamonds, peel away the paper backing and re-position all the individual pieces. Lay the applique mats on top. Fuse the pieces in place.

Fabric sandwich

3. Fabric sandwich of organza, base fabric with appliques, Vliesofix, padding, Vliesofix, interlining fabric.

The surface of the cushions are stitched, quilted and embroidered all at once. To do this you must layer and fuse almost all the fabrics together. So you do not need to tack the fabrics a number of the layers are fused together and a fabric sandwich is created. The following is a cross section of how the fabrics need to be arranged. Refer to photograph 3.

1. ....organza overlay
2. ....applique pieces fused to base cloth
3. ....base fabric
4. ———— Vliesofix
5. .... padding
6. ———— Vliesofix
7. .... interlining fabric

To set up this arrangement, follow these steps. Fuse a piece of the large Vliesofix to the wrong side of the base cloth. Peel off the backing paper and put to one side. (This gives you 2, 3 & 4.) Fuse the other large piece of the large Vliesofix to the wrong side of the interlining fabric. Peel off the backing paper. (This gives you 6 & 7.)

Lay the interfacing with Vliesofix up on the ironing surface. Lay the padding on top (5). Lay the base cloth on top of the padding, right side up. Place applique mats on top and fuse all these layers together. You may need to turn the fabric sandwich over and also fuse from the interlining side.

After fusing, lay the organza overlay on top of the appliqued base cloth. Pin in place from the centre out. You are now ready to stitch your cushion top.

Machine set up as follows for basic stitching:

foot:	applique
feed dog:	UP
stitch:	straight
stitch width:	0
stitch length:	2.5
thread upper:	black rayon machine embroidery thread
thread lower:	back rayon machine embroidery thread
tension upper:	loose
tension lower:	normal
stitching technique:	standard machine straight stitch
stitching procedure:	the stitching that you do now establishes the outline structure of the design

and anchors the

applique pieces in place. Begin the centre of the cushion and stitch up and down the diagonals of your design. Refer to photograph 4.

4. Machine embroidery – basic stitching around diamonds, freehand stitching of patterns withing diamonds, cutting back, emphasis and highlight embroidery on main design, highlight embroidery in border (optional).

You are now ready to freehand stitch your design in place.
Machine set up as follows for freehand stitching of patterns:

foot:	darning
feed dog:	down
stitch:	straight
stitch width:	0
stitch length:	0
thread upper:	black rayon machine embroidery thread
thread lower:	back rayon machine embroidery thread
tension upper:	loose
tension lower:	normal
machine speed:	fast
stitching technique:	using freehand machine embroidery, you now stitch out the patterns within each diamond shape (see diamond pattern above). You also stitch in other shapes, especially in the borders that you wish to introduce into the design. The shapes all have been stitched freely, although they may all look the same. If you feel a little nervous at trying this, turn your cushion over so that the interlining is facing you. Draw your design there and stitch with this side facing you. Do not alter the machine settings.
stitching procedure:	again begin in the centre of your design. The trick is to outline structure stitching as much as you can to continuously and invisibly travel between the diamonds. Decide on the sequence and combination of motifs over which colours before you begin to stitch your design. You want to keep the shapes clean because you will be cutting back some of them. Stitch around shapes several times. Refer to photograph 4.

Cutting back: Working with a small pair of sharp pointed embroidery scissors, snip back the top layer of organza in selected places. Carefully slide the blade of the scissors underneath the organza and cut. Again it is important for you to decide on the sequence of exposed shapes and those that remain covered. This part of the work can seem a little slow but it is exciting as the design begins to change and emerge. Don't forget to include the design shapes of your border if you have them. Refer to photograph 4.

Further machine embroidery: The purpose of this lot of stitching is to secure the edges of the shapes you have exposed and to give emphasis to different areas of your design through further stitching. You can do this by contrasting the colours of the shapes as you stitch around them, i.e. the burgundy motifs are stitched with teal highlights and vice versa. It is up to you. Gabriella has suggested a gold bobbin contrast and if you follow the set up instructions you should get gold thread coming through on to the right side of the cushion in sprinkles.

Machine set up as follows for emphasis embroidery:

foot:	darning
feed dog:	down
stitch:	straight
stitch width:	0
stitch length:	0
thread upper:	burgundy or teal rayon machine embroidery thread
thread lower:	metallic gold machine embroidery thread No. 40
tension upper:	normal
tension lower:	loosen up slightly $1/4 - 1/2$ turn to the left on your bobbin case
machine speed:	fast
stitching technique:	using freehand machine embroidery, you now stitch back over the entire cushion top changing the colour of the thread when each colour section is complete. For the best effect, stitch around each shape several times. These settings should give you a metallic flicker of gold on the stitching line.
stitching procedure:	again try to make your stitching a continuous flowing line. Use the outline structure stitching as much as you can to continuously and invisibly travel between the diamonds.

Beading, tassels and finishing

The beads and sequins are stitched on by hand in whatever arrangement you prefer. A little backstitch is worked before each bead is stitched to secure its position. Attach tassels in the four corners with hand stitching.

Make up the cushion cover using fabric for back and overlapping opening well, then joining front and back with the edging braid wedged between.

Highlights in borders: This step is optional. It involves stitching with a slightly heavier and more textured gold thread as a stitching highlight in the border. You may need to alter the bobbin tension significantly for the procedure. A second bobbin case is recommended.

Machine set up as follows for highlights in borders

foot:	darning
feed dog:	down
stitch:	straight
stitch width:	0
stitch length:	0
thread upper:	black rayon machine embroidery thread
thread lower:	metallic gold machine embroidery thread Madeira FS12 or 15
tension upper:	normal
tension lower:	loosen up slightly $1/2 - 3/4$ turn to the left on your bobbin case
machine speed:	fast
stitching technique:	as the thread is on the bobbin, the cushion top is turned over so that the interlining is facing you as you stitch. All the previous stitching is there as a guide line to let you know where to stitch. Using a freehand machine embroidery straight stitch, you now stitch the contrast thread where you would like it featured. Refer to photograph 4.

Woven Floorcoverings

Beth Hatton

The craft of weaving is kept alive by a sturdy band of devotees, and is often associated with the craft of spinning, in particular of traditional fibres such as wool and cotton, but also the 'newer' fibres of alpaca, cashmere, mohair.

Beth Hatton weaves works from rags in cotton, denim and wool, as well as offcuts of other materials, such as kangaroo skins, to create her sturdy rugs, continuing a tradition which arose in the past from necessity. Her works range from bright, light and simple in design, to rugs which reflect the colours of the outback and some which elucidate environmental issues of today, including a series on endangered animals. These latter rugs are intense and graphic in design.

Beth is well-recognised world-wide, not only for her rugs, but for her essays in such magazines as *Textile Fibre Forum* for which she contributes a regular column.

Oriental pink

This rug is woven in a four-end block weave also known as summer and winter, which produces a reversed image on the other side of the rug. Because of its narrow sett, this is a weft-faced rug. Its finished size is 152.5cm x 84cm (60" X 33").

Requirements

four-shaft six-treadle loom,
#6 reed at least 92cm (36") wide (or use a #12 reed and skip every other dent)
three shuttles — two for plain weave and one for block weave.
warp: natural linen — 3-ply sailmakers' or seine twine or 3-ply linen rug warp

Imprint 2
rag rug in wool and kangaroo skin offcuts152.5cm x 92cm (60" x 36")

Beth Hatton

weft: the bulk of the weft is cotton muslin dyed in two shades of soft pink. The inlay blocks are made of corduroy and velvet, some of which were dyed to achieve gradations of colour. A similar effect can be created by choosing fabrics in like colours.

Take-up

About 10 per cent in length.

Draw-in

About 8 per cent in width.

Warping

Wind 220 warp threads in total for a width of 92cm (36") at six epi plus two extra threads at each selvage. The finished rug measures 84 cm (33") wide when off the loom.

Threading and tie-up

Thread 1–3, 2–3, 1–3, 2–3...for 16 threads to create the border, then 1 – 4, 2 – 4, 1 – 4, 2 – 4...for 12 threads to create the first block, then 1 – 3, 2 – 3, 1 – 3, 2 – 3... for 12 threads to create the second block, then 1 – 4, 2 – 4, 1 – 4, 2 – 4... for 12 threads to create the third block, repeat until you have threaded 15 blocks before ending with 1 – 3, 2 – 3, 1 – 3, 2 – 3...for 16 threads to create the second border.

Sleying

Six epi with two extra threads at the selvages.

Weft preparation

Cut or tear fabrics into 1cm (about 1/2") strips. If the fabric is very heavy, such as denim, cut narrower strips 5mm (about 1/4") wide. If the fabric is very lightweight, such as muslin, cut the strips wider to 1.5cm – 2.5cm (^{3}/4" – 1").

Imprint 4
rag rug in wool and
kangaroo skin offcuts
100cm x 250cm
(40" x 100")

Weaving

Wind two shuttles for plain weave, each with one of the two shades of pink fabric. The two shades of pink are alternated in the weaving to create richness in the background colour. Weave a 7.5cm (3") plain border, treadling 1 – 2, 3 – 4, 1 – 2, 3 – 4, etc. Then wind the third shuttle with beige rag and lay in the first block, treadling <u>1 – 3</u>, 1 – 2, 3 – 4, <u>2 – 3</u>, 1 – 2, 3 – 4, etc. (The underlining indicates the shed for the pattern weft of beige rag.) Twelve passes of the beige shuttle will complete the beige block. While working through the blocks, extra rows of plain-weave must be laid in at each border to compensate for the fact that the blocks are not going right to the edge of the weaving. Starting from, say, the left hand selvage treadle 1 – 2, weave to the edge of the closest block, treadle 3 – 4, return to the left hand selvage, treadle 1 – 2, weave across to the right hand selvage, treadle 3 – 4, weave to the edge of the closest block, treadle 1 – 2, return to right hand selvage, treadle 3 – 4, weave back across to left hand selvage. After completing the beige block go on to a beige and yellow mixed weft, treadling <u>1 – 4</u>, 1 – 2, – 4, <u>2 – 4</u>, 1 – 2, 3 – 4, etc. Continue weaving, following this sequence and changing colours as appropriate to make the blocks. Finish with a 7.5cm (3") plain-weave border.

Finishing

A Damascus edge keeps the rug weft firmly in place. Working from left to right with a passive warp thread in the left hand and an active thread in the right, knot over and up. Upon reaching the opposite edge of the rug, turn it over and work across again. Then take a long needle and darn each warp thread into the body of the rug for at least 5cm – 7.5cm (2" – 3"). Trim thread ends flush with the surface of the rug.

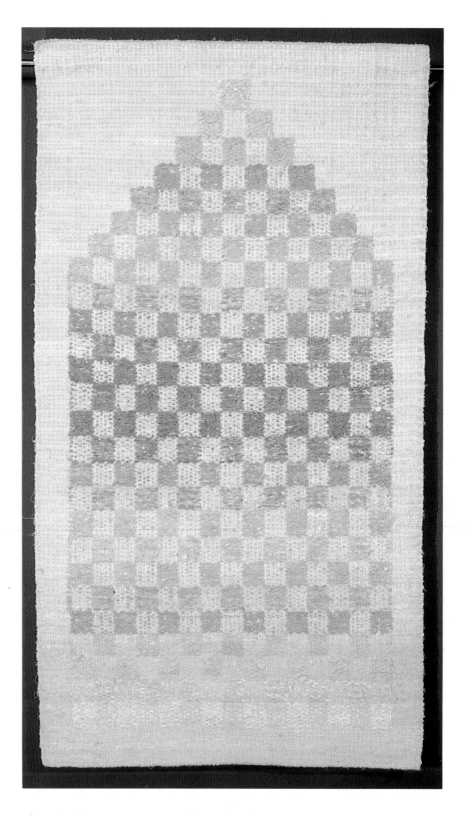

Oriental pink – rag rug in cottons, velvets and corduroys
152.5cm x 84cm (60" X 33")

Above: *Sunflowers at Midnight - a proggy rug 155cm x 100cm*

Right: *Compass 155cm x 75cm (30" x 62")*

Rag Rugs

Miriam Miller

Miriam Miller has transformed the traditional craft of rag rugging into a modern form of artistic expression. She remembers her grandmother making rag rugs to cover the floors in her childhood home in the north of England, but in those days the rugs were drab, made of old clothes and considered a craft of the poor.

Miriam has lovingly restored her historic home on the south coast of New South Wales, Australia, and decided to revive the family tradition in order to furnish the rooms of the main home as well as the cottages. In the process she has created a remarkable body of work, and has inspired others to share her passion for rag rugging. Her output is prolific and her love of colour and texture shines in her rugs and her handspun, hand-dyed woollen knits – another passion.

Miriam uses both the 'proggy' and 'hooky' methods in stunning combinations of colour and texture to create her beautifully vibrant rugs. She cuts out all sorts of fabrics, including gabardine, denim and jersey sweatshirting. They are cut into strips which Miriam sometimes overdyes to improve colour.

Proggy Rug – Compass

Requirements

2 metres hessian (harn, or greencloth may be used)

proggy tool (see photograph above right)

scissors

ruler

tape measure

marker pens in two colours

rug frame (see construction details)

trestles

assortment of clothing and fabrics

large eye sewing needle

string or strong thread

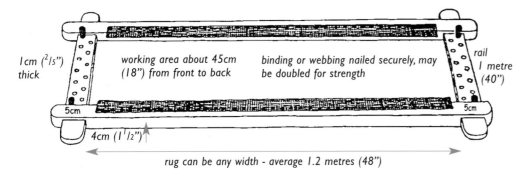

1cm (²/5") thick

working area about 45cm (18") from front to back

binding or webbing nailed securely, may be doubled for strength

rail 1 metre (40")

5cm

5cm

4cm (1¹/2")

rug can be any width - average 1.2 metres (48")

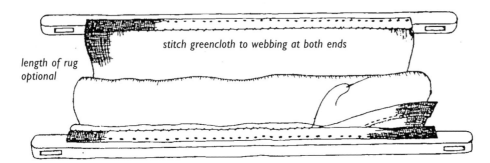

length of rug optional

stitch greencloth to webbing at both ends

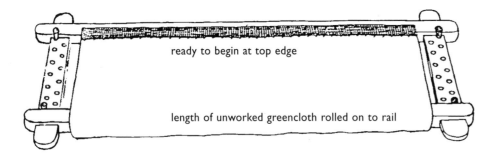

ready to begin at top edge

length of unworked greencloth rolled on to rail

The rug frame

The frame used for hooky and proggy rugs consists of two long wooden bars with slots at each end. Two flat pieces, called rails, in which holes are drilled to take pegs, slide through these slots. Each long bar has a piece of strong binding or webbing tacked or nailed on to it.

Hessian or greencloth

This can be bought by the metre or you can use old sacking. Miriam used to use up old hessian bags from around the farm, but now she uses greencloth after seeing how some old rugs had decayed over the years. The greencloth is stronger and more durable.

Attach the greencloth to the frame by stitching it to the webbing on the rails, sewing it with fine string, linen thread or synthetic thread.

Wind the greencloth around one of the bars. Leave about 45cm (18") of cloth unwound. Slot the two flat rails through the bars and wedge them in place by putting the pegs in the appropriate holes. The greencloth must be taut.

Actual size
75cm x 155cm
(30" x 62")

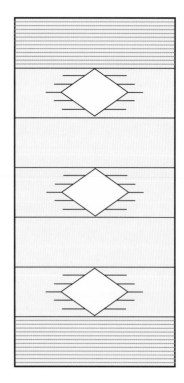

Fabrics

Prepare your old clothing and fabrics by washing before cutting it into strips. The best fabrics are non-fraying woollens, serge, worsted, coat and dress materials and old socks. Knitted, man made materials are very useful. Miriam has used mostly track suit and t-shirt material in her rug.

To work the proggy rug

Following the design provided, draw a rectangle 75cm x 155cm (30" x 62") on your hessian using a marker pen. Allow a border area of 8cm – 10cm (3" – 4") for the hem. Draw the design by using one marker pen to draw a grid and another colour pen for the design. Any design can be drawn on the hessian using a grid method to transfer the design. This rug would look good in any colour combination. Simple designs are best for proggy rugs but more

Porkies Pumpkin -
a hooky rug
from a design by
John Butler
155cm x 120cm

detailed designs are needed for the hooky method.

1. Insert the greencloth into your frame. Note that for this rug the wrong side of the rug is facing you. The fabric is pushed or progged through.

2. Cut the rags into strips approximately 6cm – 7cm ($2^1/_2$ – 3") long and 2cm ($^4/_5$") wide.

3. With a progger poke a hole in the corner of the greencloth. Using the progger push one end of a strip of material through the first hole.

4. Make a second hole 1cm ($^2/_5$") to the side of the first hole and push the other end through this hole. Make sure both ends are equal.

5. Take another piece of material and push one end of it also through the second hole.

6. Make a third hole 1cm ($^2/_5$") further on and push the other end of the second piece of material through this third hole.

7. Carry on like this, taking care to keep the strips as close as possible as this helps to stop them coming loose.

The finished pile of the rug should be about 3cm ($1^1/_5$") in length. Trim to equal lengths if necessary.

To finish the rug, turn under the hem allowance and sew with a large eyed needle, such as a bagging needle and string or very tough thread, taking care to stitch through the hessian or greencloth and not the fabric worked into it.

These rugs are floor rugs, but if you wish you could fix an envelope of material to the top of the rug, and thread a dowel through so that you can hang your rug.

Proggy rugs are not covered at the back so, if a piece of fabric comes loose it is simple to poke it back in again.

To work a hooky rug

A hooky rug is made with the right side of the rug facing you, and the fabric is cut into long strips 1cm – 2cm ($^1/_5$" – $^2/_55$") wide. If the material is thin it can be doubled. Make a hole at one corner and, holding a strip of fabric underneath the greencloth, pull the first end up through the hole. Poke a second hole with the hook 1cm ($^2/_5$") further on, and catch hold of the strip underneath. Pull it through, making a loop which stands about 1.5cm ($^1/_2$") high. Continue in this way. Start a new strip as close as possible to the last.

For the hooky rugs only, brush the back with latex (obtainable at carpet stores). Cut a piece of backing greencloth, place it on the back and hem over the top of this.

Artists' Biographies

Linda Benson 137
Selbourne, Tas.
Born Ouse, Tas. 1959
Studied: Diploma of Art, Textiles Major, Tas. State Institute of Technology 1981-83.
Teaching experience: Community Youth Support Scheme, Launceston, Youth Arts Project for International Year of Youth 1985; Alanvale College, Launceston, teacher's aide, Art department 1986-87; tutoring in bearmaking techniques, Sydney, Gold Coast, Canberra, Melbourne and Hobart 1994-2000.
Exhibitions and awards: Group Textiles Exhibition, 'Women of the Cloth', JamFactory, Adelaide 1984; Two Best in Sections, Australian Bear Affair, Sydney 1999.

Christine Bishop 99
Hawthorn, SA
Born SA 1953
Studied: TAFE course in dressmaking 1984; completed Embroiderers' Guild of SA Inc Certificate Course specialising in perforated fabric and surface stitches; attended Embroiderers' Guild of SA Inc courses in: contemporary stumpwork, design, handkerchiefs, cutwork, Mountmellick, Carrickmacross, box making.
Teaching experience: workshops and classes for Embroiderers' Guild of SA Inc headquarters and branches; Nunyara residential school; Country Conference of Embroiderers' Guild of SA Inc 1998; Embroiderers' Guild of SA Inc branches - Millicent, Bordertown (2), Mt Gambier (4), Barossa Valley, Gawler, Eyre Peninsula, Flinders and Riverland; Embroiderers' Guild of Vic. Summer School 1998-2000; Sovereign Needlework, Ballarat; National Embroiderers' Conference 1999; Quilt and Threads, Modbury 1997-99; Embroiderers' Guild of ACT 1996 and 1999; Bustle and Bows Melbourne 1998; lecturing in Certificate Course Embroiderers' Guild of SA Inc and Certificate Course Embroiderers' Guild of ACT; Embroiderers' Guild of Vic., historical embroideries 1998-99.
Judging: Royal Canberra Show embroidery 1997, cross stitch 1999; Certificate Course Embroiderers' Guild of SA Inc.
Publications: author book Schwalm Embroidery 1999; magazine projects.

Jenny Bradford 53
Canberra, ACT
Born Surrey, England 1936
In Australia since 1964
Studied: Teaching diploma from Cambridge University.
Teaching experience: Taught in schools in England, USA and in Australia with Vic. Department of Education and Adult Education; private classes and tutoring as well as seminars in all aspects of embroidery; Embroiderers' Guild of ACT.
Exhibitions: Canberra 1986; Narrabri 1989.
Publications: Author of 13 books since 1988 on silk ribbon embroidery, textured embroidery, bullion stitch embroidery, smocking, silk and wool embroidery and teddy bears, selling in excess of 330 000 copies to date; magazine articles and projects; embroidery kits.

Gary Clarke 71
Stitching Heirlooms
Launceston, Tas.
Born Tas. 1953
Studied: Launceston Matriculation and Art Colleges; 12 month apprenticeship as textile designer; self-taught embroiderer using techniques from other art and design mediums.
Other relevant experience: textile designer Universal Textiles, Hobart, Tas.; careers in display, interior design (award winner), store manager, Pastor, writer and illustrator.
Teaching experience: currently teaching, lecturing and demonstrating around Australia.
Publications: books including Embroidery and candlewicking, Cats inspiration for needlework, Bouquet Bows and bugs, Candlewicking and beyond, Simply flowers; articles and projects for magazines; designing embroidery kits.

Judith Coombe 91
Judith & Kathryn Designs
Adelaide, SA
Born Kapunda, SA 1950
Studied: SA School of Art/Western Teachers College, Adv. Dip. Teaching (Art) 1968-71.
Teaching experience: art teaching 1972-74.
(See also Judith & Kathryn Designs below)

Susan Dickens 87
South Yarra, Vic
Born Albury, NSW 1943
Studied: trained as a nurse, Royal Melbourne Hospital; studied Ceramics, Wales, UK 1970; studied Textiles, Pittsburgh, USA 1971.
Teaching experience: taught embroidery for 4 years followed by tasselmaking workshops throughout Australia, NZ, UK and USA.
Publications: author books The Art of Tassel Making 1994 and Tassels 2000; contributing artist to all of Kaye Pykes' books (see below); subject of several magazine feature articles.

Helen Eriksson 79
Adelaide, SA
Born Whyalla, SA 1945
Studied: Adult education in: Jewellery making, Whyalla 1973; China painting, Adelaide 1978; wood carving, Adelaide 1979; porcelain doll making, Adelaide 1984.
Teaching experience: private classes 1992-2000; workshops in Brisbane, Melbourne, Perth, Grafton, ACT; Victor Harbour Quilting Show 1997; Horsham Learning centre 1999; Grafton Arts Festival 1999; Whyalla 1996-99; 'Beating around the Bush' 2000.
Exhibitions and awards: Readers' Choice Craft Award for Excellence, Embroidery and Cross Stitch, Express Publications 1998; work for book Ribbon Renaissance exhibited at Melbourne 1999; Country Bumpkin 2000.
Publications: Book Ribbon Renaissance 1999; numerous articles and projects for magazines; embroidery kits.

June Fiford 85
Goonellabah, New South Wales
Born Lismore, New South Wales 1947
Studied: attended many workshops with recognised tutors in different techniques of embroidery, including design and drawing and Commercial Needlecraft Certificate Course, Lismore TAFE 1987-92; Correspondence Course in Creative Embroidery, Embroiderers' Guild, NSW 1987-90; personal embroidery study tour of England and attendance at several classes and courses during seven weeks including Certificate of Attendance from Royal School of Needlework which includes instruction in basics of Goldwork 1989; Proficiency Certificate of NSW Embroiderers' Guild, metal thread embroidery 1991; accreditation from Embroiderers' Guild in technique of Surface Stitchery 1995.
Teaching experience: tutor at residential workshop for Creative Embroiders Inc 1993; tutor of Embroiderers' Guild of NSW including Summer Schools, Winter School, 1996 Festival of Embroidery 1992-98; tutor of embroidery under name of Larodee Needlearts in Lismore 1990 - .
Exhibitions: Northern Rivers Craft art shows 1988-91; regular exhibitor with Embroiderers' Guild NSW, Sydney from 1988; Sydney Creative Embroiderers, University of Wollongong 1991; Creative Embroiderers' Images exhibition, Woolloomooloo Gallery, Sydney 1993; travelling exhibitions of Creative Embroiders 1993-94; Arts Tarts, Tree Tops Gallery, Murwillumbah, NSW 1996; Relative Values - Common Ground, Lismore Regional Art Gallery 1998.
Publications: subject of articles in Textile Fibre Forum and newspapers.

Wendy Findlay 31
Mosman, NSW
Born Adelaide 1940
Studied: Degree in Liberal Arts, Hartley CAE, SA 1983
Related experience: Audiovisual Librarian, Barker College, NSW 1984-91; Audiovisual Librarian, Cranbrook School, NSW 1991 - ; Founder Smocking Arts Guild of NSW.
Teaching experience: private classes and workshops in both smocking and garment constructions; tutor, Smocking Arts Guild of NSW.
Exhibitions: regular group exhibitions.

Dianne Firth 147
Canberra, ACT
Born Australia 1945
Studied: Degrees in Landscape Architecture, Education and Science; basically self-taught in sewing apart from informal workshops.
Curated exhibitions include: Australian Quilts, The People and their Art 1989; Threads of Journeys 1990; Manly Museum and Art Gallery 1992, 93, 97, 98, 99; National Wool Museum 1995, 97, 2000; Australia Dreaming 1995; Beds and Beyond 1995; Making their Mark 1996; Australian Quilts in Public Places 1997; Yokohama 1997; Dare to Differ 1999; Australian Quilts 2000; Refabricating the Future Awards 2000; Horizons 2000; Australian Bounty 2000.
Awards: Mary Durack Outback Craft Award, Brisbane (2nd prize) 1995; Sheep and Wool Show, Melbourne 1996; Towards the New Millennium, Adelaide 1998; European Quilt Expo VII, Strasbourg, Oceania Prize 2000.
Collections: Museum of Australia 1987; University of Canberra Art Collection 1995; Vice Chancellor's Collection, University of Canberra 1996.

Kerry Gavin 152
Canberra, ACT
Born Yass 1950
Studied: dressmaking 1968; patchwork and quilting with Judy Turner 1983; workshops with Judy Turner, Julie Filmer, Pamela Tawton, Susan Denton, Dianne Newman, Lyn Inall, Lee Cleland, Pamela Taylor, Fiona Gavens, Dianne Finnegan, Jody Hooworth, Elizabeth Busch, Beryl Hodges and Nancy Crow 1983 - 2000.
Teaching experience: regular workshops and classes 1990 - .
Related experience: member Canberra Quilters Inc, president 1996, 97 and 98; member The Quilter's Guild Inc and American Quilter's Society, USA.
Exhibitions and awards: numerous, including: annual exhibitions of Canberra Quilters Inc, 1984-2000; annual exhibition of Quilters Guild Inc, Sydney 1989-2000; Individual Differences, Five Canberra Quiltmakers 2000; has exhibited at American Quilters Society Annual Exhibition, Paducah, Kentucky, USA 1993, 94; Houston Quilt Festival, USA 1994; numerous awards at Canberra Quilters, Quilters Guild, Sydney, Royal Canberra Show, Berinba Arts Festival (Yass).
Publications: work represented in several books including Quilt a Koala by Margaret Rolfe, Quilts to Make for Children by Margaret Rolfe, Piece by Piece by Dianne Finnegan; Quiltmakers of Australia by Karen Fail, Australian Quilt Heritage by Margaret Rolfe, Spectacular Scraps by Judy Hooworth and Margaret Rolfe; in magazines including Craft Arts, Australian Patchwork and Quilting and Down Under Quilts.

Glenys Gudgeon 171
Byron Bay, NSW
Born Ballarat, Vic. 1946
Studied: Teachers Certificate, Ballarat Teachers College 1964-65; Proficiency Certificate in Machine Embroidery, Embroiderers' Guild of NSW 1993.
Teaching experience: Murwillumbah TAFE 1992-96; Embroiderers Guild NSW 1994-2000; Adult education and private classes 1991- .
Exhibitions and awards: Lismore Regional Art Gallery, Tweed River Regional Art Gallery travelling exhibitions; Embroiderers Guild of NSW.
Commissions and collections: Southern Cross University Ceremonial Gowns; Embroiderers Guild of NSW; private collections.

Jan Hanlon 129
Brady's Bears
Rosevears, Tas.
Born England 1950
Studied: trained in bookkeeping and accounting; self-taught bear maker 1993.
Related experience: full-time bearmaker from 1994.
Awards: numerous since 1995 including Section winner, Melbourne Doll show 1996; 'Bear of the Fair' and Section winner, Tas. Bear Fair, Hobart 1996; Category winner and category runner-up, Tas. Bear Fair, Hobart 1997; Category winner, Sydney Teddy Bear Festival 1998; Grand Champion Bear, Albury Bear Fair, Vic. 1998; People's Choice Award, Tas. Bear Fair, Hobart 1998; Grand Champion Bear, Burnie Doll and Bear Affair, Tas. 1999.
Publications: bears displayed, patterns published and profiles included in magazines and journals in Australia and UK.

Christine Harris 73
Sydney, NSW
Born Sydney 1947
Studied: Medical Technology; self-taught needlework and sewing
Teaching experience: Orana Community College, Coonamble (TAFE), teacher School of Fashion (adult education); Community Education and Employment Programme, Coonamble; Western College of Adult Education, Dubbo, area coordinator and teacher; teaching needlework to groups and individuals throughout Australia for more than 20 years.
Related experience: worked in pathology as a medical biochemist; technical writer for software company; assistant editor needlework magazine.
Publications: author books Wool Embroidery for Babies 1992; French Knot Pictures 1994; Embroidered Initials 1996; numerous magazine articles and projects.

Beth Hatton 183
Sydney, NSW
Born Saskatchewan, Canada 1943
Arrived in Australia 1976
Studied: original Canadian degree in Literature; basically self-taught in weaving apart from adult education classes in England and informal workshops in Australia; post-graduate Diploma in Professional Art Studies, College of Fine Arts, Sydney 1981-82.
Related experience: columnist for Object Magazine, Craft Arts and regularly for Textile Fibre Forum.
Exhibitions: solo: Rag Rugs, Beaver Galleries 1988; numerous group including recent: Text(Aisles), Tin Sheds; Devotion, Casula Powerhouse; Hobart Art Prize, Carnegie Gallery; Thylacine, Tas. Museum and Art Gallery; twice exhibited at Kyoto Museum, Japan (Australian Works in Paper 1983, Australian Craft 1991); twice exhibited in USA in Re-Visions, Handweavers Guild of America 1994 and Ragtime, Madison Morgan Cultural Centre 1998.
Awards: Australian Stockman's Hall of Fame Outback Craft Award (2nd prize) 1995; first prize 1996, 1999; Living without Violence (3rd prize) 1999; Fibres and Fabrics Award 1999.

Furze Hewitt 111
Oaks Estate, ACT
Born Cornwall, UK 1924
Arrived in Australia 1946
Related experience: anti-aircraft plotter in Army with Auxiliary Territorial Service; married Australian pilot; widowed in 1952; remarried Australian Air Force Officer; established and operated antique shop for 12 years during which time researched and collected patterns for lace knitting and began knitting from these, continuing to collect, with friend Billie Daley, more than 200 patterns for the first of her books.
Publications: author of eight books (last to be published in 2001): Motifs, Borders and Trims in Classic Knitted Cotton (with Billie Daley); Classic Knitted Cotton Edgings (with Billie Daley); Knit One, Make One in Classic Knitted Cotton; Heirloom Knitting for Dolls; High Fashion Knitting for Dolls; Traditional Knitting for Children and Bears; Traditional Lace Edgings; Aromatic Gifts in Classic Knitted Cotton.

Beryl Hodges 151
Canberra, ACT
Born Melbourne, Vic.
Studied: Vic. Teaching Certificate; Bachelor of Education Studies, University of Qld.; Design Units – Claremont School of Art, WA and Canberra School of Art.
Teaching experience: Infants and primary schools; adult quiltmaking classes from 1982.
Awards and exhibitions: Prizewinner – Best use of colour, Quilters' Guild of NSW 1997; Group exhibitions from 1980 in Canberra, Sydney, Perth, Melbourne, Armidale; exhibitions in USA and Canada; Individual Differences, Five Canberra Quiltmakers, Canberra Museum and Gallery 2000.
Publications: author (with Margaret Rolfe) of book Australian Houses in Patchwork 1991.

Wendy Holland 170
Mount Wilson, NSW
Studied: National Art School, Sydney 1965-69; Diploma of Education, Art, Sydney Teachers' College.
Teaching experience: art teacher, secondary schools 1973-76; began giving slide presentations and workshops in 1985.
Related experience: worked with theatrical costumes, sewing, painting, dyeing, printing etc 1970-71; worked full time with fabrics 1977-78; began making quilts 1980.
Exhibitions: numerous since 1981 including recent: Stanthorpe Arts Festival, Qld. 1996; Australian Quilt and Craft festival, Melbourne 1996; 17th National Craft Acquisition Award, Museum and Art Gallery of the NT 1997; Braemar Springwood, NSW 1998, 99; Fairfield City Museum and Gallery, NSW 2000

Judith & Kathryn Designs 91
(see also Judith Coombe and Kathryn Thompson)
Established 1980
Exhibitions and Awards: Brisbane, Sydney, Melbourne, Canberra, Hobart, Adelaide, Perth 1980 –; London Knitting and Needlework Show 1996; Houston Quilt Festival USA 1996; Los Angeles 'I Love Needlework Show' 1998; ASPAT Seoul, Korea 1999; Craft and Sewing Industry Award of Excellence 1998 in recognition of the outstanding contribution made to the Australian Craft Industry.

Diana Lampe 17
Canberra, ACT
Born Coonamble, NSW 1945
Studied: art and textiles; basically self-taught in needlework and botany, attending occasional classes and studying texts.
Teaching experience: has taught needlework throughout Australia, NZ and South Africa, mostly through needlework and specialty shops, but also through other craft groups, and at home.
Publications: author books Embroidered Garden Flowers 1991 with Jane Fisk; More Embroidered Garden Flowers 1993; Embroidery from the Garden 1997; Little Book of Embroidered Garden Flowers 1999; numerous magazine articles and projects; designs and distributes embroidery kits.
Exhibitions and awards: numerous, most recent: DMC 250th Birthday Celebrations 1996; craft shows 1991-99; Australian Open Garden Scheme, ACT 1996-97; Floriade ACT 1998; Word Festival, Canberra 1999.

Marie Laurie 105
Gloucester, NSW
Born Gloucester, NSW
Studied: nursing Royal North Shore Hospital Sydney; interest in embroidery, crochet and knitting; Branscombe tape with Mrs Susan Cox, English Lace School, Tiverton, UK 1982; other trips overseas to study: Hollie Point and Zele, UK; lace from Belgium; Limerick and Carrickmacross, Ireland; Youghal lace with Mrs Veronica Stuart who had researched the old laces from the Presentation Convent, Youghal, Ireland; Halas, Kiskunhalas, Hungary; Rosemary Shepherd's Correspondence course for Torchon bobbin lace; as well as other private reading and research.
Teaching experience: has conducted workshops throughout Australia and Ireland and is an accredited needlelace tutor for the Embroiderers' Guild of NSW and the Country Women's Association; holds a handcraft judging badge from the CWA.
Exhibitions and awards: lacework has been exhibited in many countries overseas as well as locally, with many prizes awarded including John Bull from UK; numerous annual state awards from CWA; Dame Nancy Buttfield highly commended; exhibited at Sydney Royal Show for many years with impressive success including four Standard of Excellence Awards; second prize award in First World Lace Exhibition, Hungary 1998.

Susie McMahon 143
Exeter, Tas
Born Adelaide, SA 1952
Studied: Teacher's Diploma of Art, Tas. School of Art 1971; Associate Diploma in Music, Tas. State Institute of Technology, Launceston 1986.
Related experience: teacher of school art 1976; itinerant craft teacher in schools 1976-83; itinerant music teacher 1983-92; teacher of art, craft and design, Georgetown 1987-92; part time art education assistant,

Prospect High School 1994 - ; invited to judge Santa Fe Doll Art 1998, 2000.
Exhibitions and awards: numerous exhibitions since 1976 including: Best in section award, Sydney Doll Show 1989; Runner-up Best Working Exhibitor, Deloraine Craft Fair 1991, award 1995; Best Doll, Circular Head Arts Festival, Stanley 1991; two Best in section awards for original dolls, Sydney Doll Show 1991, 93; work selected for exhibition Dame Nancy Buttfield Exhibition, SA 1992, 93; two Best in section awards for original dolls, Melbourne Doll show 1993; work selected for use on Australia Post stamp set 1997; Australian Doll of the Year Award (category 4 and 5: Cloth and Polymer Clay) 1997; Australian Doll of the Year Award (Category 6: Any other Medium) 1995, 96, 97, 98; Santa Fe Doll Art Award for Best Cloth Doll 1997; invited to exhibit in Edith Lambert Gallery, International Exhibition, Santa Fe, New Mexico 1998, 99; invited to exhibit in The Poetry of Dolls International Exhibition, Alburquerque, New Mexico 2000; awarded William Wiley Award for Creative Excellence in World of Dolls, Santa Fe Doll Art Show, Alburquerque, New Mexico 2000.
Publications: subject of feature articles in magazines and journals including Contemporary Doll Collector (USA); Dolls, Bears and Collectables; Pastimes Magazine.

Annemieke Mein 165
Sale, Vic.
Born Holland 1944
Arrived in Australia 1951
Teaching experience: tutor, Fibre Forum Conference 1982; tutor, Australia Pacific Embroidery Festival 1984; tutor, Gippsland Summer School of Art & Textiles 1987; tutor, Gwen Webb Arts Activity Centre, Sale 1987; tutor, Stitches and Craft Show 1992.
Related experience: member of council of Crafts Council of Vic. 1980-83; steering committee member then committee member Gippsland Division of Crafts Council of Vic. 1980-84.
Awards: Coats Patons/Family Circle Award 1978; Hoechst Australia Ltd Textile Award in Australian Crafts 1980 Centenary Exhibition; winner of A.F.T.A. 'Thread Affair' 1983; Enterprise Award, Vic.'s 150th Celebrations 1985; Order of Australia Medal 1988; Textile Award Wildlife Artists Society of Australasia 1988; VIP Listing, City of Sale 1992.
Collections and commissions: historical bas relief sculpture commissioned by City of Sale 1984; designer of Pictorial Postmarker, Australia Post 1987; bronze commission for Bishop of Sandhurst, Bendigo, 'Dr Henry Backhaus' 1987; designer of wine labels for Narkoojee Winery 1993; bronze commission for Bishop of Gippsland, Sale, 'Mary MacKillop' 1994; textiles represented in: National Gallery of Vic.; Art Gallery of Qld; Museum of Applied Arts and Sciences, Sydney; Ararat Art Gallery; Gippsland Art Gallery, Sale; City of Box Hill Collection; Benalla Art Gallery; West Gippsland Arts Centre, Warragul; Sculpture Gallery, Metung; Hoechst International Collection; Penguin Threads International Collection; private collections in Australia, Holland, USA, UK, Japan, Canada, New Zealand, Sweden and Germany.
Exhibitions: more than 50 since 1980 including: National Gallery of Vic., Environmental Textiles 1981; Gippsland Art Gallery, Sale 1980-2000; Waverley City Gallery 1992; Tourist Information Centre, Sale 1992-97; Royal Botanic Gardens, The Fabric of Nature 1996; Ballarat Fine Art Gallery, The Art of Annemieke 2000.
Publications: subject of scores of articles in magazines, journals and books including Fibre Forum Magazine, Craft Australia. Author book Annemieke Mein, Wildlife Artist in Textiles 1992; Art of Annemieke Mein Calender 1994, 95 and 97; limited edition prints: Thornbills 1993, Splash 1995, Sea Gar 1996.

Miriam Miller 187
Milton, NSW
Born North England 1935
Arrived in Australia 1948
Taught rug making by her father and remembers rugs made by her grandmother in N.E. England. Has made proggy and hooky rugs for nearly 30 years, developing her own style.
Teaching experience: founding member and teacher with the Narrawilly Proggy Rag Ruggers since 1994; informal teaching when requested to any interested group around Australia of rag rug making, creative knitting and wool dyeing.
Exhibitions: various solo and group exhibitions in NSW, latest joint exhibition of rugs and hand dyed knits with painter John Butler 1999.

Effie Mitrofanis 173
Sydney, NSW
Studied: Secretarial certificate Lismore TAFE 1956; pattern and dressmaking certificate Lismore TAFE 1957-60; Proficiency Certificate canvas embroidery, Embroiderers' Guild of NSW 1980; Proficiency Certificate surface stitchery, Embroiderers' Guild of NSW 1981; Assoc. Dip. Fine Art, St George College of TAFE, Sydney 1990-91; Master of Visual and Performing Arts research student, Charles Sturt University, Wagga Wagga 1997-99; local workshops with Australian and visiting artists; overseas research trips as follows: Athens; Greek costume and embroidery 1989; UK various workshops including Embroiderers' Guild 1989; Embroidery collections in England and Scotland 1993; textiles of India (with UK Guild) 1995; research studies into cutwork, reticella, punto in aria needlelace, Italy – museums and collections in Florence, Sienna and Venice, UK – museums and collections including Vic. and Albert Museum, Ruskin work, Cumbria, Gawthorpe Hall, Embroiderers' Guild, Hampton Court 1997.
Teaching experience: numerous workshops throughout Australia and NZ, Scotland and UK; through Embroiderers' Guilds, Textile Fibre Forum, Adult Education and Kuring-gai Community Arts Centre as well as private classes.
Related experience: product manager, promotions and production manager, DMC Australia 1993-95.
Exhibitions and awards: Embroiderers' Guilds of NSW 1973-98; Sydney Creative Embroiderers 1980-92; Dame Nancy Buttfield Embroidery, Adelaide 1992-96; DMC France - Exposition Internationale, Paris and Japan 1994 and 95 as well as others; inaugural recipient of Jean Vere Scholarship by the Embroiderers' Guild of NSW 1997-98.
Publications: author books Creative Canvas Embroidery 1990; Tassels and Trimmings; 1992; Decorative Tassels and Cords 1995; Casalguidi Style Linen Embroidery 1996; numerous magazine articles and essays including World of Embroidery Magazine UK and Textile Fibre Forum.

Jane Nicholas 37
Bowral, NSW
Studied: Sydney University and Sydney Teachers College; Textile Fibre Forum courses, Sturt Craft Centre, Mittagong NSW 1991-96.
Related experience: owner Chelsea Fabrics, fabric and haberdashery store 1975 - .
Teaching experience: for specialty and needlework stores throughout Australia and NZ 1993 –; conferences and for Embroiderers' Guilds in Australia and NZ as well as the USA and Canada; recent conferences include: Seminar 1996 – San Francisco Embroiderers' Guild of America; Autumn Retreat Embroiderers' Guild of NSW 1997; Okataina Winter Warm Up NZ Embroiderers' Guild 1997 and '98; Seminar 1998 – Kentucky Embroiderers' Guild of America 1998; The Great Escape – Keri Keri NZ Embroiderers' Guild 1999; Taking Threads - Seminar '99 Embroiderers' Association of Canada 1999; Wanaka Embroidery School Otago Embroiderers' Guild, NZ; Seminar 2000 - Orlando, Florida Embroiderers' Guild of America.
Exhibitions and awards: include Bicentennial Sydney Royal Easter Show - First Prizes in Applique – Hand Sewn and Embroidery – Gold Work and Francis Binnie Special Award as well as Bicentennial Medallion for most successful needlework exhibitor 1988; Embroiderers' Guild of NSW Third Festival of Embroidery Exhibition/competition – Viewers Choice Award 1992; Dame Nancy Buttfield Embroiderers Exhibition 1993 and '95; Berrima (Bowral) District Art Society Exhibition 1994; Churchill Fellowship to research seventeenth century needlework.
Publications: author books Stumpwork Embroidery – A Collection of Fruits, Flowers and Insects for Contemporary Raised Embroidery 1995; Stumpwork Embroidery – Designs and Projects 1998; Stumpwork Dragonflies 2000; articles and projects.

Stephaney Packham 125
Wentworth Falls, NSW
Born Sydney 1939
Studied: Nursing: Psychiatric - Callan Park Hospital, General – Repatriation General Hospital, Concord, Retardation – Marsden Hospital, Westmead.; tatting from husband's elderly aunt during 2 weeks 1985, self taught after this; bobbin lacemaking through private lessons with Annette Pollard 1990-95.
Teaching experience: informal teaching when requested at Australian Lace Guild Lace Days.; several workshops associated with local businesses and a number of private students.
Exhibitions and awards: Numerous composite Lace Guild exhibitions; awarded first prizes at each of very few shows entered.

Kaye Pyke 84
Port Melbourne, Vic.
Born Vic. 1943
Studied: self taught post secondary school; experimented with calico and designs with wool on calico, then ribbon.
Teaching experience: teaching embroidery and sewing and decorating for 30 years, private classes and seminars throughout Australia.
Relevant experience: worked in decorating, operated strip furniture shop for restoration of furniture for 10 years; sewing at home; sold work in Greece and Florence 1975; operated design, decorating and embroidery shop 1984-2000.
Publications: author books Elegant Embroidery, Classic Cushions, Sumptuous Settings; numerous magazine articles and projects.

Jenny Rees 117
Canberra, ACT
Born Molong, Vic. 1956
Studied: Bachelor Science and Diploma of Education, Australian National University, Canberra; basically self-taught lacemaker.
Teaching experience: Secondary schools in ACT, science and special education in mathematics, science and reading; private tutor in lacemaking.
Exhibitions and awards: Lace Guild exhibitions; Prize at Triennial Lace Awards of Australian Lace Guild 1994 and 97; Winner 6 times Lace Section Canberra Times Craft Expo at Canberra Show.

Annette Rich 61
Coonamble, NSW
Born Coonamble 1935
Studied: TAFE: Fine Needlework Course 1, 1980, 81, Developing Creative Craft; B.M.I. Staff Development Course 1987; NSW Embroiderers' Guild practical teaching skills course 1999 (High Distinction); NSW Embroiderers' Guild Certificate as Accredited Guild Tutor in area of surface stitchery and modern dimensional embroidery.
Teaching experience: NSW Embroiderers' Guild 1995-97; conducted workshops at many affiliated groups including Dubbo, Narrabri, Gunnedah; classes and workshops in needlecraft shops including Wagga, Mosman, Oatley; demonstrations at craft shows.
Publications: author books Wildflower Embroidery 1994, Botanical Embroidery 1999.

Margaret Rolfe 155
Canberra, ACT
Born Melbourne 1994
Studied: Bachelor of Arts, Diploma of Education, Melbourne University 1962-65, Art History (single subjects to make a major) Australian National University, Canberra 1981-87.
Related experience: Teacher and Psychometrician, Melbourne and Toronto Canada 1966-69; since 1981 has researched the history of quilting in Australia; Historic Quilts Coordinator for the Quilters Guild, Inc., for the historic quilts at the Bicentennial quilt exhibition, Quilt Australia 88.
Teaching experience: taught patchwork and quilting since 1980, in Canberra, widely throughout Australia, and also in Canada, NZ and the United states; recent international teaching includes Quilting-by-the-Lake 1994, Pacific International Quilt Festival 111 1994, Quilting-by-the-Sound 1996, Houston International Quilt Festival 1996, Pacific Connections Vancouver 1998.
Exhibitions: from 1980 quilts exhibited in the annual exhibitions of the Canberra Quilters and Quilters' Guild, Sydney; numerous other exhibitions including most recently Colours of Australia, Sydney 1995, and subsequent tour around Australia, Wool quilts, Meat Market, Melbourne 1997, exhibition of animal quilts, World Quilt and Textile, Greensboro, North Carolina 1999, Individual Differences - Five Canberra Quiltmakers, Canberra Museum and Art Gallery 2000.
Publications: author books Australian Patchwork 1985, Quilt a Koala 1986, Patchwork Quilts in Australia 1987; Quilts to make for Children 1989; Kimono: Straight-line patchwork on a Japanese theme 1991, Australian Houses in Patchwork (with Beryl Hodges) 1991; Go Wild with Quilts: Fourteen North American Birds and Animals 1993, Metric Quilt making 1993, Go Wild with Quilts – Again: 10 New Bird and Animal Designs 1996, A Quilter's Ark 1997, Australian Quilt Heritage 1998, Spectacular scraps (with Judy Hooworth) 1999; numerous articles, papers and projects for magazines and conferences.
1976 - founder and life member of Canberra Quilters Inc (formerly the Patchwork Group).

Jenny Saladine 67
Perth, WA
Born Sydney 1949
Studied: 6 year informal apprenticeship with couturier Dorothy
Stephen, making and embellishing clothes for wealthy and influential
clients; dressmaking at home; self-taught fine embroidery when
preparing own baby's clothes.
Relevant experience: embroidery for Mary and Heather McClure.
Teaching experience: various needlework shops including Antique
Rose in Perth, Country Bumpkin in Adelaide and Affinity Plus in
Canberra 1985 –.
Exhibitions and awards: Prize Winner fine embroidery Campbelltown
Show several times during 1980s; various craft shows and DMC 250
years exhibitions.
Publications: numerous magazine articles and projects; designing
embroidery kits; distributing painted picture kits.

Alison Snepp 27
Mosman Needlecraft
Sydney, Australia
Born Australia 1954
Studied: Bachelor of Arts, University of NSW 1975; Proficiency
Certificate with Distinction, Embroiderers' Guild of NSW 1981;
Editing Small Publications, University of New England 1992.
Teaching experience: freelance embroidery teacher to community
groups, guilds, technical colleges and colleges of advanced education
1981-89; in own shop 1998 – .
Related experience: manager large specialist embroidery store in
Sydney 1979-81; operated specialist embroidery finishing business
1981-89; embroidery judge at Royal Easter Show 1984, 85 and 89 as
well as at Embroiderers' Guilds and craft organisations; senior product
manager with DMC Needlecraft 1989-92; freelance embroidery writer
and editor 1992-93; craft editor Murdoch Books 1994-95; assessor
Proficiency certificate Embroiderers' Guild of NSW 1993, 95;
freelance embroidery writer, designer, specialist embroidery finisher
and embroiderer 1995-98; owner speciality shop 1998 – .
Publications: author of seven books including Creative Home
Furnishing and A Kid's First Book of Sewing; craft editor of two books;
writer of numerous articles and instructional projects in Handmade
magazine and Better Homes and Gardens.

Ruth Stoneley 161
Patchwork Supplies
Brisbane, Qld
Born Qld 1940
Self-taught. Crafts Board Professional Development Grant 1982;
Churchill Fellowship to USA 1986.
Related experience: craft teacher in rehabilitation unit 1976-81;
experimented there with simple quilts; established patchwork supply
shop 1982; textile designs 1995, 98.
Teaching experience: teaching regularly in own shop 1982 - ; has
conducted workshops in all Australian states except WA; USA;
Salzburg, Austria 1988; Abu Dhabi, UAE 2000; artist in residence Peace
Quilt Project, Community arts Board, Brisbane.
Exhibitions and awards: numerous including most recent: solo:
Brisbane City Gallery, Brisbane City Hall; 46 group from 1974 -
including: Fairfield Fashion Show, Houston, Texas, USA 1990, 93, 98;
Houston Quilt Festival, Texas 1995; David Jones Gallery, Brisbane
1990, 93; Flowers of Mainau, Quilts in Bloom Exhibition, Germany
1999; Wedlock, University of Southern Queensland 2000; Special Merit
Award for Contemporary Textiles, World Craft Conference Council,
Jakarta, Indonesia.
Collections and commissions: Art Gallery of WA, Qld Art Gallery,
Brisbane, Tamworth Regional Art Gallery, University of Southern Qld;
commissioned quilt for Government House Brisbane 1982; design and
execution of ecclesiastical vestments for St Stephen's Catholic
Cathedral, Brisbane 1989.

Kathryn Thompson 91
Adelaide, SA
Born Christchurch, NZ 1949
In Australia since 1954
Studied: University of Adelaide Bachelor of Arts; SA School of
Art/Western Teachers College, Adv. Dip. Teaching (Art) 1968-71.
Teaching experience: School art teaching 1972-77.

Awards: Laura Emily Waterhouse Award for Needlework 1971.
(see also Judith & Kathryn Designs above)

Judy Turner 153
Canberra, ACT
Born Wagga Wagga, NSW 1947
Studied: non-certificate course in dressmaking and soft furnishing,
TAFE, Wagga Wagga 1968-69; patchwork classes with Margaret Rolfe,
Wendy Saclier, Elizabeth Kruger 1981; more than 50 different
patchwork and quilting workshops 1982–99; Design and Colour for
Crafts People with Carol Newman 1981.
Teaching experience: more than 50 different workshop locations
throughout Australia 1982– ; Accredited Teacher with Canberra
Quilters Inc 1983 – ; SA Regional Retreat 1990, 91, 92, 96; Waverley
Patchworkers' Mini Symposium 1991; New Zealand 5th National
Quilting Symposium 1993; Artist in Residence Bellerive Community
Art Centre 1993, 99; The Calico House, Perth 1993, 94, 95, 96, 97, 98;
Quiltskills, Sydney 1994, 98; Patchworkers and Quilters of the
Hawkesbury, Quilt Camp 1995, 96; Dookie Quilt Camp, Vic. 1997, 98;
International Quilt Festival, Houston, Texas 1997.
Related experience: member Canberra Quilters Inc; Quilters' Guild
Inc, Sydney; American Quilters' Society; Australian Forum for Textile
arts; judge Sydney Quilters' Guild exhibitions 1989, 1994; Queensland
Quilt Competition 1990; Melbourne Quilt Exhibition 1994.
Exhibitions and awards: more than 50 exhibitions in Australia and
overseas since 1983 including most recently: From the Desert to the
Sea, Grobenzell, Germany 1999; The New Quilt, More or Less, Manly
Art Gallery, Sydney 1999; One Step Further, Vic. Quilters' Association,
Wangaratta, Vic. 1999; Individual Differences, Five Canberra Quilters,
Canberra 2000; numerous awards from Canberra Quilters Inc and
Sydney Quilters' Guild Inc; J.B. Fairfax Press Acquisition Award,
Quilter's Guild Exhibition, Sydney 1998.
Collections and commissions: more than 20 quilts sold to private
collectors in Australia and the USA; Corporate Collection J.B. Fairfax
Press, Sydney.
Publications: work displayed and projects included many magazines
and journals; author book Awash with Colour 1997.

Gabriella Verstraeten 177
Melbourne, Vic.
Studied: Bachelor Education Art & Craft (metalcraft and textiles
majors) Melbourne State College 1979-82; Bachelor of Design Textiles,
RMIT 1985-87; CAD Training, APS Design Systems, Atlanta, Georgia,
USA 1996; part time study Advanced Diploma of Electronic Design,
Vic University of Technology 2000–.
Teaching experience: secondary schools 1987- ; Institutes of TAFE
1988- present, including Box Hill Applied Art and Design Department
and Fashion Department
1995 - ; private classes conducted at own studio in design
fundamentals, machine embroidery, creative textiles, fabric
manipulation 1987– ; artist-in- residencies: numerous since 1983
including Melbourne Zoological Gardens 1983; Camperdown
Community 1997; guest lecturer, tutor and demonstrator at craft
shows 1989, 90, 91, 92, 93; tour of New Zealand 1992, 94, 99;
professional organisations such as Fibre Forum, MacGregor Summer
School, Winter Whirl and other 1989-99.
Related experience: established freelance design studio 1989; studio
based at the Metro Craft Centre (formerly the Meat Market Craft
Centre) 1993-99; design and production work for Sheridan Textiles;
Australian Ballet; Hemden Shirts; Myers and others; international study
tour escort, Art and Textiles to China 1997, 98, 2000.
Exhibition and awards: recent highlights: Australian textile artists
exhibition, Fashion and Embroidery Show, Harrogate, UK 1998;
Textiles 21, Voirrey Institute, Wirral, UK 1999; Masters of Technique,
Monash Gallery of Art and touring 1999 - 2000; grand prize and
overall winner of Stitches magazine, USA 1996; 2nd and 3rd prize
winner of Eurostitch Magazine, Amsterdam, Netherlands 1998.
Publications: textile and design work published in magazines as well as
several videos.

Judy Wilford 45
Youmanii Studios
Armidale, NSW
Born Perth, WA 1941
Studied: Design Diploma, Perth Technical College Correspondence
1973; Creative Embroidery Correspondence, Embroiderers' Guild of
NSW 1982-84; Proficiency Certificate, Applique, Embroiderers' Guild
of NSW 1985; BMI Certificate, TAFE 1991; various workshops and
Summer Schools in Australia, England and Europe.
Teaching experience: various workshops in pottery, drawing and
textiles for adults and children at Kununurra, WA; 1972–84; various
workshops of 3D flowers and landscapes 1989-93; Armidale NSW
TAFE, Commercial Needlecrafts Course T.I.C. 1989-93; Accredited
Tutor, Embroiderers' Guild of NSW 1992; since 1994 has taught
various workshops and classes for Embroiderers' Guilds and other
organisations throughout Australia including most recently National
Embroiderers' Conference, Adelaide 1999; MacGregor School,
Toowoomba Qld 2000.
Related experience: founding and life member Kimberley Arts
Council; nominated Citizen of the Year in community 1982;
Churchill Fellowship Award to study ancient and contemporary
narrative embroidery 1999.
Exhibitions: exhibitor with Australian Craft Shows Sydney and
Brisbane 1989-2000; Dame Nancy Buttfield Award, Adelaide 1991,
93, 95; Bungendore Woodworks Gallery (embroidery and wood -
with husband)1995, 96, 98, 2000; Narek Galleries, ACT 1992;
Mulgara Gallery, Ayers Rock 1993, 94; New England Regional
Gallery 1998; Kimberley Fine Diamonds, Kununurra, WA 1998.
Collections: private collections in Australia; Taiwan; Hong Kong;
Japan; Germany; France; England; USA; gifts for dignitaries: Sir
James Rowland, NSW Transport Commission; Takesha Fukuda,
Mayor Kauma City, Japan and others.
Publications: book a Burble of Birds – paintings 1992; articles in
magazines and journals.

Jan Woodman 30
Stansbury, SA
Born Adelaide, SA 1940
Studied: Embroidery Certificate at School of Art, North Adelaide
1972–74; Design Certificate Course, Department of Further
Education 1975–76; studied flower painting using medium of pure
watercolour 1983-87; studied in State Herbarium 1986-87.
Exhibitions: solo: Festival of Embroidery, Adelaide 1986; Yarrabee
Gallery, Botanic Gardens, Adelaide 1987, 88, 97; Grand Cru Estate
Gallery, Springton, SA 1990; group: Bonython-Meadmore Gallery,
Nth Adelaide 1987; David Jones Gallery 1988; Annual Tapestry
Exhibition, Boxhill, Vic., by invitation Anti-Cancer Council of Vic.
1993, 94, 96; Friends of Botanic Gardens, Melbourne, invitation for
sesquicentenary celebrations, National Herbarium, Vic 1996; Waite
Arboretum 1998; Royal Botanic Gardens, Melbourne 1998;
Riddoch Art Gallery, Mt Gambier, SA 1999; many other displays of
paintings and embroideries by invitation from various associations.
Publications: cross stitch embroidery books: Australian
Wildflowers for Embroiderers 1986; Floral Emblems of Australia
1988; Bushland Magic 1991; Australian Bushland Friends 1993;
posters of SA wildflowers: Wildflowers of Southern Mt Lofty
Range 1985; Wildflowers of the Flinders Ranges 1986; Wildflowers
of Coastal SA 1992; 8 designs for greeting cards; 2 perpetual
wildflower calendars; limited edition prints: Adelaide Hills
Wildflowers; Mallee Wildflowers; 20 cross stitch and embroidery
kits.

Photo credits

All photography by Andrew Sikorski unless detailed below.

Andrew Dunbar, photo of Helen Eriksson p79

Andrew Elton, p36

F.A. Kennely, photo of Judy Turner, p153

Effie Mitrofanis, p172, p174, p175

Georgina Smith, photo of Furze Hewitt, p111

John Tucker, p152

Ben Wrigley, photo of Jenny Bradford, p53

MasterWorks